STRANGE MYSTERIES

Tom Slemen

The Tom Slemen Press

Copyright © 2013 Tom Slemen

All rights reserved.

ISBN-10: 1494766167
ISBN-13: **978-1494766160**

DEDICATION

For all lovers of mystery

CONTENTS

Introduction	1
Did Joan of Arc Escape the Flames?	6
The Turin Shroud	13
The A38 Hitch-hiker	21
The Boy from Nowhere	26
The Ukraine's Giant Spider	37
Was Homer a Woman?	42
The Scottish Prophet	47
Did Shakespeare Exist?	51
The Mysterious Mr Cavendish	56
Who's on Our Moon?	62
The Murder that Wasn't	74
The Ghost that Helped Kojak	79

The Crown Jewels Theft Mystery	84
The Song that can Kill	89
Was Bruce Lee Assassinated?	93
Spring-Heeled Jack	99
Was Poe a Murderer?	110
A Victorian Sorcerer	116
An 18th Century Spaceman	123
The Phantom Writers	127
He Flew Before the Wright Brothers	133
The Teenager who Divided a Nation	137
The American Levitator	143
Visions of Death	149
The Real Frankenstein	153
The Elusive Monarch	159
The Man in the Velvet Mask	167
The Vanished Lord	172
The Incredible Healer	178

The Men in Black	183
Holy Man of the Himalayas	196
Was Richard III Really Bad?	200
Swift's Martian Moons	204
Mother Shipton's Prophecies	208
The Long Man of Wilmington	213
Was Tchaikovsky Murdered?	218
The Cheshire Prophet	223
Robin Hood	228
The Man they Couldn't Hang	231
The Lincoln Conspiracy	237
Murder of an English Warlock	248
Adolf Hitler – Black Magician?	256
A Man of Two Worlds	271
The Atlanteans	279
The Green Children	292
An Extraordinary Gambler	298

The Man in the Iron Tube	305
What Happened to Buster?	309
The Mystery Airships	317
Tales of the Undead	330
Doppelgängers	343
The Tunguska Alien	351
The Zodiac Killer	361
Pope Joan	394
The Thing in Berkeley Square	398
Murder Repeats Itself	404
The *Titanic's* Frozen Lady	411
Beware the Ides of March	416
The Akashic Records	420
Old Testament UFOs	425
Was Jesus an Extraterrestrial?	447
Execution in a Railway Tunnel	462
The Mystery of the *Mary Celeste* – Solved?	465

The Ultimate Mystery	474
Other books by the author	480

INTRODUCTION

We all love a mystery, and I positively thrive on them, whether it's the ultimate ontological mystery of why the Universe is in existence (see the chapter entitled "The Ultimate Mystery" at your own risk of going insane), or some trivial yet intriguing mystery which seems insoluble, and of these latter types of mysteries, I can quote many examples, such as: why did Walt Disney suddenly write down the name of the actor Kurt Russell just before he died in 1966? At the time of the legendary filmmaker's death, Russell was a child actor signed to Disney Studios, and he was even taken in to Walt's office by senior employees of the Disney corporation to see his name scrawled in the late animator's notebook for himself, but just why Walt Disney wrote down Russell's name is still unknown.

While researching this book, I unearthed a lot of information on mysterious people that was maddeningly too scanty. One such example is Jechiele, a French rabbi who had an electric light - in the thirteenth century! The chroniclers of his time merely give us a tantalizing glimpse of this strange man when they tell us that Jechiele discouraged unwanted visitors from knocking on his door by sending a "fiery blue spark" from a curious apparatus in his study to the door-knocker via a wire. Callers who were unfortunate enough to be holding the knocker when the blue spark was crackling would be thrown back from the doorstep by the invisible power. Through his window at night, Jechiele could be seen in his study, working by the light of "a peculiar blue lamp that had neither oil nor wick". What's more, this lamp lit itself. What was Jechiele working on in his study? The chroniclers never answered that question. Jechiele is just one of the many mysterious geniuses who have been omitted from the history books, and there are striking omissions as far as ordinary people are concerned too. Take the case of the first woman into space. The history books record that Russian cosmonaut Valentina Tereshkova was the first female to orbit the earth (48 times) in June 1963, but two years before, on February 17th, 1961, tracking stations around the world picked up the launch of a manned space probe from the USSR, and one of the cosmonauts who was heard chatting to her colleagues in the craft was a woman who never identified herself. The Russians didn't even announce the launch of the craft, which orbited the earth in the erratic trajectory. The following enigmatic comment was made by the female cosmonaut: "It's difficult . . . [static] ... if we don't get out, the world will never hear about it . . ."

Seven days later, the radio telescopes at the tracking stations of Uppsala, Bochum, Turin and Meudon picked up the final horrifying transmission from the ill-starred cosmonauts. It is alleged that the tapes of the distressing dialog have never been released. Space experts and military scientists who analyzed the bizarre trajectory of the doomed spaceship conjectured that the craft had made an unsuccessful attempt to orbit the Moon, but had lacked sufficient speed to break away from the Earth's gravitational pull. Whatever the cause of the tragedy, the unknown Russian space pioneers remain anonymous in death.

Another example of a mysterious person on whom we have scarcely any data is the "M4 Girl" - a young woman who was found wandering in a confused state along the hard shoulder of the M4 motorway near the Severn Bridge in the west of England in November 1988. She failed to respond to questioning by the police and several doctors. The silent woman was taken to a Bristol hospital and a description of her was circulated to police forces throughout Britain. Shortly afterward, a man and a woman from Crediton, near Exeter, in Devon, came forward saying they were the girl's parents. They took the girl home and it was never revealed who she was or why she was walking along a motorway 80 miles from home, because the couple from Devon requested anonymity and, for some inexplicable reason, a phalanx of hard-boiled journalists who had been keenly following the case, quickly dropped the story. The autistic-like girl later became something of a cult figure when the pop group Marillion released their concept album *Brave*, which was inspired by the incident.

Another mysterious individual who has provided us with insufficient data is the young man in a white T-shirt who apparently walked through a solid door in a Lancashire nightclub in the north of England. If this strange feat had not been captured on a security video camera, it would certainly have been dismissed as an incredible yarn, but the video tape has been analyzed by BBC television technicians, and they have declared it genuine.

This eerie incident unfolded in the early hours of October 27th, 1991, at the Butterflies nightclub in Oldham. The time was precisely 4.32 a.m., and the club was deserted, when the burglar alarm went off. At that precise moment, the thing that had triggered the alarm was captured on a security video camera: it was a semi-transparent young man in a white T-shirt coming through a solid locked door. The brief footage shows him prowling the corridors of the empty club like a thief in the night. But this was no ordinary prowler, for when the police and the club's manager and assistant manager arrived at the locked-up premises, there were no physical signs of a break-in, and there was no trace of the spectral burglar. When the police viewed the tape of the translucent intruder, they were amazed at the sight of the figure passing through the closed door. The tape was taken to the BBC and handed over to a group of technicians who employed a simple test to discover whether the tape was a hoax. Using the latest micro-chip technology they found that there was only one video signal on the tape — and this meant that no one had tampered with it. So the tape was genuine — but who was the intruder? No one knows. It was naturally assumed at the time that he was a ghost, but the nightclub has no history of hauntings. The anonymous prowler, consigned to the supernatural dustbin, is yet another example of those shadowy individuals featured in this book - the mysterious people.

> Tom Slemen
> Liverpool,
> England

DID JOAN OF ARC ESCAPE THE FLAMES?

Joan of Arc was born in the picturesque village of Domremy in 1412. She was not really French, as Domremy was in those times an independent duchy of Bar, in Lorraine - which did not join the Kingdom of France until 1776. Joan did not even regard herself as a Frenchwoman, yet today the 'Maid of Orleans' as she later became known, remains France's most celebrated heroine.

Joan was one of five children. She had three brothers and a sister who died at an early age. Joan's name was not d'Arc, as some official sources still state, but Tare - the former version of the name arose from a misspelling made by a sixteenth-century poet. Jacques Tare, Joan's father, was Domremy's leading citizen and prosperous enough to be a co-renter of a large chateau, as well as the keeper of the local cattle pound. Most accounts of Joan's life repeat the fallacy of the hard-working peasant girl, but although Joan was not over-cossetted, her parents looked after her well and she led something of a sheltered life. Her mother, Isabelle, was very religious and taught Joan her prayers and encouraged her attempts at embroidery.

As young Joan stitched away at her needlework, the Hundred Years' War between England and France, which began in 1337, was still raging. The conflict originated in English claims to the French crown during the reign of Edward III, and war finally broke out when Philip VI of France confiscated Gascony from Edward, who retaliated by siding with the Flemish rebels against Count Louis (a French ally) and by invading northern France. After Edward's archers and men-at-arms destroyed the French fleet at the battle of Sluys in June 1340, the King of England and his eldest son, the Black Prince, were attacked by the French army as they led their forces into Ponthieu. Although they were greatly outnumbered, the English were victorious because of their superior tactical expertise and the deployment of skilled archers who used the Welsh longbow - a much-feared weapon that was lighter and more accurate than the traditional crossbow.

Edward went on to take Calais, and a seven-year truce followed. The next phase of the war commenced with English raids in northern France, Languedoc and Normandy. A decisive victory was won by the Black Prince at Poitiers, but Edward did not follow up his advantage, so intermittent fighting ensued, and resulted in 20 years of an uneasy peace, punctuated by short battles. Then, in 1415, Henry V renewed the English claim to the French crown. In his first martial undertaking, Henry seized the strategically important town of Harfleur, and in the following month he revived England's military prestige when his army of 5,700 fought 25,000 French soldiers at Agincourt. The latter were undisciplined, and Henry's bowmen killed 8,000 of them. The English only lost around 400.

By 1419 the English had conquered Normandy, and the Treaty of Troyes in May 1420, arranging Henry's marriage to Catherine de Valois, made him heir to the French throne. After the premature death of Henry, in 1422, the English made further conquests, and the French people needed a saviour. They were to get one in the form of a softly-spoken teenage girl.

At the age of 13, Joan Tare was in her father's garden when she heard a strange disembodied voice coming from somewhere above her in the air, close by the local church. She heard the voice three times, and told her parents it had been that of St Michael, the Archangel. According to the teenager, the first time she had heard the voice of the Archangel, he had simply said, "Be a good girl and God will help you".

Joan's parents were naturally concerned about their daughter's farfetched story, and nervously dismissed the tale as the invention of a lonely adolescent. But Joan continued to hear the supernatural voices, and later told her mother and father that the beings who were communicating with her had now started to reveal themselves by materialising in the form of crowned heads. Joan claimed that she had recently touched the beings, and savoured their sweet scent and had even made a vow of chastity to St Michael. Then came the astounding message from the Archangel: "You will come to the aid of the King of France."

Joan was baffled and upset by the angel's prediction, but she listened carefully to the unearthly visitant's other commands. St Michael told her that she must go into France to the fortress town of Vaucouleurs. There she would find Robert de Baudricourt, the captain of that place, and he would give her the people who would follow her.

"But I do not even know how to ride a horse, never mind make war," Joan replied, yet over the rest of the week she felt a growing urge to carry out the angel's commands.

She finally decided that she must go to Vaucouleurs, despite her father's dire warning that if she went to France, he would drown her with his own hands.

Joan mounted a horse, and to her surprise, managed to ride off for Vaucouleurs with little difficulty. When she arrived at the town, Robert de Baudricourt would not have anything to do with her, but Joan refused to leave, and finally persuaded him that it would benefit the French nation if he would send her to the Dauphin (Charles VII) at Chinon. Baudricourt relented, and sent her to Charles, who she quickly convinced of her divine mission.

Joan underwent an incredible transformation, literally overnight. She cropped her hair, dressed in male attire and suddenly became a skilled horsewoman - a knight of France. Joan led the troops to Orleans, and on 8 May 1429, after four days of intense battle, relieved the town. The English panicked and withdrew, and Joan rode into Orleans in triumph. More victories followed at Jargeau, Beaugency and Patay (where the English army were routed), and Troyes.

On 17 July of that fateful year, which proved to be a turning point in the Hundred Years' War, the Dauphin was crowned and consecrated in Reims Cathedral. Joan Tare stood beside Charles throughout the ceremony with her battle standard in her hand, dressed in a green tunic and a rich mantle of red and gold. When the anointed king later rode in procession around the city, accompanied by Joan, thousands flocked to see him, and many who lined the procession route bowed at the teenage girl and touched her feet. She had done so much at such a young age, but dark days lay ahead.

In May 1430, she made an attempt to relieve John of Luxembourg's siege of Compiegne, but was captured after being knocked from her horse. She was imprisoned at Beaurevoir and then at Rouen, where she was put on trial in March 1431. Accused of heresy and witchcraft, Joan stood before Pierre Cauchon, the bishop of Beauvais, and Jean Le Maistre, the vice-inquisitor of France. After being found guilty, Joan was taken to a local cemetery, where a scaffold had been constructed, but she was not burned. Instead, she was forced to give a full confession and abjuration of her heresies, and the seriously ill and confused girl, thinking she was about to meet her death, confessed to worshipping evil spirits and invoking them. The guards then took her from the scaffold and put her back in a prison cell.

On 30 May 1431, the 19-year-old girl received confession before she was escorted to the market place in Rouen and declared a 'relapsed excommunicate and heretic'. She was tied to a stake nailed to a high platform, and the faggots of wood beneath it were set alight. Joan was cremated alive before a crowd of ten thousand. When the executioner later prodded about in the ashes, he shuddered when he found Joan's heart, completely intact.

And that, according to the history books, is where the story of Joan of Arc ends. But in May 1436, exactly five years after Joan was burnt as a heretic, a young woman who bore an incredible likeness to the Maid of Orleans turned up in the French town of Metz. What's more, this damsel claimed that she was Joan, but the first citizens who met the young woman called her an impostor. When Joan Tare's two younger brothers, Petit-Jean and Pierre heard of the woman who was impersonating their deceased sister, they rode off at once to track her down. At the village of La-Grange-aux-Ormes, two miles south of Metz, they watched in amazement as a knight in full armour rode across a field where a tournament was being held, expertly pulling stakes out of the ground. The brothers galloped up to the knight and Petit-Jean said, "Who are you?"

The knight raised her visor and the two brothers recoiled as they saw that it was Joan Tare. Petit-Jean and Pierre were struck dumb at the sight of their sister, and they suddenly noticed that most of the people at the tournament were soldiers who had served under Joan. The king's chamberlain, Nicole Lowe, was present, as was John of Metz, one of the maid's most loyal supporters. But how was this so? Joan had surely perished in the flames at Rouen. The returned martyr gave no explanation, but simply smiled enigmatically at her brothers.

Later, she accompanied them on a journey to Vaucouleurs, where she stayed for a week and went to see Robert de Baudricourt, who was naturally shocked at the sight of the girl who was supposed to have been burnt alive five years before. He took a close look at her face and trembled.

Around this time, Petit-Jean went to visit the king and told him that his sister was still alive. The king didn't seem too surprised, and instead of summoning Joan to his court, ordered his treasurer to pay Petit-Jean one hundred francs. According to the nineteenth-century historian Jules Quicherat, in his five-volume Trial and Rehabilitation of Joan of Arc (1841), the treasury accounts of Orleans for 9 August 1436 record that the council paid a courier who had brought letters from Joan the Maid. Quicherat also reveals that Joan's doppelganger met the king at Paris in 1440. Shortly before her arrival at his court, the king asked one of his men to impersonate him, but when Joan turned up, she was not taken in by the ruse, and demanded to see the real monarch. When the real king came out of hiding, Joan knelt at his feet, and the king said, "You are welcomed back in the name of God."

But Quicherat states that after the king and Joan had talked at length in private, the monarch suddenly declared that she was an impostor, although he never explained just how he had come to this conclusion. The woman who was identified as being Joan Tare by Petit-Jean and Pierre Tare, and the many soldiers who served under the Maid of Orleans, soon left Paris and was never heard from again. Was she really Joan of Arc? and if so, how did she escape the flames? To this day, no one has been able to answer these tantalising questions.

THE TURIN SHROUD

After the Crusades, the wandering mendicant friars of Europe were like travelling salesman dealing in holy relics. Pieces of the Virgin's gown, fragments of crusts from the Last Supper, and even the knuckle bones of St Peter were peddled in every town. Reformers such as John Calvin and Martin Luther condemned the religious pedlars, but relics were big business. One critic of the day calculated that a replica of Noah's Ark could have been built with all the pieces of Christ's cross that had been sold to the gullible!

The Roman Catholic Church also condemned the relic merchants, and at the end of the nineteenth century, the Vatican issued a proclamation stating that: 'No relic, be it the most sacred in Christendom, can be regarded as authentic'. Even today, 32 'genuine' nails from Christ's cross, and three corpses of Mary Magdalene, are venerated around the world!

One of the most famous alleged relics is the burial cloth, or shroud, of Christ. Its early history is unknown, but the cloth was said to have been kept hidden for three hundred years after the crucifixion of Jesus, during the Christian persecutions. It was later acquired by the treasury of the Byzantine rulers of

Constantinople. When the city was sacked in 1204, the Crusaders took the shroud to France, where it was kept at Besancon Cathedral, in the province of Doubs. After narrowly being destroyed by a fire at the cathedral in 1349, the shroud was presented to the Dukes of Savoy in 1432. Another fire almost consumed the cloth at the ducal palace, but the flames failed to do any serious damage to the strange image of a man displayed on the shroud. The relic was taken to Turin, where the dukes had another residence, and there it has been kept since 1578. Every 33 years (the supposed age of Christ when he died), the Holy Shroud of Turin was put on display for the thousands of pilgrims who flocked to see it.

Scientists and most learned men in the nineteenth century naturally regarded the cloth as a pathetic forgery, and who could blame them? Science and the Church were moving in separate directions - Darwin had virtually proven that man had evolved from the same ancestors as the primates, and the pieced-together fossil remains of dinosaurs were painting a very different picture of the earth's past from the halcyon tales of Eden in the Book of Genesis.

Then, in 1898, a rectangular strip of linen, four metres long by one metre wide, sent out shockwaves that were to rock the religious and scientific world for the next century. That year, Secondo Pia, a Turin photographer, was commissioned to take the first photographs of the cloth, which was said to be the burial shroud of Jesus of Nazareth.

On the so-called Shroud of Turin all Secondo could see was a ghostly, faint, yellowish-brown imprint of a human figure who was naked and bearded. Secondo thought nothing of the photographic subject - until he was developing the plates in his darkroom. On the plates was the crisp image of a man, not in negative - but in positive. Secondo was so shocked by the revelation, that he dropped one of the plates. The Shroud of Turin was apparently a photographic negative.

At the French Academy of Sciences, Dr Yves Delage, a brilliant physicist and zoologist, made it his goal to discover how the negative image of a man could have been put on the cloth, centuries before the advent of photography. Delage spent three years on his project, and tried a myriad of ways to reproduce an identical shroud. He employed fine artists, but even the most skilled ones could not recreate the image's exact tones. The artists even experimented with mediaeval pigments, but had to call it a day in the end. Delage was forced to admit defeat, but he thought that the formation of the image may have had something to do with the way the Jews of Christ's time treated their dead. Their most frequently used burial ointments were myrrh and aloes, and Delage conjectured that these compounds, reacting with the urea given off in sweat by a dead body, may have caused an ammonia-based substance which stained the shroud.

Delage, who was renowned for being an agnostic and a militant anti-Catholic, caused quite a stir when he presented his findings to the Academy of Sciences in 1902. He told his colleagues that the cloth had indeed been Christ's shroud, but this claim was greeted by an uneasy silence. His findings were rejected and the Academy even took the unprecedented step of refusing to print Delage's carefully presented evidence in their minutes.

For 30 years, Delage's findings were only discussed by learned men in private - none of them would go on record to discuss the shroud. It was left to another Frenchman - Dr Pierre Barbet - a forensic pathologist, to take a further look into the controversial relic, this time from a medical viewpoint. Barbet was intrigued by the clues in the image. He noted that the nail wounds were located in the wrists of the man in the shroud. Most traditional paintings of the crucifixion depicted Jesus with the nails driven through his palms. This was curious. Barbet got permission to experiment with dead bodies. When he nailed a body to a cross by its hands, he discovered that the weight of the body simply caused the corpse to fall from the cross. The hands could not support the weight. But when Barbet drove the nails through the wrists of a dead body, it was easily supported. And he learned one other strange fact from these experiments. When the nail pierced the wrist, it damaged the median nerve, which caused the thumb to retract into the palm - and the man in the shroud had retracted thumbs.

But the Shroud of Turin yielded its most astounding secrets in the 1970s, when two top European scientists were allowed to have a go at dating the cloth. They weren't permitted to use the Carbon 14 dating method, because that would have involved destroying a piece of the shroud in the process, so Professor Max Frei, a Swiss forensic scientist, and Professor Gilbert Raes, a Belgian authority on fabric, were forced to use their pooled deductive skills to throw some light on the shroud's age and origin.

Frei recovered 48 different samples of pollen from

the cloth. Pollen grains last indefinitely, and are one of the most helpful indicators of an object's age in forensic science. Most of the grains were from France and Northern Italy, which was to be expected - but seven pollen grains were from halophylic plants usually found in the Dead Sea region and other parts of Palestine. Gilbert Raes, meanwhile, had determined that the threads in the shroud derived from Middle-Eastern cotton plants. He also discovered that the threads - which were woven into a herring-bone twill weave - had been bleached before weaving. This was an extremely archaic practice.

All the new evidence seemed to signify that the shroud was authentic, and in 1974, another important discovery came to light. John Jackson and Eric Jumper, two US Air Force scientists, placed pictures of the shroud under a VP18 image analyser - a complex computerised device designed to generate three-dimensional images from two-dimensional photographs of the moon's surface.

The results were breathtaking. When viewed under the VP18 scanner, the face of the figure in the shroud literally popped up off the cloth. It was the face of a bearded man who looked remarkably like the traditional pictures of Jesus. The find unearthed a new mystery - how could a two-dimensional image contain so much three-dimensional information? This question was never answered satisfactorily.

Finally, in the 1980s, scientists were given permission to cut samples from the shroud to solve the mystery once and for all. In October 1988, these scientists announced that the Shroud of Turin could not be the burial cloth of Christ, because three independent carbon-dating tests had proved that the shroud's linen was made from flax cut between AD 1260 and 1390.

Many believers in the shroud were devastated, and some naturally questioned the reliability of the dating method employed by the scientific investigators. But the radiocarbon dating test of the shroud was impeccable in its execution. Minute pieces of the linen were delivered to laboratories in Arizona, Zurich and Oxford, along with control samples of linen that were known to belong to the Middle Ages, and to ensure that the tests were carried out without any bias, only the co-ordinator of the experiment knew which samples were genuine.

Although the results of the dating test proved that the shroud did not originate from the first century, there are still many unanswered questions. If the image on the shroud is not a depiction of Jesus, who does it represent? And if it is a fake, by what process was the image applied to the cloth? Scientists are still at loggerheads over the procedure that a thirteenth-century artist could have employed to create the shroud's realistic representation of a man who has undergone crucifixion. Even under the electron microscope there are no definite traces of the hypothetical artist's brushstrokes. Furthermore, the argument that the shroud is a mediaeval forgery fails to explain why the image on the cloth shows a man who had nails hammered through his wrists. All other mediaeval painters believed (wrongly) that Christ was nailed through the palms. How did the shroud-forger know the truth? How did he know that Christ did not wear a crown, but a cap of thorns - as depicted in the shroud? Consider, also that the man in the shroud is naked, and it was considered blasphemous to depict Christ in such a way in mediaeval times.

Here are three logical possibilities. Firstly that the scientists are not telling us the truth, perhaps because they have proved that the shroud is genuine, and therefore must admit that Jesus did exist and that he was a very unusual man. Perhaps fearing the ideological controversy that would ensue, they chose to discredit their own findings. The second possibility is that the shroud depicts a person who is not Christ, but some extraordinary man (perhaps a follower of Jesus) who was crucified between 1260 and 1390. This theory is unlikely, as no nation in the Middle East used crucifixion as an execution method during that period.

The remaining possibility is that the shroud was created by an artistic genius with a detailed knowledge of antiquity. Which artist in the late thirteenth to early fourteenth century fits the bill? The great 'Renaissance Man', Leonardo Da Vinci, was not born until 1452, and the first sighting of the shroud occurred at Constantinople in 1203, some 249 years before his birth. Yet this first mention of the shroud by military chronicler, Robert de Clari, does not tally with the time window given by the scientists. De Clari says he saw the 'sydoine' (shroud) bearing 'the figure of our Lord' during the sacking of Constantinople by the Christian knights of the Fourth Crusade. According to de Clari, the shroud was snatched by someone during the turmoil and never seen again. But this first historical mention of the cloth suggests that the estimated date of the shroud's manufacture by the scientists who carbon-dated it is erroneous. They are at least 57 years out. And the description de Clari gives of the shroud in Constantinople compares well with the shroud in Turin.

Another sinister aspect of the shroud is that the image suggests that blood was still flowing after the body was wrapped in it. Some think it suggests that Jesus was not dead when he was taken from the cross. There have also been hypothetical discussions recently among genetic engineers who think it may be possible to tackle the shroud mystery by analysing the genetic information that may be found in microscopic samples scraped from the holy cloth's bloodstains. This sampling could possibly provide a genetic profile of the man on the shroud that would give his ethnic origin, eye colour, and many more physical characteristics. A yet more controversial possibility would be the cloning of the shroud man, using a genetic technology similar to that depicted in the sci-fi film *Jurassic Park*. It could happen in the not-too-distant future.

THE A38 HITCH-HIKER

During the early hours of a rainy autumn morning in 1958, Harry Unsworth, a long-distance truck-driver, was driving his vehicle along the A38 towards a depot in Cullompton in Devon, when he noticed the silhouette of a man about 300 yards in front of him, standing in the middle of the road.

Unsworth slowed down and stared beyond his busy windshield wipers at the figure up ahead. He was middle-aged, with a mop of curly grey hair, and he wore a saturated grey raincoat. The man produced a torch from his pocket and flashed it straight at Unsworth, who responded by braking hard and pulling up his truck. Unsworth wound his side window down to get a better look at the hitch-hiker.

The man just stood there on the road, looking up at the driver in his cab with a dripping, expressionless face.

"Come on then!" Unsworth shouted impatiently. "Get in if you're going to!"

The man then slowly climbed into the driver's cab, and in a well-spoken voice asked Unsworth to drop him off four miles down the road at the old bridge at Holcombe. As they drove on into the night down the deserted road, the hitch-hiker suddenly started chuckling to himself. Unsworth glanced at him to try and find out what he was laughing at, but the stranger turned his face away and looked out of the passenger window, still sniggering to himself for no apparent reason. Unsworth asked him what was so funny, and the man suddenly turned towards him, his face contorted into an eerie smile.

"Did you know there was a real tragic pile-up here a few years ago?" he asked. "Arms and legs everywhere, and blood all over the road - horrible!"

He continued to recount grisly stories about all the traffic accidents that he'd witnessed on that stretch of road. Unsworth had seen a few disturbing automobile crashes himself in his time, but the hitch-hiker's gruesome blow-by-blow accounts of the injuries and fatalities really turned his stomach. He eventually told him to shut up, and was only too glad to be rid of his morbid passenger when the truck reached the agreed drop-off point at the old bridge. Three days later, Mr Unsworth was driving his truck through the dead of night along the same section of the A38, when he came across the same hitch-hiker once again. As before, he stood right in the middle of the road, flashing a torch and waving his arm.

With a sickening sense of deja vu, and a deep sense of foreboding, Unsworth pulled up beside the man, who again asked to be dropped off at the old bridge at Holcombe. This time the man said nothing throughout the journey, but kept smiling to himself and looking at Unsworth out of the corner of his eye. His sneaky behaviour made the truck-driver's flesh creep. When the man got out at the bridge, he didn't offer a word of thanks and walked away into the darkness.

A month after that, Unsworth was again heading along the A38 to the truck depot when he saw the dreaded hitch-hiker again, standing in the same stretch of road as before. Even the weather was the same as it had been on the two previous occasions: torrential rain. And the hitch-hiker's request? To be dropped off four miles down the road at the old bridge.

Understandably, Unsworth was decidedly reluctant to give the man a lift, but decided to take him to the confounded bridge for one last time. This time, the hitch-hiker remained silent during most of the journey, but occasionally burst out laughing.

On the following night, Harry Unsworth was again on the same route to the depot. As his vehicle neared the section of the A38 where the oddball had a habit of appearing, he anxiously scanned the road ahead. But on this occasion, the hitch-hiker was nowhere to be seen.

There was then a gap of three months before Unsworth found himself driving along the A38 again. He was whistling in his cab as he approached the place where he had first set eyes upon the hitch-hiker. He remembers smiling to himself as he thought about the crazy man with the torch. He also remembers the sight that wiped the smile off his face. Standing in the pouring rain in the middle of the road was the grey-haired man, waving his torch frantically.

Unsworth stopped next to the lunatic and wound

down his window, and was astonished to hear the same hackneyed request. At this point Unsworth was more intrigued than scared, and he dropped off the man at the bridge again - but this time the hitch-hiker broke the repetitive pattern by asking him to wait whilst he went to "collect some suitcases", because he wanted to go to a destination further down the road this time.

The best part of 20 minutes elapsed and the man still hadn't returned to the truck, and as Unsworth was running to a tight schedule he couldn't afford to wait any longer. So he started up the vehicle and drove on.

Three miles down the road, Unsworth's heart jumped when he saw the hitch-hiker waving his torch in the middle of the road again. He was baffled as to how the man could possibly have travelled such a distance in so short a time. He obviously hadn't hitched a lift, for no vehicles had passed along the deserted road, and this realisation gave Unsworth the creeps. He tried to steer around the sinister figure, but as he did so, the hitch-hiker dived head-first into the path of his truck!

Unsworth slammed on the brakes and almost jack-knifed his vehicle. He leapt out of his cab expecting to find a flattened corpse, but there was nothing there. Forty feet away stood the hitch-hiker, swearing at the lorry-driver. He started to jump up and down with derision and waved his first at Unsworth. And then - he simply melted back into the night!

Unsworth ran back to his vehicle and drove off at high speed. He never encountered the A38 apparition again, but the solid-looking ghost continues to appear to other unfortunate motorists.

In December 1991, a woman driving to Taunton on the A38 was rounding a bend near the village of Rumwell, when she saw a man in a grey raincoat flashing a torch at her in the middle of the road. She couldn't brake in time and was forced to swerve her vehicle into a ditch. She was fuming as she got out of her car, ready to give the suicidal jaywalker a piece of her mind, but was amazed to find that the road was completely deserted in both directions. The man with the torch had mysteriously disappeared. The same figure has been seen on the same stretch of the motorway as recently as 2010, but why the ghost goes through the same unending cycle is still unknown. People who fail to confront some fear or to acknowledge some traumatic event often relive it over and over in recurring nightmares, and I feel that this is the case with the troubled, and apparently earthbound spirit which haunts the A38; he is probably some solid-looking carnate essence of one of the numerous people who have perished in car accidents on that dangerous stretch of road over the years.

THE BOY FROM NOWHERE

In the secluded fairytale state of Bavaria on the Whit Monday morning of 26 May 1828, a youth of about 17 years of age came hobbling down the almost deserted cobblestoned streets of Nuremberg. A cobbler named George Weichmann watched the young stranger, who was dressed in tattered clothes and was walking with a stiff-legged lurch through Unschlitt Square. The teenager made a pathetic moaning sound as he limped by, and the shoemaker, suspecting that he was ill, approached and offered him help. The boy seemed very confused, and mumbled something unintelligible before holding out a letter to Weichmann. The letter was addressed to 'The Captain of the 4th Squadron, 6th Cavalry Regiment, in Nuremberg'.

The cobbler was so intrigued by the bedraggled boy and his letter that he took time out to locate the captain of the 4th Squadron. He made enquiries at the New Gate guardroom, and was given the captain's address by an official. When Weichmann called at the military man's house, a servant said that his master was not home, but admitted the cobbler and the scruffily-dressed boy and offered them refreshments. The servant and the cobbler watched spellbound as the youth attacked a loaf of bread, devouring it like a wild animal. He also guzzled down a pitcher of water, but for some reason shied away from the ham and beer on the table. A candle which illuminated the gloomy side of the room soon caught the waif's attention. He walked over to it, mesmerised, and attempted to pick up the flame, and let out a scream when he burned his fingers.

The cobbler and the servant repeatedly quizzed the boy, but his only answer to every question was "Weiss nicht" (Don't know).

The other servants of the captain's household came down to look at the strange boy. They watched with amusement as he trembled in fear upon seeing the swinging pendulum of the old grandfather clock. He backed away from the timepiece in trepidation, seeming to regard it as if it were alive.

When Captain Wessenig finally arrived home, he found his servants standing in a circle around the boy, and asked what all the commotion was about. When he was told, he asked to see the letter that he carried. Its contents were two, badly-spelled, clumsily-phrased notes, fastened together. The first note read:

Honoured Captain,

I send you a lad who wishes to serve his king in the Army. He was brought to me on October 7th, 1812. I am but a poor labourer with children of my own to rear. His mother asked me to bring up the boy, and so I thought I would rear him as my own son. Since then, I have never let him go one step outside the house, so no one knows where he was reared. He, himself, does not know the name of the place, or where it is.

You may question him, Honoured Captain, but he will not be able to tell you where I live. I brought him out at night. He cannot find his way back. He has not a penny, for I have nothing myself. If you will not keep him, you must strike him dead or hang him.

The second note was dated October 1812, and ran:

This child has been baptised. His name is Kaspar; you must give him his second name yourself. I ask you to take care of him. His father was a cavalry soldier. When he is seventeen, take him to Nuremberg, to the Sixth Cavalry Regiment; his father belonged to it. I beg you to keep him until he is seventeen. He was born on April 30th, 1812. I am a poor girl; I can't take care of him. His father is dead.

As Wessenig perused the letters, the boy suddenly perked up and smiled at the captain. He then shouted out two intriguing sentences: "I want to be a soldier like my father!" and "Horse! Horse!"

Captain Wessenig was baffled by the letters, and dismissed the young ragamuffin as "either a primitive savage, or an imbecile". He had the boy taken to the police station, where what seemed to be a breakthrough occurred when the foundling was given a pencil and a sheet of paper. The policeman told the boy to write his name, and he obediently scrawled two legible words in upper case that read: 'Kaspar Hauser'. Further prodding from the policeman to continue, merely prompted the boy to say, "Don't know".

Police Sergeant Wust recorded a detailed description of the boy in a notebook. According to Wust, Kaspar Hauser was a sturdy, broad-shouldered lad of around 17 or 18 years, with a healthy complexion, light-brown hair, blue eyes, and rather small hands and feet. His clumsy gait was caused by the cluster of blisters on the soles of his unusually tender feet, presumably caused by walking a long distance. His worn-out clothes didn't seem to belong to him - the old hat, baggy trousers and badly-torn shirt were much too large, and his boots, which were reinforced with horseshoes, were too tight. The boy's toes - which protruded from them - were caked in clotted blood.

Sergeant Wust's search of the boy's clothes resulted in some curious finds. In the trouser pockets he found a packet of salt, a rosary, and two printed religious tracts, none of which provided the faintest clue to the abandoned lad's identity.

Not knowing what to do next, the police lodged Hauser in a cell. The jailer who watched him all night told Wust, "He can sit for hours without moving a limb. He does not pace the floor, nor does he try to sleep. He sits rigidly without growing in the least uncomfortable. Also, he prefers darkness to light, and can move about in it like a cat."

A physician who later examined the boy claimed that the youth's ability to sit motionless for hours was due to a distortion of his knee joints, caused by lengthy periods spent sitting with his legs straight in front of him when young, and this would account for the shaky gait he exhibited when he walked. The doctor also said that the youth was neither insane nor dull-witted, but had apparently been forcibly prevented in the most disastrous way from attaining any personal or social development. The doctor's inspection of Hauser also confirmed that the boy could see in the dark better than in daylight, and revealed that his senses of hearing and smell were outstanding. The boy could identify animals by their scent alone, and distinguish trees by the scent of their leaves.

As the story of the mysterious teenager spread, hundreds of curious Nurembergers gathered outside Hauser's cell. They scrambled for a view through the barred window to see the oddity eat, drink, sleep and defecate.

As the weeks went by, Hauser's vocabulary seemed to expand steadily, and he was soon able to offer a fairly detailed account of his past life. This account was printed and circulated around the city as a pamphlet entitled, Bulletin Number One - concerning the Child of Nuremberg. The leaflet, which was signed by Burgomaster Binder of Nuremberg, stated:

He neither knows who he is, nor where he came from, for it was only at Nuremberg that he came into the world. He always lived in a hole, where he sat on straw on the ground; he never heard a sound, nor saw a vivid light. He awoke and slept and awoke again; when he awoke he found a loaf of bread and a pitcher of water beside him. Sometimes the water tasted nasty, and then he fell asleep again, and when he woke up he found a clean shirt on; he never saw the face of the man who came to him. He had two wooden horses and some ribbons to play with; he was never ill, never unhappy in his hole, because he simply didn't know of any other type of existence ...

One day the man came into his room and put a table over his feet; something white lay on the table, and on this the man made black marks with a pencil which he put in Kaspar's fingers. This the man did several times, and when he was gone, Kaspar imitated what he had done. At last he taught him to stand and to walk, and finally carried him out of his hole. Of what happened next Kaspar has no very clear idea, until he found himself in Nuremberg with a letter in his hand.

The pamphlet turned Hauser into a celebrity overnight. He was talked about all over Europe. Who was he? Where was he from? were the questions on everybody's lips. The town press of Nuremberg printed thousands of handbills bearing Mauser's image, each carrying an appeal that read, "Anyone possessing knowledge of his true identity, or any intelligence pertaining to the same, should immediately come forward to inform the authorities and collect a cash reward."

As the handbills were being distributed, police agents were making a thorough search throughout Bavaria for the place were Hauser had been imprisoned. But no one ever came forward to collect the reward on offer, and the drawn-out police search ultimately proved futile. Anselm Ritter von Feuerbach, an eminent jurist and criminologist from Germany, visited Hauser and interrogated him for hours, and concluded that the boy's account of his early life up to his arrival in Nuremberg was genuine. The renowned lawyer also hinted that he had solved the Hauser enigma and intimated that it involved an epic scandal, but he refused to go into more detail and quickly left the city.

Rumours abounded naming Kaspar Hauser as the illegitimate son of almost every aristocratic rake of

Europe. The theory went that Hauser had been kept hidden away by his high-born parent for 16 years before finally being turned loose when it was judged that time had eradicated the danger of a scandal.

Professor George Friedrich Daumer, a distinguished educationalist and philosopher, was appointed to be Hauser's guardian. Daumer was fascinated by the boy's incredible naivety. He watched an amused Hauser look behind a mirror after glancing into it, and on another occasion saw him stroke a ball that had bounced into his lap, as if he regarded it as an animate being. Daumer also discovered that Hauser was ambidextrous and had some artistic talent. This artistic faculty was soon developed under Daumer's guidance, and within a matter of months, Hauser was executing exquisite pencil drawings of still life and rural scenes.

In the summer of 1829, Professor Daumer helped his protégé write his autobiography. In the August of that year the book was published, but it proved to be something of an anti-climax, for the autobiographical work threw no new light on the Hauser mystery. It looked as if the people of Nuremberg were losing interest in their lionised citizen, but their interest was rekindled in a most dramatic way when reports circulated of an attack on Hauser.

On the afternoon of 7 October 1829, the teenager was found prostrate in Professor Daumer's cellar. He was unconscious, his shirt was torn to the waist, and he was bleeding from a gash in his forehead. He was carried upstairs and put to bed, where he gradually regained consciousness and Daumer was able to ask him to give an account of what had happened. Hauser said that he had been attacked by a tall, sinister-looking assailant wearing a top hat, black silken mask, dark clothes, and black leather gloves. The masked man had struck Hauser once with a heavy cosh, and then fled.

What was the motive behind the attack? This was just another unanswered question of the Hauser enigma. When several people came forward saying they had seen a suspicious-looking character leaving Daumer's house, the police combed the area, but the attacker was never found. The authorities now believed that Hauser was in danger, and moved him from Daumer's house to the home of a certain Freiherr von Tucher. The jurist Anselm Ritter von Feuerbach was summoned to become his new guardian. Two police constables were also assigned to be Hauser's bodyguards, and they both slept in the same room as him.

In May 1833, von Feuerbach suffered a paralytic stroke and died. He had been compiling a detailed report on his ward, and many thought the chronicle would finally reveal the answers to the Hauser mystery. The report, entitled Example of a Crime Against the Life of the Soul of a Man, stated that Hauser was a legitimate child, because no one would go to such lengths to hide a bastard offspring. Therefore, von Feuerbach speculated, Kaspar Hauser had to be in line of succession to a very high position - a position exalted enough to facilitate Hauser's removal and cruel confinement. Since Hauser's confinement was voluntarily brought to an end after a certain period of time, it followed that some other person had taken over the position formerly usurped from Hauser. And according to von Feuerbach, the only position that was exalted enough to justify such clandestine manipulations was a royal one.

After his controversial conclusion, von Feuerbach left the pages blank, because as a lawyer he knew he would be libelling the crown (a most serious offence in the nineteenth century) if he so much as pointed the finger of suspicion at any particular royal family member. Von Feuerbach's thesis was translated into most European languages, and was followed by rumours claiming that von Feuerbach had not died from a stroke at all, but had been poisoned by people in high places who thought the German criminologist was getting too close to the truth.

Curiously, the eccentric English aristocrat Lord Stanhope suddenly took an interest in the Hauser case. He visited Germany and convinced the Nuremberg Council to give him permission to lodge the teenager in the town of Ansbach, some 25 miles away from Hauser's then residence. A friend of Lord Stanhope, Dr Meyer, was appointed as Hauser's tutor, and Captain Hickel, a military officer, was given the task of protecting the boy. Hickel must have been somewhat embarrassed when, on the afternoon of 11 December 1833, the boy he was supposed to be shielding from harm came staggering through the doorway with a deep knife-wound in his abdomen. Hauser had gone out earlier that day to enjoy a walk through the deserted, snow-covered Hofgarten, Ansbach's public park.

"Man ... stabbed!" gasped the mortally wounded Hauser. "Knife! Hofgarten ... gave purse ... Go look ... quickly!"

Dr Meyer and his wife came running to the teenager's aid, and Captain Hickel raced to Hofgarten, hoping for a confrontation with the assailant. Hickel only saw Hauser's set of footprints as he trudged through the snow in the park, but he found the silk purse Hauser had mentioned. He picked it up and opened it. It contained a baffling note written backwards in mirror writing:

Hauser will be able to tell you how 1 look, whence I came from, and who I am. To spare him that task, I will tell you myself. I am from ... On the Bavarian border ... On the River ... My name is "M.L.O."

But contrary to the note's claims, Hauser did not know who the man was, or where he was from. But from his deathbed he managed to tell an interesting story about that fateful day. He said he had gone to the park to meet a man who had contacted him earlier by sending a message through a labourer. The man, who was described as tall, with dark whiskers and wearing a black cloak, approached him in the park with the question, "Are you Kaspar Hauser?" When Hauser nodded, the stranger handed him a silk purse. As Hauser opened it, the man suddenly stabbed him before running off. Kaspar dropped the purse and stumbled homeward through the snow.

A massive manhunt quickly got underway, but the tall, dark-whiskered man was never caught, and some wondered if he had ever existed, for he left no tracks at the scene of the crime.

Until Kaspar Hauser slipped into a coma on the afternoon of 17 December, Dr Meyer continually asked him if he had inflicted the wound himself to get attention, and Hauser's persistent answer had been a shake of his head. Later that day, minutes before Hauser passed away, he was heard to say, "I didn't do it myself".

The post-mortem, performed by three doctors, revealed that a sharp instrument had come through the diaphragm just below the ribcage and had been thrust upwards until it penetrated the heart. Two of the doctors were certain that the murderer had been left-handed, and one said he was absolutely sure that Kaspar Hauser could not have stabbed himself.

Today, the debate still rages. Some think Hauser was a hoaxer who craved attention, while others think he was the victim of a conspiracy. A monument now stands marking the spot in the Ansbach park where Hauser was stabbed, and the Latin inscription upon it states: On this place, for mysterious reasons, one mysterious figure was murdered by another mysterious figure.

Not far away from the monument, in Ansbach Cemetery, the epitaph on Hauser's gravestone reads: Here lies the Riddle of our Time. His Birth was Unknown, his Death, Mysterious.

THE UKRAINE'S GIANT SPIDER

The following creepy tale has been buzzing around the Internet for years and has also appeared in various tabloid newspapers in Europe, but has never been reported in the British or American press.

In the summer of 1990, police in Russia found a resident in a block of flats in the Ukraine, lying dead on the floor of an elevator. The man had two puncture holes in the side of his neck, which was badly bruised yellow and blue. At the post-mortem, the coroner established that the man in the elevator had died through shock and loss of blood. About 1.5 litres of blood were missing from the body, yet there had been no bloodstains in the elevator. It was as if something had sucked the blood straight out of the dead man, but the Russian police couldn't accept such an outlandish explanation.

A month later, the police were called to the same block of flats because a girl of 13 was trapped in the elevator, which was stuck between the fourth and fifth floors. Residents had heard the girl screaming frantically, and when the police arrived with three members of the local fire service and gained access to the elevator her screams had stopped. They found the child lying on the floor of the elevator. She was dead, and two small puncture marks were later found on the girl's left breast, which was heavily bruised. The residents understandably refused to use the faulty elevator, and were convinced that a vampire, or some other blood sucking creature was at large in the block of flats.

Police attempted to play down the seemingly unsolvable deaths, and one former KGB propaganda minister suggested that the girl had probably died after injecting heroin, but the dead girl's parents threatened to sue the official, because their daughter had never taken drugs and no syringe was found in the elevator.

To try and get to the bottom of the matter, a Russian detective and a sergeant entered the lift and rode it continuously up and down. The two men were armed with pistols and carried flashlights and two-way radios.

But nothing happened until three days later, when the lift was travelling upwards and it suddenly halted between the fifth and sixth floors of the building. The lights went out, so the men switched on their torches and two-way radios to alert their colleagues, who were playing cards in a police van in the street below. The two trapped men waited apprehensively, perhaps wondering if some ghostly vampire was about to materialise. There was complete silence for about three minutes; then they heard something scuttling about above their heads. Something was moving along the roof of the elevator. The detective noticed a black square - almost a foot across - set in the roof of the elevator, where an access panel had come away. The lift was so old that the panel had probably fallen off because of rust. He shone his torch through the square hole in the roof, and the beam from his torch lit up the lift shaft above and the steel cables supporting the lift. Something peered back through that hole that made the detective's blood turn to ice. A black, hairy head, the size of an orange, with a bunch of black, gleaming eyes, the size of grapes, peered down at him.

The sergeant was revolted by the freakish-looking animal and raised his Beretta and aimed it at the thing, but the detective calmly ordered him not to fire yet.

"What the hell is it?" said the petrified police sergeant, trembling, almost dropping his torch with nerves.

"Turn your torch off," hissed the detective.

"What? No way! I'm sorry, sir, but I'm not taking my eyes of that, that - thing," the sergeant protested, sweating heavily.

"You can tell it doesn't like light," said the detective. "You keep your torch on, then, and I'll turn mine off. Don't make any sudden moves, and tell the men downstairs to stand by."

The detective switched off his light, and watched as first one long, hairy leg and then another, slid further into the lift. Suddenly, the sergeant's nerves got the better of him, because he had three phobias: fear of the dark; fear of enclosed spaces; and arachnophobia - a fear of spiders - and that horrible thing hanging through the hole in the ceiling looked like a hideous overgrown spider. So the sergeant freaked out and in his panic he dropped his torch - and his nerves cost him his life. The torch hit the floor and smashed. Before the detective could switch on his torch, the enormous hairy black spider had dropped into the lift with lightning agility, and had bitten the only thing in the lift that was moving excitedly. The spider sank its giant fangs into the unfortunate sergeant's face, and hung on like a vice as it sucked out his blood.

The detective switched on his torch and watched in impotent horror as the whole nightmarish drama unfolded. The sergeant was screaming hysterically, and the spider was like some alien creature from another planet. Its body was the size of a Jack Russell dog, and its eight hairy legs were almost three feet long. The freak insect's mouthparts were still embedded into the sergeant's face, and as it drained his life-blood, the spider's body throbbed and turned a deep rubric red.

The terrified detective forced himself to act. He took aim and shot twice at the sickening spider. The first shot missed, and the second bullet blasted one of the spider's legs off, but when the bullet ricocheted off the wall, it bounced back and smashed the torch bulb. The lift was once again plunged into absolute darkness. The sergeant suddenly stopped screaming and his body hit the floor with a dull thump, and the detective felt sick as he felt bristly hairs brushing against him as the wounded spider scrambled past and climbed back up to its lair through the hole in the elevator's roof.

When the police and firemen opened the elevator, they found the dead sergeant, whose terror-stricken face was bruised and bloody - and on the floor, in the corner, sat the traumatised detective. Nearby on the elevator floor was the long, hairy, black leg of the spider, still twitching. The detective remained speechless for a while, then blurted out the incredible story.

The Russian authorities quickly hushed up the incident, but news of the story leaked out via the Internet, and a version of the story also appeared in a Turkish newspaper, but was quickly denounced as an fabrication or at least, exaggeration.

It was claimed by some that the giant spider was a deformed black widow spider that had been mutated by the radioactive fallout from the recent Chernobyl nuclear plant disaster. Later reports on the Internet said Russian troops had destroyed the spider with a flame-thrower, and had then discovered that the insect had laid dozens of eggs in a large cocoon at the top of the lift shaft.

WAS HOMER A WOMAN?

The stirring tales of the *Iliad* and the *Odyssey* have been thrilling readers since they were penned by a blind Greek poet named Homer in the eighth century BC. But what do we know of Homer? Not much, according to the historians. They say that it is quite possible that the Ionian poet never existed; Homer may have been the name of a group of writers who collectively wrote the *Iliad* and the *Odyssey*, as well as the mock-heroic Greek poem, *The Battle of the Frogs and The Mice*, and the so-called Homeric hymns.

The Iliad and the *Odyssey* as we know them today are based on texts that were edited in the sixth century BC. The Athenians tampered with a considerable proportion of the *Iliad* text to increase their role in it, and in the second century BC, two scholars - Aristarchus of Samothrace and Aristophanes of Byzantium - meddled with the wording of the *Iliad* in Alexandria. The extant texts are substantially those of Aristarchus.

So much for the classical texts, but what information do we have on the man who is supposed to have authored them? The Greek historian Herodotus (c485-425 BC) tells us that Homer's mother, Critheis, an impoverished orphan, lived in Smyrna, Asia Minor. After becoming pregnant out of wedlock, she left Asia Minor and settled at a place near the River Meles in Greece, where she gave birth to a son whom she named Melesigenes (after the river). Melesigenes was known in his later years by the nickname of 'Homer' - which means 'blind man' in Greek. Critheis later returned to Smyrna and secured employment as a housekeeper to a music and literature teacher named Phemius, whom she later married. Phemius took to his stepson as if he were of his own flesh and blood, and tutored him daily in music and the written word. As a result, young Homer excelled at school and upon the death of his stepfather was appointed to run it, soon gaining the status of a local celebrity. He later became friends with a wealthy traveller from Leukas named Mentes and accompanied him on a tour of Italy, but upon reaching Ithaca, he caught an eye infection that worsened until he was almost blind. Mentes reluctantly left his friend in the care of a doctor called Mentor, and continued on his journey. Mentor had a vast knowledge of the legendary exploits of Odysseus and the Trojan War, and Homer, being a good listener, took in every detail of the doctor's tales. When the *Odyssey* was written many years later, Homer immortalised Mentor by naming the teacher of Odysseus's son after him.

Mentor could not find a remedy for Homer's eye infection, and Homer decided to make an attempt to return home before his predicament worsened, but he had only got as far as Colophon, in Asia Minor, when he became totally blind. He was taken back to Smyrna, where he decided to dedicate himself to poetry, and having no school to provide him with any financial support, set out to live the life of a wandering poet. Homer's meanderings brought him to a place called the New Wall (Neon Teichos) where he earned a meagre living by reciting verse. He later drifted to Cumae, where he begged the town council to support him for his poetry recitals, but one waspish councillor complained that if Cumae fed every blind man who came to the city, the people would soon be overrun with vagrants.

The council decided not to fund Homer, who left and travelled from town to town for many years, until he finally settled at Chios, where he was employed to teach the children of a wealthy man. Homer became so well-liked at Chios that the inhabitants later claimed that Homer had been born among them. Tales of the blind poet's wisdom reached Greece, and when Homer visited the island of Samos, he was regarded as a sort of godlike figure, and was asked to take part in the religious festivals. He left Samos, bound for Athens, but upon reaching the island of Ios, he suddenly became seriously ill and died from what was probably a stroke.

After Homer's death, stories of the legendary poet travelled throughout Greece, Italy and Spain, and the bards of those countries began to recite Homer's poems. The *Odyssey* and *Iliad* were suddenly held in such esteem that they were recited and re-enacted every four years at the Panathenaea festivals in Athens.

That then, is a summary of Homer's life, according to Herodotus, a historian who has been criticised for credulity and reckless interpolation, but admired for his charming narrative. Herodotus named the bird of immortality 'Phoenix' after confusing the mythical creature with 'phoinix' - the Greek name for the palm tree which the bird was said to sit upon. It is no wonder then, that many scholars have treated the Greek historian's account of Homer's life with caution; some students of history regard his version of the bard's life as an outright work of speculation based on legends and figments of his imagination.

One such notable person was the English satirist, novelist and translator, Samuel Butler (1835-1902). Butler stunned the literary world in 1897 with the publication of his book, The Authoress of the *Odyssey*, in which he defended his long-held conviction that Homer was a woman. What led the writer to this unusual conclusion? Well, Butler re-read the *Odyssey*, and while perusing the part of the book that describes the enchantress, Circe, he was struck by the depth of her character in comparison with the stilted, almost wooden males of the work. Butler suspected that a woman, and a young one at that, may have been the elusive author, and not the blind old man of legend. Butler read on and began to see more clues in the text, such as in the description of a rudder on the front of a ship, which suggested that the authoress had no idea of seamanship - a male skill. Homer clearly wasn't too familiar with woodwork either, because he (or she) tells us how seasoned timber was cut from a growing tree. Butler noted these errors and many more to back up his 'Homera' hypothesis, and concluded his work by identifying Princess Nausicaa, the daughter of the *Odyssey*'s Queen Arete, as Homer. Butler also deduced that Nausicaa's home town was Trapani, on the west coast of Sicily, a conclusion he reached after sifting through the text of the *Odyssey* for geographical details.

Butler's book was largely ignored by the scholars of his day. Professor Benjamin Jowett, Oxford's celebrated expert on Ancient Greece unashamedly admitted that he had not even bothered to glance at Butler's book. Despite rejection from the cognoscenti, Butler managed to convince George Bernard Shaw, Robert Graves and many other writers that the person who laid the foundation stone of western literature was a woman. Although Butler's theory is entirely plausible, it has been almost totally ignored by modern scholars.

A STRANGE SCOTTISH PROPHET

In the year 1600, Coinneach (Kenneth in Gaelic) Odhar was born on the Isle of Lewis in the Outer Hebrides. Odhar was a poor farm labourer until tales of his prophetic powers reached the ears of his feudal overlord, Lord Mackenzie of Kintail. Lord Mackenzie was so intrigued by the stories of the Scot's mysterious talent that he summoned Coinneach to live on his land at Brahan Castle, near the Firth of Cromarty. Shortly after Coinneach's arrival on the Brahan lands, Lord Mackenzie died, and was succeeded by one of the Earls of Seaforth.

The 'Brahan Seer', as Coinneach was known, was taken on as a resident prophet of the Seaforth family, and he lodged in a sod-roofed cottage on the Brahan estate. Some doubted his purported powers of second sight, and one such doubter, an elderly man named Duncan Macrae of Glenshiel, asked the Brahan Seer to tell him how he would end his days. Coinneach Odhar told Macrae that he would die by the sword. Many laughed at this prediction; after all, who would stoop to killing an old man with a sword?

But years later, in 1654, the English General George Monck was leading a troop of Parliamentary soldiers up towards Kintail, and a company of his men encountered old Duncan Macrae, who was walking across the hills to his home. The soldiers challenged Macrae - who was unfamiliar with the English tongue - and he panicked and reached for his broadsword. A nervous English soldier reacted to the old man's sudden movement by hacking him to death with a sword - exactly as the Brahan Seer had predicted years previously.

In 1630, the Seer was crossing a vast expanse of moorland when he suddenly stopped and soliloquised: "Oh! Drummrossie, thy bleak moor shall, ere many generations have passed away, be stained with the best blood of the Highlands. Glad I am that I will not see the day! Heads will be lopped off by the score, and no mercy shall be shown."

The Brahan Seer was accurately describing the battle of Culloden that would be fought in the area 116 years later, when the Duke of Cumberland's Royal troops completely routed the Highlanders of the Young Pretender, and many heads were indeed lopped off. Cumberland's barbaric tactics at Culloden earned him the title of 'Butcher'.

Another of the Seer's predictions that was regarded as nonsense at the time, was his assertion that, one day, strings of black carriages, horseless and bridleless, would pass through the Highlands, drawn by a fiery chariot. That was the only language available to the seventeenth-century oracle to describe the railways, and their colossal, fire-burning steam engines, that were to come to the Highlands in the Victorian era.

The Brahan Seer also declared that ships would one day sail round the back of Tomnahurich Hill. Those who laughed at the seemingly ridiculous prophecy never lived to see the construction of Thomas Telford's Caledonian Canal, which linked the North Sea with the Irish Sea, via the Great Glen. The great canal cut a path round the back of Tomnahurich Hill, and so it came to pass that ships, or at least barges, were able to sail behind the hill - 150 years after the Brahan Seer prophesied that it would be so.

The Celtic soothsayer also foresaw three Scottish ecological disasters. The first of these has already come to pass. The Seer predicted that a Loch above Beauly would burst its banks and destroy, in its rush, a village in its vicinity.

In 1967, an unusually heavy rain storm was responsible for causing the hydro-electric dam at Torachilty to overflow, and this in turn caused the River Conlon to burst its banks. The ensuing flood destroyed buildings, cattle and crops, and created havoc for the village of Conlon Bridge, which is only five miles from Beauly. The second, as yet unfulfilled prophecy of the Brahan Seer states that when 'Loch Shiel in Kintail shall become so narrow that a man shall leap across it, the salmon shall desert the Loch and the River Shiel.'

The third bleak prophecy concerned 'horrid black rains' that will fall on the land. Perhaps the Seer is describing a type of acid rain, or perhaps even fallout from an atomic war, or a nuclear-power plant disaster, like the one that occurred in the 1980s at Chernobyl.

In the end, the Brahan Seer sealed his own fate with one of his prophecies when he told the Countess of Seaforth that her husband had a mistress in Paris. The Seer was correct about the adulterous affair, but the Countess was so outraged by the information, that she ordered that the psychic should be boiled in tar as a warlock. A classic case of shooting the messenger.

The Seer was taken to Chanonry Point on the Moray Firth to be executed, but shortly before he was cruelly boiled alive in a barrel of molten tar he made his last prediction, which concerned the future of the Seaforth family. He said that the last of the Seaforth line would be deaf and dumb, and added that the inheritor would be a 'white-hooded lassie' who would kill her sister.

One hundred and fifty years later, in January 1815, Francis Mackenzie, the last of the line, died of a sinister illness that left him deaf and dumb, and two years afterwards, his eldest surviving daughter, Mary, who inherited his estate, was wearing the traditional white hood to mark the recent death of her husband as she drove a carriage through woods. With her was her sister Caroline, and during the journey, the ponies bolted and the carriage overturned, injuring Mary and killing Caroline. So the Brahan seer's last predictions also proved to be true.

DID SHAKESPEARE EXIST?

What do the following eminent individuals have in common? Charles Dickens, Sigmund Freud, Charles de Gaulle, Daphne du Maurier, Mark Twain, Walt Whitman, Benjamin Disraeli and Charles Chaplin.

The answer is that none of them believed that the 38 plays attributed to Shakespeare were actually written by the great bard. Freud thought that Shakespeare had nothing to justify his claims, and believed that the real author of *Hamlet* and *King Lear* was the Seventeenth Earl of Oxford, Edward de Vere.

It is somewhat ironic that Mark Twain and Charlie Chaplain held the view that Shakespeare could not have produced the plays credited to him because he was a mere country bumpkin, lacking in education. Yet Twain himself was born in a small frontier village and left school at eleven years of age, while Chaplin, who experienced an impoverished childhood after his father died, received his first taste of education at the Hanwell poor law institution!

One of the first people to doubt that Shakespeare existed at all was a Dr James Wilmot, an associate of Samuel Johnson and a fellow of Trinity College, Oxford. Wilmot researched the Bard of Stratford for four years, and in 1785 reached the conclusion that the plays of Shakespeare were penned by none other than Sir Francis Bacon. Just what led him to this conclusion will never be known, for upon Wilmot's death, his housekeeper for some reason threw the fruit of his researches onto the fire.

Anyone who has slogged their way through one of Bacon's scientific essays will scoff at Wilmot's claim, but adherents to the Bacon theory (who call themselves Baconians) assert that their candidate certainly had the educational background to produce the plays and chose the name 'Shakespeare' as a mere nom de plume. They point out that Shakespeare's works indicate that the author was a true Renaissance Man, with a vast knowledge of law, history, seamanship, medicine and the Continent - just like Bacon.

If we are to believe that the Baconians have a case, then there must have been a gigantic conspiracy in the late sixteenth century, and the conspirators would have included the rector of the Stratford church where the records of Shakespeare's birth, marriage and death are kept, along with the baptismal records of his children. Other individuals would also have been implicated in the Bacon Conspiracy: people like Ben Johnson, King James, Queen Elizabeth I, the Second Earl of Southampton, the Second Earl of Essex, and the 26 members of Shakespeare's acting troupe, the King's Men.

Far fetched? Not according to the Baconians, who cite two pieces of information to back up their argument. The first piece of 'evidence' concerns an enigmatic inscription on Shakespeare's monument in Poet's Corner at Westminster Abbey. Upon the monument's marble scroll, there is an inscribed quotation from The Tempest, Shakespeare's last play. The quotation has been hacked about and is laced with apparently intentional spelling mistakes, but a line in the middle of the inscription stands out, because, for some unaccountable reason, it contains only two words: 'Shall Dissolve'. Cryptologists have now discovered that if the letters of those two words are set out in the 13 squares of a well-known seventeenth-century cipher, they do indeed spell out: Francis Bacon.

Alexander Pope, who had a hand in the erection of the Shakespeare monument in 1741, was a master of cipher, and was probably behind the encoded message on the marble scroll. If so, what was he trying to say? That Bacon was Shakespeare?

Another curious fact came to light in 1989 when a producer from Yorkshire Television's documentary programme, *First Tuesday*, obtained permission to X-ray Shakespeare's grave in Stratford's Holy Trinity Church, which is visited by thousands of tourists every year. The results of the X-ray proved, beyond a shadow of a doubt, that Shakespeare's 'grave' was completely empty. Nothing was there - not even the slightest trace of the bard's bones.

In March 1994, a book called *The Shakespeare*

Controversy by Graham Phillips and Martin Keatman was published. The book claimed that the most famous playwright of all time was a secret agent who used his theatrical career as a cover. In a nutshell, the authors' theory is that through his fellow playwrights, Christopher Marlowe and Anthony Munday, Shakespeare was embroiled in a network of spies, informers and saboteurs led by Sir Walter Raleigh and Sir Francis Walsingham, a puritanical Protestant and one of Queen Elizabeth's principal Secretaries of State. The authors point out that the idea of Shakespeare as an agent in the Elizabethan Secret Service is not as absurd as it first seems. So many in his circle certainly were - people like Munday, Marlowe, and Shakespeare's patron, Lord Strange, who was involved with the government network of spies. Lord Strange informed Sir William Cecil of the Hesketh Plot, a planned Catholic conspiracy to overthrow the government.

The authors of the book go on to say that William Shakespeare's sudden death in 1616 was probably the result of being poisoned by Raleigh, who had just been released from the Tower. Raleigh had been imprisoned after being accused of being a spy by a mysterious agent named William Hall - perhaps an alias for Shakespeare? So upon his release, Raleigh quickly sought out the agent who had put him behind bars and exacted his revenge.

What are we to make of all this? Are the Baconians right? Was Shakespeare a spy? And does it really matter in the end? Whoever he was, he left us with a magnificent legacy of plays and sonnets which are still performed and read all over the world. As the Bard himself wrote in *Romeo and Juliet*: 'What's in a name? That which we call a rose, by any other name would smell as sweet.'

THE MYSTERIOUS MR CAVENDISH

History records that Sir Henry Cavendish, the English scientist and natural philosopher, was born in Nice in 1710, but the exact circumstances of his birth were said at the time to be bizarre - and some apocryphal sources say that a child substitution took place.

The great genius of the eighteenth century studied at Cambridge University, but decided to leave in February 1753 without earning a degree, because at that time, in order to be awarded a degree, students at the famous university had to declare that they were believing Christians and practising members of the Church of England. Cavendish was not prepared to lie, and admitted that he could see no logic in religion and so could not receive a degree.

Now for the first mystery regarding this unusual man. Despite having no degree, and without having written a single scientific paper, Sir Henry was warmly welcomed as a member of the prestigious Royal Academy of Science in 1760, at the age of 29. Cavendish's entry into the highly respected Academy was unprecedented, and no one has since entered the scientific fraternity without a degree.

Thirteen years after he became a member of the Academy, Cavendish suddenly became fabulously rich, literally overnight. The source of this vast wealth has never been traced - some contemporaries of the scientist thought the money was an inheritance, while others hinted that the fortune was accrued from an aristocrat as payment for a lucrative alchemical process that Cavendish had discovered. When Cavendish's bank heard of his newly-acquired wealth, his banker immediately wrote to him, advising him to invest the huge sum. Cavendish wrote back, warning the banker: "Sir, my private financial affairs are my own business. Kindly look after the sum of money I have already deposited with you. If you bother me again, I will take out all my money!"

As far as his banker was concerned, Cavendish was wasting his money by giving it away to numerous charitable causes. For instance, one day Cavendish heard that the young student who catalogued the books in his library was experiencing dire financial troubles, and immediately sent the young man a draft for ten thousand pounds sterling. An excessive gesture by anyone's standards!

This was by no means an isolated act of philanthropy. Cavendish literally gave away millions of pounds to hundreds of impoverished individuals - yet still had millions left in his coffers when he died. He bequeathed most of his riches - which included ownership of a canal and several grand buildings - to his distantly related heirs.

Upon his death it also transpired that Cavendish had

been a principal stockholder of the Bank of England. But around the time that he acquired his mysterious wealth, his behaviour had become increasingly bizarre. He settled in London at a house in the street that nowadays bears his name, close to Clapham Common. At the rear of his house he had a stairway built which was meant to be used by the female staff. Cavendish apparently thought that women were an incompatible species, and the maids were given strict orders to stay out of his sight - if he chanced to bump into a female domestic at his house, he would fire her immediately. He shunned contact with almost everybody, and resorted to leaving his staff specific instructions regarding his well-being on written notes left on his hall table.

With virtually no interruptions, the solitary Cavendish could devote all his time to his remarkable scientific experiments. He made a number of breakthroughs in the field of chemistry, and in 1798 he even constructed an ingenious device consisting of suspended metal balls, a mirror and a candle, that allowed him to calculate the weight of the earth for the first time in history. Cavendish also formulated a hypothesis about the deviation of light rays in the vicinity of the sun's mass. This theory was corroborated centuries later by Einstein's Theory of Relativity.

The neurotic genius also experimented with electricity, and long before Volta and Galvani, he told disbelieving colleagues at the Royal Academy of Science that electricity was the means by which the brain controlled muscles, and he also predicted that this mysterious force would change the world. But the scientific fellows at the Academy only laughed at the strange hermit. They thought that he was mad because he rejected Christianity in favour of Hindu philosophy, and eccentric because of the array of seemingly empty glass tubes that he was continually hoarding. In 1921, researchers discovered these tubes in Cavendish's laboratory and found them to be filled with rare inert gases.

One strange-looking tube containing argon had electrodes fitted at each end, suggesting that Cavendish had passed an electric charge through it to make the tube of gas light up like the modern neon-light tube. Another tube had elaborate mirrored electrodes inside, which suggests that he was on the brink of creating an argon laser. Fortunately, Cavendish did not let his prototype death-ray see the light of day in 1777. Perhaps he envisioned the horrific consequences of a laser-armed British Empire. The year 1777 was a turning point in the War of American Independence, and the battle of Stillwater would have had a very different outcome if General Burgoyne had deployed an argon laser cannon!

Sir Henry was also fascinated with space, and seemed to sink into a kind of hypnotic trance whenever he looked at the face of the moon. He would stare at the lunar disc for hours, perhaps with a burning desire to explore that beckoning globe. One night, during the Royal Society Club dinner, a crowd of scientists were looking out of a window, smiling and chatting about something that had caught their attention. Cavendish, who was seated on the other side of the room, presumed that the scientists were observing the moon, so he got up and joined them, only to see, to his disgust, that the learned men were enthralled with the sight of a beautiful young woman who was leaning out of a window in the house opposite. Cavendish turned abruptly and marched back to his seat with his jaw set and his head bowed. Shortly before his death in March 1819, Cavendish rang a bell to summon his servant. When the servant arrived at his sickbed, Cavendish said, "Listen carefully to what I have to tell you. I'm going to die. When I am dead, but not before, go and tell Lord George Cavendish." The servant was shocked by this bald statement, and, concerned about the fate of his master's soul, presently returned to his bedside and nervously mentioned the administration of the last sacrament. Cavendish seemed puzzled by this suggestion and simply replied, "I don't know what you mean. Bring me some lavender water and come back when I am dead."

Within the hour, Sir Henry Cavendish was dead. In his will he left millions to his heirs, as well as a set of specific instructions regarding his interment. He recorded in his will that he should be buried in a specially-built vault in Derby Cathedral (without any examination or post-mortem). The vault was to be walled up immediately and no inscriptions were to be made to identify the tomb. These strange instructions were carried out by his heirs on 12 March 1810.

Today, we have hundreds of Sir Henry's papers written in a strange, symbolic shorthand which form but a rudimentary sketch of a peculiar individual who was seemingly born centuries too early. Where did a man who had no university degree get his extraordinary futuristic technological insights from?

And, for that matter, why has no one ever been able to trace the source of Cavendish's incredible wealth? Hundreds of years after his death, the lonesome scientist still remains a fascinating enigma.

WHO'S ON OUR MOON?

According to present estimates, the moon was probably formed around the same time as the Earth and the other planets of the solar system, around 4,600 million years ago. During the first 700 million years the moon was bombarded by gargantuan rocks from space - the interplanetary debris left over from the solar system's formation. These impacts were responsible for the massive craters we now see in the NASA photographs of the lunar surface. It's thought that this continual bombardment in the moon's early history melted its outer crust, and that when the barrage of mountain-sized meteorites had diminished, the molten rock gradually cooled at the top and became solidified in the almost absolute cold of space. This solidified top stratum contains abundant traces of feldspar, zircon, pyroxene, olivine, aluminium, calcium and sodium, as well as small amounts of magnesium, iron, and even radioactive uranium.

There is also a surprising amount of oxygen contained in moonrock. If we treated two and a half tonnes of the stuff with a chemical reducing agent, it would release a tonne of oxygen - sufficient to keep a lunar settler alive for three years. Although oxygen and other gases are locked up in the lunar crust, the moon, unlike Earth, does not have any protective atmosphere, and so the surface is exposed to dramatic temperature extremes (-180°C in the shade to +110°C in direct sunlight). In short, according to the astronomical textbooks, the moon is a hostile, airless globe, completely devoid of any life. But this doesn't seem to be the case at all when we take into consideration the hundreds of well-documented reports from astronomers and astronauts who have seen strange things on the surface of our closest celestial neighbour. Only in recent years has the term, 'transient lunar phenomena' (invented by the British astronomer Sir Patrick Moore) been included in astronomy textbooks. Transient lunar phenomena, or TLP, is a term used by astronomers to label the host of strange objects that have been observed on the moon over the centuries.

One early example of TLP was recorded in the eighteenth century by William Herschel, the brilliant British astronomer who discovered the planet Uranus. On 18 August 1787, Herschel looked through his telescope and sighted a red sparkling glow on the dark half of the crescent moon that resembled 'slowly burning charcoal, thinly covered with ashes'. On 12 November that same year, two other astronomers witnessed bolts of lightning on the moon.

A little under a year later, on 26 September 1788, the German astronomer Johann Heronymus Schroter, saw a dazzling white point of light shining among the peaks of the lunar Alps near to the crater Plato, which lasted for 15 minutes. Seven further sightings of activity on the lunar surface by professional moon-gazers are noted in Volumes XXVI and XXVII of *The*

Philosophical Transactions of the Royal Society. One of these controversial reports was penned by none other than the Astronomer Royal, the Reverend Nevil Maskelyne, who saw a strange cluster of lights moving across the dark half of the lunar disc.

In July 1821, the German astronomer, Franz Gruithuisen - the originator of the meteoric impact theory of lunar cratering - saw brilliant flashing points of light on the surface of the moon. When he announced that he had discovered a lunar city, his colleagues ridiculed him, and Gruithuisen burned the notes of his observations. Five years later, on the night of 12 April 1826, a professional astronomer named Emmet recorded a sighting of an enormous black cloud moving across the moon's Sea of Crises, or Mare Crisium.

Over half a century after this sighting, another odd lunar spectacle was observed by several independent astronomers: a 'luminous cable' which gradually stretched from west to east, until it completely spanned the crater Eudoxus. The line of light lasted for almost an hour, then blinked out.

Lights and clouds are not the only inexplicable things that have been seen on the moon. On 4 July 1881, two 'pyramidal protuberances' appeared on the moon's limb (the outer edge of the lunar disc), but as the world's most powerful telescopes were scrutinising these gigantic structures, they seemed to fade away. A year after this bizarre 'mirage', moving and stationary shadows were sighted in the vicinity of the crater Aristotle. The shadows seemed to be cast by an enormous object that was difficult to make out because it was the same colour as the lunar crust.

On 31 January 1915, astronomers were shocked to see a luminous shape in the Littrow crater that resembled the Greek letter gamma. This same luminous shape was later spotted near the crater Birt, and an account of it was printed in the highly respected Astronomical Register in London.

Other 'glyphs' have been seen too. A radiant 'X' has been seen in the shadows of the crater Eratosthenes many times over the years, and a strange, glowing, chequered shape has been sighted in the Plato crater on more than one occasion.

In 1899, another mystery of lunar origin was created when the scientific genius Nikola Tesla began broadcasting high-powered radio signals into space from his laboratories in Colorado Springs. Seconds after the experimental broadcasts, the dials of Tesla's radio equipment began to register an intelligent sequence of radio signals. Tesla had heard the howls and static from the aurora borealis and solar disturbances, but the signals he now heard were clear and suggested a mathematical order. Furthermore, they were definitely not echoes of Tesla's original signals. Tesla pondered on the meaning of the signals, and later wrote, 'The feeling is constantly growing on me that I have been the first to hear the greeting of one planet from another.'

Besides Marconi, no one else in the world had the technology to broadcast such radio signals in 1899. Tesla initially suspected that intelligence on Mars was the culprit, but upon further consideration concluded that the speed of the reply to his own signals suggested somewhere much closer, and the moon seemed to be the only logical answer. A radio signal from the moon takes around one and a quarter seconds to arrive, whereas from Mars, because it is so far away, it takes up to 23 minutes.

Strangely enough, around the time Tesla was apparently receiving signals from an extraterrestrial source, Marconi was transmitting the letter 'V, in Morse code, to his assistants 50 miles away, when something inexplicable happened. Marconi also received a signal of unknown origin, which seemed to be in some sort of code similar to Morse.

He wrote down the mysterious message and saw that the code contained the Morse code for 'V, as if something was replying to his original transmission. Marconi believed the signal had been broadcast from space, but kept his opinion to himself for years. When he finally told the New York Times about the signals, the reaction of members of the public was to either be frightened, or amused, by the claims.

More unearthly signals were picked up at the dawn of the radio age. In the 1920s and early 1930s, mystifying radio bursts were received from the moon, the most spectacular signals being the ones received by Dr Van der Pol in October 1929. Dr Van der Pol, of the Philips Research Institute at Eindhoven in Holland, had transmitted radio call-signs of different durations at 30-second intervals in September 1928. Three weeks after the transmissions, Van der Pol was flabbergasted to receive echoes of his original transmissions.

Curiously, something had happened to the original signals - they now contained delay intervals (in seconds) of 8, 11, 15, 3, 8, 8, 12, 15, 13, 8 and 8. More echoes of this transmission were received throughout

February 1929 on radio sets all over the world, and the same transmission was picked up again in October 1929. It was even heard for the fourth time in the 1940s, all of which defies explanation. The Van der Pol echoes suggest that the original message had been intercepted, interpreted and re-broadcast by something out in space. The general consensus in the 1930s was that the signals were of lunar origin. In July 1953, a spectacular change occurred on the moon's surface that was witnessed by astronomers all over the world. An enormous 'bridge-like structure', of over 12 miles in length, was seen stretching across part of the Sea of Crises. John J O'Neil, the former science editor of the *New York Herald Tribune* was one of the first to see it, and he was at a loss to explain it, because no astronomer had sighted such a bridge before. Another witness to the strange spectacle was the eminent British astronomer and lunar expert HP Wilkins, who was interviewed by BBC Radio about the bridge. He struck fear into listeners by remarking, "It looks artificial. It looks almost like an engineering job. It's very straight and definitely solid, as it casts a shadow."

The bridge across the Sea of Crises is now nowhere to be seen. It has vanished as mysteriously as it appeared.

In 1956, a year before the start of the Space Race, radio telescopes around the world reported a code-like chatter coming from the moon. In October 1958, the same radio emissions were heard, but on this occasion, the culprit was spotted by American, British and Soviet astronomers through optical telescopes as well. A small globular object was spotted whizzing towards the moon at 25,000 miles per hour. Some astronomers said the object was a meteorite, but that such an object would not have been able to transmit high-powered radio signals.

Ten years later, on 21 December 1968, two more unidentified interplanetary objects were tracked by the optical and radio telescopes of the world. The two saucer-shaped objects in question were apparently accompanying Apollo VIII as it orbited the moon. It is alleged that Borman, Lovell and Anders - the three astronauts on board Apollo VIII - saw the UFOs at close quarters, and also heard weird, unintelligible voices which broke in on the special channel used to communicate with mission control. The UFOs later darted away from the American spacecraft and descended towards the lunar surface. It has been alleged for many years that most of the astronauts on the Apollo missions encountered UFOs on and around the moon, but NASA has always strenuously denied the claims. All the same, manned and unmanned lunar exploration has produced many unanswered questions.

A year after Apollo XI had landed on the moon, the following article appeared in the *Daily Telegraph* on 10 July 1970:

MYSTERY OF THE MOON SPIRES
From our New York Staff

Photographs of the lunar surface have revealed objects that appear to have been placed there by intelligent beings, it was claimed yesterday.

Mysterious spires on the Moon were said to have been revealed by Russia's Luna 9 and America's Orbiter 2 spacecraft four years ago.

The claims were made in the *Argosy* magazine, which said the Russian and American spacecraft had photographed groups of solid objects at two widely separated locations.

The two groups of objects are arranged in definite geometric patterns and appear to have been placed there by intelligent beings.

The photographs taken by Orbiter 2 showed what appeared to be the shadows of eight-pointed spires shaped like Cleopatra's Needle.

The Russians believed that their probe, Luna 9, had photographed some sort of monument, but NASA wouldn't confirm this verdict. The spires stood in the Ocean of Storms in a formation almost identical to the 'abaka' alignment that the ancient Egyptians used. In fact, the spires were arranged in precisely the same way as the three great Egyptian pyramids on Earth.

After studying TLP for decades, two Russian scientists, Mikhail Vasin and Alexander Shcherbakov, came to the controversial conclusion that the moon was an artificial satellite of the Earth that had been put into orbit about our planet at some time in the distant past by intelligent beings from another solar system. This unusual hypothesis was instantly dismissed as nonsensical by the international scientific community, but unknown to the two Russian freethinkers, a much-respected American astronomer and astrophysicist named Morris Jessup had come to the conclusion in the 1950s that the Moon was a base for UFOs. Jessup too had scoured astronomical records for references to lights and other strange phenomena seen on the moon, and noticed that the strange lunar activity corresponded with UFO activity on Earth. He published his theories in 1955, but no one took him seriously. Some naturally regarded him as a crank, but this 'crank' had discovered many double stars, and as well as teaching astronomy and mathematics at Drake University, had erected and supervised the largest refractor telescope in the southern hemisphere for the University of Michigan.

Alas, in 1959, Jessup was found dead in his estate wagon in Dade County Park, Florida. A hose leading into the car had been attached to the exhaust pipe. It looked like suicide, but close friends of the scientist strenuously argued that Jessup was not the sort of person who would kill himself, and shortly after his death there were rumours that he had been disposed of by sinister individuals because he had found out too much about UFOs. Strangely enough, shortly before his untimely death, Jessup had announced that he had made a breakthrough regarding the UFO problem.

According to Vasin and Shcherbakov, the Moon would be found to be a hollow metal sphere which housed enormous atomic engines and other mechanical workings. They also asserted that the metallic hull of the 'spaceship' moon - estimated to be about 40 miles thick - had been cratered by collisions with asteroids during its wanderings through the cosmos.

Oddly enough, there is now evidence which suggests that the moon does indeed have a metallic shell. This finding was made in November 1969, when several highly sensitive seismometers were set up by the Apollo XII astronauts on the moon's Sea of Storms to measure lunar tremors, or 'moonquakes'. Shortly afterwards, when the Lunar Module ascent stage had taken the astronauts back up to the orbiting Command Module, the astronauts sent the discarded ascent stage of the Lunar Module back down to the lunar surface. The disused spacecraft impacted into the moon's surface and was smashed to pieces. The shock wave from the impact was picked up from the lunar seismometers on the moon's surface, and when NASA scientists back on Earth heard the data transmissions, they couldn't believe their ears. The moon's crust was ringing like a gigantic bell, and continued to ring for nearly an hour. When all of the seismological data had been fed through the computers at Houston, NASA admitted that the Moon seemed to be behaving like a hollow sphere with a metallic layer some 30 to 40 miles deep.

NASA created more artificial moonquakes to retest their lunar seismometers in April 1970, when the spent third stage of the Saturn V booster rocket, from the ill-fated Apollo XIII, was sent crashing into the moon. The booster rocket hit the lunar surface and exploded with a force equal to 11 tonnes of TNT, just over 87 miles from the site where the seismometers had been set up. Again, the moon's crust emitted a ringing sound, this time for an incredible duration of 90 minutes. NASA rechecked the seismological data, and again established that the data indicated that the moon had a metal shell.

The moon held another surprise for the Apollo programme. The orbits of spacecraft about the moon were often distorted by areas of the lunar surface where the moon's gravity field was particularly intense. NASA called these puzzling high-gravity areas 'mascons' - short for mass concentrations. What causes these mascons is still a mystery.

Even today, in these post-Apollo, post-Space Shuttle times, the moon remains a mysterious but alluring place. There is still no consensus regarding its origin, or age, and strange lights and other inexplicable phenomena are still regularly seen on the lunar surface. In 1996, it was reported that the Pentagon had sent a number of military probes to the moon in the late 1980s and early 1990s. There were rumours that the US military had been testing nuclear weapons on the lunar surface, but the Pentagon furiously denied the claims.

According to a February 1996 feature in Britain's *UFO Magazine*, the Pentagon's military lunar probes had been sent to photograph strange structures on the moon from close quarters with complex hi-tech cameras. The magazine published an astonishing photograph of a tower-like object on the moon's surface near the crater Ukert, estimated to be over two miles in height. The photograph had allegedly been leaked from the Pentagon's files and released to the public via the Internet. It is claimed that the tower, which is said to be nicknamed 'the Shard' by Pentagon officials, was constructed by UFO occupants who use the moon as a base, but as expected, the US military denies that the photograph was sent back by their probes. What then, is the purpose of the Pentagon's lunar probes? That information is still classified, say the officials in the US Defence Department - leaving us to speculate just what secrets the moon still holds.

China landed an unmanned six-wheeled 120 kilogram lunar rover probe named Yutu – "Jade Rabbit" – on 14 December 2013. It was the first soft-landing of a probe on the Moon since 1976, and Jade Rabbit is the first mobile probe to roam the lunar surface since the Soviet Lunokhod shut down in May 1973. Jade Rabbit has ground-penetrating radar which will investigate the top soil and to a depth of around 98 feet and the radar will also probe the structure of the lunar crust to several hundred meters. The probe has two panoramic cameras to scan the lunar surface in 3D and it also carries a host of other scientific instruments, including spectrometers for the infrared and X Ray regions of the spectrum. China's next goal is to send astronauts to the Moon, and this might hopefully re-ignite another Space Race, as the exploration of the Cosmos in general has become rather lethargic in the East and West in recent decades. Many private firms are now eyeing the Moon and the asteroids and nearer planets as tourist destinations and also sources of minerals and other materials. Perhaps when the new invasion of our natural satellite begins, we will finally discover the truth about the strange activity that has been taking place on our Moon, and who knows, we may finally come face to face with the "Lunarians" – I hope they are friendly.

THE MURDER THAT WASN'T

On August 16th, 1660, 70-year-old William Harrison, conscientious steward to Lady Campden, set out on a three-mile walk from the English town of Chipping Campden to Charringworth in the Cotswold hills. He was off to collect rents for Lady Campden, and had told his wife that he expected to return home by early evening at the latest.

By 8 p.m., Harrison's wife was still waiting for him to return. She had a strange feeling that something had happened to her husband, so she sent out a servant named John Perry to look for him. The hours dragged by, but there was still no news of Harrison — or Perry. By 3 a.m., Mrs Harrison was frantic with worry and sent her son Edward out to look for the missing men. Edward met John Perry on the road leading to Charringworth, and the servant said he had looked everywhere for Mr Harrison but that he was nowhere to be seen. Edward and Perry embarked on another search of the surrounding countryside, but failed to find any trace of the missing man.

On their way back from the futile search, they met a man who told them that William Harrison's hat and collar had been found covered in blood at a roadside. Both articles had been slashed with a blade.

News of the suspected murder swept through the town of Chipping Campden, and a massive search party headed out of the town and into the countryside. The woods were thoroughly searched, and every ditch was inspected, but no traces of Harrison nor any vestiges of a murder were found.

The traumatized Mrs Harrison started yelling at John Perry, calling him a murderer and a robber. Perry was brought before the magistrate on the following morning and interrogated about his movements on the day of the disappearance. Perry admitted that he had not searched for Mr Harrison as Mrs Harrison had instructed him because he was scared to go into the countryside on his own in the dark, but he had been too ashamed to return to the village to admit his fear. He had spent the night hiding in a henroost until midnight, when a full moon came out from behind the clouds to light up the countryside. Perry said he had then mustered up enough guts to begin a search, but became lost in a thick mist and ended up sleeping under a hedge.

The magistrate was angered by the unbelievable yarn, and Perry was kept in custody for a week while another search was made for Harrison. But this hunt was also in vain. It was as if William Harrison had vanished into thin air.

Perry suddenly announced that he had information relating to the mysterious disappearance of his master, but was only prepared to communicate his knowledge to the magistrate. The judge agreed to his wish, and Perry told the magistrate that he knew for sure that Harrison had been murdered, but could not reveal the identity of the killer for personal reasons. The magistrate demanded to know the murderer's identity and grilled the servant for hours, until finally, Perry confessed that his own mother and brother had killed the missing man.

The magistrate was furious. He had known the servant's mother for years, and refused to believe John Perry's accusation. But the servant was adamant that he was telling the truth, and started to elaborate on the causes of the murder. He said, "Ever since I took up my post at the Harrison household, my family have been urging me to steal little things for them. They recently started to become interested in when the rents were being collected by Mr Harrison so that they could waylay him. I told them I would not become involved with such a crime, but my mother kept reminding me how poor the family was. They pressured me so hard that I told them what they wanted to know - what routes Harrison took at certain times, and the amount he would be carrying. They planned to knock him unconscious before making off with the rent money, but the old man cried out for help, and my brother panicked and strangled him. He and my mother dumped the body in a field before making off with the money."

"Then how did they forget to hide the hat and collar that was found?" asked the magistrate.

Perry told him that his mother and brother had deliberately left the items at the roadside to mislead any searchers.

Joan Perry and her son Richard were arrested, and although no body was found at the spot in the field specified by the servant, Joan and Richard had no alibi for the time of the murder.

In September, Joan, Richard - and John Perry, were brought before Sir Christopher Tumor at Gloucester Assizes. The judge said that as there was no body, there was no evidence that a murder had been committed. But as Joan and Richard sighed with relief at the judge's ruling, another case was introduced against them - a separate case of robbery. A year earlier, William Harrison's house had been broken into and the thieves - who were never caught - made off with a sum of £140. In the light of the murder accusation, the Perrys seemed to be the only natural suspects. They were advised to confess to the robbery without fear of any punishment, because of the Act of Pardon and Oblivion issued by King Charles II. This unusual act was introduced to forgive the horrors perpetrated during the Civil Wars, and it covered any crimes prior to May 1660. So, with the act in mind, the Perrys decided to confess to the robbery, knowing that they would be pardoned. They were, but the judge then placed the murder case before Sir Robert Hyde. In March 1661, Hyde sentenced John Perry and his mother and brother to death. It had been a peculiar case. John Perry had changed his testimony, saying that he had been in a state of insanity when he made his original statement. He swore that he had made up the story about his mother and brother killing Harrison, but the court assumed that the servant was simply trying to talk his way out of hanging.

On Broadway Hill, the Perrys were hanged one after the other. Until the noose broke their necks, they screamed that they were innocent. Not one of the jeering spectators believed their desperate claims. So imagine how these people felt when William Harrison turned up in good health a year later.

Harrison strolled into Chipping Campden two years after his supposed murder and told his wife that he had spent the last couple of years working as a slave in Turkey! On the day of his disappearance, he had been attacked by three men who took him on horseback across England to Deal in Kent, where he was put on board a ship. The ship sailed off, but weeks into the voyage, it was chased and captured by Turkish pirates, who took all the passengers to a slave market. Old Harrison was purchased by a wealthy 80-year-old Turkish doctor who employed the Englishman as a servant in his house. After a year in the service of the doctor, Harrison saw that his master's health was worsening, and when the doctor dropped dead, Harrison sold his deceased master's belongings and made enough money to pay for the passage home.

Nobody believed this incredible far-fetched tale, but Harrison stuck by his story for the rest of his days.

Could it be that Harrison really spent his two missing years trying to start a new life — perhaps with a mistress? This would have been out of character for a man who faithfully served Lady Campden and cherished his wife. But surely his exotic adventure was purely a romantic invention - unless, as the old saying goes, stranger things happen at sea.

THE GHOST THAT HELPED KOJAK

Shortly after 3 a.m. on the morning of February 27th, 1957, the late American actor Telly Savalas - famous for his role as Theo Kojak in the eponymous television series of the 1970s - was driving home from his cousin's house on Long Island, New York. Halfway through the homeward journey, Savalas heard the engine of his car splutter, before stalling, and he realized he'd ran out of gas.

The actor left the car and walked through heavy rain to the red neon-sign burning in the distance. It turned out to be an all-night diner. A young man at the counter told Savalas how to get to the nearest garage. He walked outside and pointed to a poorly-lit lane, and told him, "Walk right down there, sir, and you will come to a freeway. Turn right at the freeway and you will see a gas station about three hundred yards away."

Savalas thanked the man and set off down the dark secluded lane. He was halfway down the lane when he heard a noise behind him. Savalas turned, and saw a black Cadillac crawling along the road with its headlights off. The driver wound his side window down and shouted in a high-pitched voice, "Do you want a lift?"

Savalas was obviously wary about accepting lifts from strangers in the dead of night in New York - especially from drivers snaking about with no lights - but there was something trustworthy about the driver. He seemed quite sane and decent, and the rain was heavy, so Savalas decided to accept the stranger's kind offer. He got in the vehicle and sat in the front passenger seat.

"Where do you want to go?" asked the driver.

"Er, the nearest gas station, please. You turn right at the end of this lane and it's three hundred yards down the freeway," Savalas replied.

The man didn't speak, and there was an eeriness about him that unnerved Savalas. The man never tried to make conversation at all. He just sat and looked over the wheel and didn't seem to blink. He stared at the lane ahead with a grave look.

"Where are you headed yourself?" the actor asked, as he surveyed the man's smart attire: a black tuxedo, white silk shirt and a black bowtie. His raven hair was oiled and slicked back, and he had a little well-trimmed toothbrush mustache.

"To the crossroads - to meet my destiny," came the curious reply.

Savalas just said, "Oh," and assumed the man was mad or even drunk. He was beginning to regret taking the lift from the stranger, but the journey continued without any more dialog. Even so, Savalas was only too eager to leave the uncommunicative driver when the gas station loomed through the rain-lashed windshield. But before he left the car, Savalas felt compelled to offer the man a couple of dollars for giving him the lift. It was then that Savalas realized to his embarrassment that he had left his wallet at his cousin's house. Still, he was keen to pay the man at a later time, so he asked the driver for his name and address.

The man was very reluctant and strangely nervous

about giving the details, but he finally told the actor that his name was Harry Agannis, and he gave a South Manhattan address and a phone number which Savalas wrote down on a piece of notepaper. He also offered a dollar bill to Savalas, and told him, "Please take it for your gas. Go on."

Savalas took the money and thanked Agannis, then ran through the downpour to the gas station. When he reached the station, he turned to wave at Agannis — but the Cadillac had gone.

Rather appropriately, Savalas had just landed a starring role in an episode of Rod Serling's *Twilight Zone* series when, a couple of days later, he found the note with Agannis's address and phone number in the inside pocket of his jacket. He decided to telephone him to say he'd be over soon to pay him.

Savalas got a busy tone the first time, so he tried again, and a woman answered, "Joan Agannis. Hello?"

The actor said, "Hi. Could I speak to Harry Agannis please?"

There was a silent pause, then in a broken voice the woman said, "What? Is this some kind of sick joke? Who are you?"

Savalas was baffled, but he calmed the woman down and told her he was serious, and the woman reacted by bursting into tears. So Savalas said, "Look, have I dialed the right number for cryin' out loud? What's wrong?"

The woman stopped sobbing and told Savalas that her husband had been dead for three years.

"That's impossible," Savalas said, and he repeated the name of the man he'd written on the note.

"That's right. Harry Agannis. He's dead. What do

you *want?*" the woman replied, and she slammed the phone down.

Savalas was intrigued - and a little scared - but he decided to drive to the woman's house. When the woman answered the door, he explained who he was and showed Mrs Agannis his Actor's Union card, and she admitted him into her home. She showed him the photograph of her deceased husband. It was the same man who had given Savalas a lift. Same toothbrush moustache and black slicked-back hairstyle. The actor shuddered when he saw the photograph. Then she told Savalas how her husband met his death. In February 1954 he had been returning from a high-school reunion party around 3 a.m. — dressed in a tuxedo as Savalas had described — when the Cadillac he was driving was involved in an horrific crash at the crossroads half a mile from the gas station where the actor had been dropped off. The Cadillac skidded into a truck and burst into flames. The truck driver survived, and even tried to free Mr Agannis from the burning wreckage of his car, but his legs were trapped. The trucker managed to retrieve a fire extinguisher from his crashed vehicle, and tried to use it to douse the flames from the burning Cadillac - but the extinguisher was faulty, and failed to work. Harry Agannis screamed as the flames rose around him. In a state of shock, the trucker punched Agannis repeatedly in the face until he was unconscious. The truck-driver said he did this so Agannis would not suffer too much. Seconds later the Cadillac erupted into a fireball which burned the trucker's face and arms.

Up until his death in 1994, Telly Savalas was haunted by the memory of that rainy night, and he refused to travel anywhere near the area of Long Island where he believed a dead man had given him a lift.

THE CROWN JEWELS
THEFT MYSTERY

1671 was a year of unlimited opportunity for two of history's greatest adventurers. In the West Indies that year, the Welsh buccaneer Sir Henry Morgan was made Deputy Governor of Jamaica, while in England, self-styled "Colonel" Thomas Blood was putting a plan into action that would result in the most daring robbery of all time: the theft of the Crown Jewels from the Tower of London. Thomas Blood (alias Ayliffe, aka Allen) was born in 1618, the son of an Irish blacksmith. Information on his early life is very scant, but it is known that he served the parliamentary cause during the English Civil War. Just exactly what Blood's role was during the war isn't known, but he seems to have been involved in espionage, and he was rewarded for his services with considerable estates in Ireland. However, when the monarchy was restored in 1660, Blood lost his lands and his position, and became an embittered terrorist with a dark genius for ruthless schemes designed to disrupt and intimidate his aristocratic enemies. But long before he fell on hard times, Blood was a mysterious individual who expressed no particular allegiance to any religion or political wing — unless it suited his own ends. It is easy to dismiss him as an adventurer, but Blood seems to have been in the pay of someone. Behind all of his "who dares wins" exploits, there are tantalizing glimpses of a man who was somebody's agent. Many suspected him of being a spy - but a spy for whom? In 1633, Blood and a group of abettors tried to kidnap the Duke of Ormonde, the Lord Lieutenant of Ireland, at Dublin Castle, but the conspirators were betrayed, and all but Blood were captured and thrown into prison. A reward was offered for Blood's capture - dead or alive - but he apparently wasn't too worried about the price on his head, for he attempted - unsuccessfully - to free his co-conspirators, and was forced to flee to Holland.

In 1639, Blood was active among the Fifth Monarchy Men, an extreme Puritan sect who literally believed that the "fifth monarchy" - foretold in the Book of Daniel - was at hand. The biblical prophecy claimed that a fifth monarchy of Christ would succeed the rule of the Assyrians, the Persians, the Greeks, and the Romans. The sect was led by Thomas Venner, a religious fanatic, who launched two abortive risings in 1657 and 1661. Venner was subsequently captured and executed but Blood got away scot-free. In fact, the Irishman had an uncanny habit of leaving rebellious groups just as they were about to be eradicated. It was the same story when he joined the Covenanters - a group of Scottish Presbyterians who opposed the introduction of Charles I's religious policies into Scotland. Blood was right behind the movement and sat at the table with the counsel, but just days before the going got tough, and a confrontation with the King's troops was imminent, Blood was suddenly nowhere to be seen.

In 1667, Blood heard that an old militant acquaintance, a Captain Mason, was being taken under guard to a prison in York. With three accomplices, Blood rode up to the soldiers and opened fire on them. Captain Mason was rescued, and a badly-wounded Blood led him to safety. The price put on Blood's head was trebled, but the Irishman still managed to evade capture.

In 1670, he turned up in central London, where he perpetrated another audacious crime. He rode up to the coach carrying the Duke of Ormonde and yanked open the door. The terrified Duke was pulled from the coach by Blood and an accomplice and thrown onto the horse of another henchman - who rode as far as Tyburn before the cry went up that the nobleman had been kidnapped. The Duke was soon rescued, but Blood and his men escaped without harm.

This brings us to the event in 1671 for which Blood is best remembered: the theft of the British Crown Jewels.

For several weeks, Thomas Blood, disguised as a parson, had been getting regularly acquainted with Talbot Edwards, the 77-year-old keeper of the Crown Jewels, in order to win his confidence. After just a few visits, the old man considered the "parson" thoroughly trustworthy and completely above suspicion.

On May 9th at seven in the morning, Blood turned up in his clergyman guise for the last time with three accomplices. The keeper's daughter was around, so to keep her attention diverted, Blood introduced her to his "nephew" - who was in fact the youngest accomplice, a fairly handsome man of about twenty-five. As the couple began to chat, Blood steered the small-talk to the subject of the Jewels, and the keeper excitedly told Blood and his accomplices to follow him to the chamber of Martin Tower, where the Jewels were kept. Upon reaching the chamber, the old man turned to lock the door behind him and the visitors, at which point Blood suddenly pulled a cloak over his head. The keeper struggled, and a gag was rammed into his mouth. Still, the old man protested, so one of the thieves battered his head with a mallet before callously plunging a dagger into his stomach.

Blood then grabbed the mallet and used it to flatten St Edward's Crown so he could stuff it in his coat. Another thief filed the sceptre in two, while the robber who had murdered the keeper put the orb down his trousers as he laughed.

Then the unexpected happened. The son of the dead keeper turned up, and bumped into Blood's "nephew", who was acting suspiciously like a lookout. The son attacked Blood's accomplice, but was coshed and gagged for his troubles.

The lookout raced to the chamber and warned the others. Blood and his men instantly made a dash out of the chamber, and in the ensuing panic, the sceptre was dropped and left behind.

The son of the murdered keeper then regained consciousness, tore the gag from his mouth, and raised the alarm, shouting, "Treason! Murder! The crown is stolen!"

Within seconds, the keeper's daughter arrived and clung to her brother with fear. One of the yeoman warders also answered the alert and challenged Blood squarely. The Colonel levelled his flintlock at him and blasted a hole in his chest, killing him instantly. As the fleeing gang headed for the Tower Wharf, they encountered another guard, but when he saw Blood and his men approaching, the yeoman got cold feet, dropped his musket and stepped aside, letting the thieves pass unchallenged.

The Tower was soon swarming with soldiers, and Blood's three accomplices were quickly captured. The Colonel's escape route was blocked by Captain Beckman, a fearless Civil War veteran, and the only man who managed to subdue the Irish daredevil. Blood was escorted to a cell in the Tower and interrogated for hours. But the prisoner insisted he would talk to no one but the king about his deeds.

Two days later Blood's request was granted, and the miscreant was taken to Whitehall, where he had a lengthy conversation with King Charles II. Blood was taken back to the Tower, but was later inexplicably released and given a Royal pardon - as well as a "pension" of £500. Blood's confiscated estates in Ireland were also restored to him. Not long after all this, the English author and diarist John Evelyn was invited to dine at the king's table. When he arrived at the dinner, he was astounded to see Thomas Blood seated near the king. This didn't make sense to Evelyn, who knew that the Irishman had served as a parliamentarian in the Civil War and had made numerous kidnap attempts on the nobility. Yet, despite these crimes of treason, the attempted theft of the Crown Jewels and the murder of the old keeper who looked after them, Blood was apparently still held in favour by the king. And therein lies the mystery that has baffled generations of historians.

THE SONG THAT CAN KILL

In December 1932, a down-and-out Hungarian named Reszo Seress was trying to make a living as a songwriter in Paris, but failing miserably. All of his compositions had failed to impress the music publishers of France, but Seress carried on chasing his dream regardless, determined to become an internationally famous songwriter. His girlfriend had constant rows with him over the insecurity of his ambitious life. She urged him to get a full-time nine to five job, but Seress was uncompromising. He told her he was to be a songwriter or a hobo, and that was that.

One afternoon, matters finally came to a head. Seress and his fiancée had a fierce row over his utter failure as a composer, and the couple parted with angry words.

On the day after the row - which happened to be a Sunday - Seress sat at the piano in his apartment, gazing morosely through the window at the Parisian skyline. Outside, storm clouds gathered in the gray sky, and soon the heavy rain began to pelt down.

"What a gloomy Sunday," Seress said to himself as he tinkled on the piano's ivories, and quite suddenly, his hands began to play a strange melancholy melody that seemed to encapsulate the way he was feeling and the dispiriting weather.

"Yes. Gloomy Sunday. That will be the title of my new song," muttered Seress, excitedly, and he grabbed a pencil and wrote the notes down on an old postcard. Thirty minutes later he had completed the song.

Seress sent his composition off to a music publisher and waited for acceptance with a lot more hope in his heart than usual. A few days later, the song-sheet was returned with a rejection note stapled to it that stated: "*Gloomy Sunday* has a weird but highly depressing melody and rhythm, and we are sorry to say that we cannot use it."

Undeterred, he sent the song to another publisher, and this time it was accepted. The music publisher told Seress that his song would soon be distributed to all the major cities of the world. The young Hungarian was ecstatic.

But a few months after *Gloomy Sunday* was published, there was a spate of strange occurrences, allegedly sparked off by the new song. In Berlin, a young man requested a band to play *Gloomy Sunday* but after the number was performed he went home and blasted himself in the head with a revolver, after complaining to relatives that he felt severely depressed by the melody of a new song which he couldn't get out of his head. That song was *Gloomy Sunday*. A week later, in the same city, a young female shop assistant was found hanging from a rope in her flat. Police who investigated the suicide found a copy of the sheet-music to *Gloomy Sunday* in the dead girl's bedroom.

Two days after that tragedy, a young secretary in

New York gassed herself, and in a suicide note she requested *Gloomy Sunday* to be played at her funeral. Weeks later, another New Yorker, aged 82, jumped to his death from the window of his seventh-story apartment after playing the "deadly" song on his piano. Around the same time, a teenager in Rome who had heard the unlucky tune jumped off a bridge to his death.

The newspapers of the world were quick to report other deaths associated with Seress's song. One newspaper covered the case of a woman in North London who had been playing a recording of *Gloomy Sunday* at full volume, infuriating and frightening her neighbours, who had read of the fatalities connected with the tune. The record-player stylus finally became trapped in a groove, and the same piece of the song played over and over. The neighbours hammered on the woman's door but there was no answer, so they forced the door open — only to find the woman dead in her chair. She had taken cyanide.

As the months went by, the steady stream of bizarre and disturbing deaths allegedly connected to *Gloomy Sunday* persuaded the chiefs at the BBC to ban the seemingly accursed song from the airwaves.

Back in France, Reszo Seress, the man who had composed the controversial song, was also to experience the adverse effects of his creation. He wrote to his ex-fiancée, pleading for a reconciliation. But several days later came the most awful, shocking news. Seress learned from the police that his sweetheart had poisoned herself. And by her side, a copy of the sheet-music to *Gloomy Sunday* was found.

At the end of the 1930s, when the world was

plunged into war against Hitler, Seress's inauspicious song was quickly forgotten in the global turmoil, but the sheet-music to the dreaded song is still available to those who are curious to know if the morbid melody can still exert its deadly influence . . .

WAS BRUCE LEE ASSASSINATED?

Bruce Lee was born in San Francisco on November 27th, 1940, but was raised in Hong Kong, where he embarked on a movie career at the age of six. During his early teens, Bruce started to develop an interest in the martial arts. To harden his fists, he would pound them on a stool every day for hours, gradually transforming his hands into ataraxic weapons.

He returned to the United States when he was 18 (to retain his American citizenship) and enrolled as a philosophy graduate at Washington University. Throughout his studies, Lee taught jeet-kune do (a hybrid discipline of kung fu and western pugilism) to provide him with an income of a few hundred dollars per week. One of his students, Linda Emery, was fascinated by her tutor, and she married him in 1964.

Lee then decided to quit his studies to rekindle his acting career in Hollywood and landed a role as Kato in *The Green Hornet* television series. He also gave martial arts lessons to some of the biggest movie stars in Los Angeles. For $150 an hour he taught some of his skills to James Coburn, Lee Marvin, James Garner and Steve McQueen.

Around this time, Warner Brothers were ready to produce *Kung Fu*, a groundbreaking television series about Kwai Chang Caine, a Buddhist monk trained in karate who flees mainland China for the West after murdering a nobleman. Lee applied for the part of Caine, but Warner thought he was too inexperienced to play the role, which went to actor-dancer David Carradine instead. *Kung Fu* proved to be a phenomenal success story in the United States and Europe, and is now highly regarded as a television cult classic.

Lee felt he had been denied stardom in the land of opportunity, so he returned to Hong Kong, where he struck up a partnership with Raymond Chow, an innovative film producer. The two men became the new wave of the Hong Kong film industry, and collaborated on some of the early kung fu blockbusters.

In 1971 Lee starred in his first Chinese action film, *The Big Boss*. He played the part of a new boy in an ice factory who helps striking workers with his breathtaking martial arts talent. The original cut was deemed to be too violent, the censors holding the film release date back for a year, and there was more trouble getting the film distributed, yet Lee continued to strive for international superstardom. He wrote, produced and directed *The Way of the Dragon* (1973), in which he cast himself as Tan Lung, an out-of-town strong-arm who is paid by a Chinese restaurant owner in Rome to sort out the local Mafia menace.

Warner Brothers learned that the films were being received well, and were soon beating a path to Lee's door. They offered major financial support for Lee's next film, *Enter the Dragon* (1973). The film proved to be the success that had eluded Lee for so long, but tragically, the rising film star never got to enjoy the benefits of his achievement. While dubbing the film in Hong Kong on May 10th, 1973, Bruce Lee collapsed. He recovered but experienced respiratory problems, finding it exhausting to breathe. He also underwent a series of convulsions which were put down to a swelling of his brain. Lee was given Mannitol, an osmotic diuretic drug, which seemed to do the trick, and a week later, he appeared as fit as ever. In Los Angeles, Dr David Reisbord examined Lee. After a brain scan, a brain-flow study, a physical check-up, and an EEC analysis, Dr Reisbord told Lee that he had probably suffered a grand mat seizure — an indication of epilepsy — yet there were no indications as to why this was so. The brain scan showed no abnormalities, and other tests confirmed that Lee was in perfect physical condition, so the sudden collapse and brain swelling were very unusual.

Lee then began to lose weight, much to the consternation of his friends, who urged him to see his doctor again. But Lee seemed too wrapped up in his work - this was the break he had dreamed of for so long. Two months after his check-up, Lee was working on a script in the Hong Kong apartment of Betty Ting-pei, his co-star, when he suddenly complained of a bad headache. The actress offered Lee an Equagesic painkiller - a two-layer tablet containing aspirin, calcium carbonate, and ethoheptazine citrate. The drug had been prescribed for Ting-pei by her doctor. Lee took the tablet and said he was going for a nap in the actress's bed. He never woke up again. At 9.30 p.m., Raymond Chow arrived at the apartment to pick the film star up for a dinner engagement. When he found he could not wake Lee, he called for a doctor, but the doctor's efforts to revive him were in vain. Bruce Lee was pronounced dead at Queen Elizabeth Hospital. The world was rocked by the news.

The circumstances surrounding Lee's death were interpreted as suspicious by many. Lee had allegedly not been taken to the nearest hospital when he was found unconscious, and traces of cannabis were found in his dead body. Many wondered how someone regarded as "the fittest man in the world" could just die without any apparent cause.

A coroner's inquest was convened on September 3rd, which uncovered two important findings. Firstly, the amount of cannabis found in Lee's body was too small to have contributed to the actor's death. Secondly, Lee had "probably" died because of a hypersensitivity to a compound in the painkiller he took — possibly the aspirin component.

The official verdict was "death by misadventure". Case closed.

But several unsavoury facts were bandied about by the media regarding Lee's behaviour on the eve of his death. It was learned that Lee had publicly attacked Lo Wei - the man who directed The Big Boss and other kung fu genre films - on the very day before he died. But the incident was quickly put down to being the climax of a long-standing feud between the two men. There were also rumours that the Chinese Mafia and the Triads had a hand in the actor's demise, and there were other exotic theories gleaned from people who had been close to the star. For instance, it came to light that during the last months of Lee's life, certain mysterious, nameless individuals had approached him and told him he was surrounded by "bad omens". Some believed these "men in black" to be members of an obscure eastern sect who had come to America to warn Lee about flaunting the closely-guarded secrets of the ancient fighting arts. These alleged visitors were said to have killed Lee with the "death-touch" or dim mak as it is known in the Far East. According to legend, a person who is trained in dim mak can dispose of his enemy by applying the briefest of pressures on the non-critical points of the victim's body. The victim does not die immediately, but succumbs after a length of time has passed. The delay period is governed by the particular nerve-points that are chosen and the amount of pressure applied to each point. It is easy to scoff at such a concept of killing by touch, but there are historical records that state that the art of dim mak was in use during the T'ang Dynasty (AD 618-906), and in Taiwan, even today, the deadly art is still alleged to be employed for "perfect murders".

The reports of Lee losing weight shortly before he died have led some students of the Eastern arts to conclude that the actor was killed by a lethal technique known as *duann mie*, which, without going into too much esoteric detail, is a way of killing an enemy by directing a blow against a specific vein, which leads to a wasting away of the victim through the ensuing disruption of specific blood vessels. Oddly enough, when Bruce Lee's body was examined by a pathologist, the blood vessels in the lungs were found to be unaccountably broken in a way described by the medical expert as "strange".

SPRING-HEELED JACK

In Victorian times, Barnes Common, an eerie, isolated tract of land on the southern bank of the Thames in London, was a place to avoid. Many travellers foolhardy enough to cross the common during twilight hours were attacked and robbed. The common was also a magnet for the suicidal. One evening in September 1837, a businessman who had been working overtime at his office decided to risk a short cut across the common on his way home. Even as he passed the railings of the adjoining cemetery, the man's thoughts did not wander onto the supernatural. His mind was too preoccupied with mundane matters relating to his business.

Suddenly a figure vaulted high over the railings of the cemetery - as if propelled from a springboard - and landed with a thud in front of him. The businessman trembled when he saw that the mysterious leaper had pointed ears, glowing eyes, and a prominent pointed nose. Without further ado, the businessman turned and fled.

Three girls encountered the same sinister figure on the following night. Again, he made his appearance by bounding over the railings of the cemetery, but on this occasion, he also displayed a violent streak. One of the girls had her coat ripped by him, but managed to flee, followed by one of her screaming companions. The remaining member of the trio tried to scream as the unearthly-looking stranger grabbed at her breasts, then began to tear her clothes off. The victim was later found unconscious at the site of the attack by a policeman.

During the following month the leaping terror struck again. This time the venue was Cut-Throat Lane, Clapham Common. After visiting her parents in Battersea, Mary Stevens, a servant, headed back to her employer's household on Lavender Hill. As she strolled through the entrance of Cut-Throat Lane, a tall figure dressed in black jumped out of the darkness and threw his arms around her, holding her in a vice-like embrace. Before she had a chance to scream, the stranger kissed her face, then dipped his hand into her cleavage, before laughing hysterically. The servant girl let out a scream, and the stranger released her and ran off into the darkness. A number of men hurried to the distressed girl, and after calming her down, listened to her account of the attack. They immediately searched the neighbourhood for the mysterious assailant, but without success, and the servant girl was simply dismissed as having an over-active imagination.

However, the following night, the attacker appeared again, not a stone's throw from the house where the servant girl worked. This time, her demonic assailant bounded out of the shadows and into the path of an approaching carriage. The horses pulling the carriage bolted in fright and a terrible crash ensued, injuring the coachman. The mayhem-maker then seemed to defy the law of gravity as he jumped effortlessly over a nine-foot-high wall. Not long after this superhuman feat, a mysterious high-jumping man with a cape attacked a woman near Clapham Churchyard, this time leaving behind a most curious clue that nowadays could have thrown some light on the secret of his amazing leaping ability: two footprints in the moist soil of the churchyard. The impressions were about three inches deep and obviously made by someone who had landed from a great height. On closer inspection, there were strange imprints within the impressions, which suggested that the attacker had been wearing some kind of apparatus on his shoes. But there were no forensic investigators in those days, and instead of making plaster casts of the intriguing impressions, the police allowed the weather to erode the evidence.

Gradually, the news of the Satanic superman spread, and the public soon gave him a name — Spring-heeled Jack. In February 1838, 18-year-old Lucy Scales and her sister Margaret were on their way home at 8.30 p.m., after a visit to their brother's house in the Limehouse area. Lucy, being the bigger of the two, impatiently marched ahead of her dawdling sister as they passed the entrance leading to Green Dragon Alley. Suddenly, the terrifying cloaked silhouette of Spring-heeled Jack leapt out of the darkness and exhaled a jet of blue flames from his mouth that blasted Lucy's face. The teenager screamed and her legs collapsed under her. She fell to the ground, blinded, and suffered a fit. Jack jumped high over his victim and her sister and landed on the roof of a house. From there he bounded off into the night.

A pattern was emerging - Jack seemed to like molesting and terrifying young females. His next attack, which took place two days later, was also on an 18-year-old girl. Her name was Jane Alsop. Jane's house was situated in Bearhind Lane, a quiet back street in the district of Bow, where she lived with her father and two sisters.

She was spending the evening reading, when suddenly, just before nine o'clock, the front-gate bell sounded. Jane answered the door and outside in the shadows stood a caped man. He said to Jane, "I'm a policeman. Bring a light! We've caught Spring-heeled Jack in the lane!"

Jane ran excitedly back into the house and returned to the police officer moments later with a candle. Upon offering the candle to the caller, she beheld a nightmarish sight. The light from the candle illuminated the face of the man purporting to be an officer of the law. It was Jack, and he grinned as he studied the girl's shocked expression. Before she could make a move he pursed his lips and spurted out a cone of phosphorescent gas which partially blinded the teenager, then he grabbed her and started to tear at her clothes. Jane punched his big nose and managed to give him the slip, but the enraged Jack bolted after her and stopped her from re-entering the house by clutching her hair. As his claw-like hands sadistically scraped her face and neck, Jane's screams alerted her sisters, who came running out of the house. By some miracle, one of them managed to drag Jane from her caped attacker. The three sisters then retreated indoors with Jack in hot pursuit a couple of feet behind them, and in the nick of time they stammed the door in Jack's face.

When Jane was quizzed by the Lambeth Police Court about the assailant's appearance, she described a very unusual person. She said, "He wore a large helmet, and a sort of tight-fitting costume that felt like oilskin. But the cape was just like the ones worn by policemen. His hands were as cold as ice, and like powerful claws. But the most frightening thing about him was his eyes. They shone like balls of fire."

Two days later, Jane's deposition was strengthened by the testament of a butcher from Limehouse. He was the brother of Lucy and Margaret Scales — the victims of the Green Dragon Alley attack.

The accounts of Spring-heeled Jack's cowardly assaults on the ladies of South London soon featured in the newspaper headlines. The reports scared some Londoners into staying indoors after dark, while others decided to organize vigilante patrols. When the 70-year-old veteran of Waterloo, the Duke of Wellington, read of Jack's string of attacks in *The Times*, he decided to come out of retirement, and armed with two pistols, mounted his steed and charged off into the night to track down the leaping villain. Alas, the supreme strategist soon discovered that even his great military prowess was no match for Jack's cunning and hyper-agility. In the end, despite many brave cat-and-mouse chases with the bounding bogeyman, the aging Duke had to call it a day.

A week after the attack on Jane Alsop, Jack called at a house in Turner Street, off Commercial Road. A servant boy answered the door, and Jack, shielding half of his face with his cloak as he stood in the shadows, asked the boy in a gruff voice if he could talk to the master of the house. The youngster was turning, about to call for his master, a Mr Ashworth, when Jack made the mistake of moving out of the shade into the lamplight. The boy recoiled in horror when he saw that the caller had bright orange eyes. As he stood there in a state of shock, the boy noticed two other details about the mysterious caller: he had claws for hands and, under his cloak, an intricate embroidered design that resembled a coat of arms. Below this design, the letter "W" was embroidered in gold. The boy had heard all the spine-chilling rumours of Jack's "eyes of Hell," and let out a terrific scream. Within seconds, windows and doors all over the immediate neighbourhood were opening. Jack waved his fist threateningly at the boy, then rocketed over the roofs of Commercial Road. When the boy regained his senses, he was cross-questioned and interrogated repeatedly by the authorities about his hair-raising encounter. His inquisitors wondered about the significance of the embroidered "W", and some conjectured that the glyph was the initial of the Marquis of Waterford, an individual widely known as a mischievous prankster who had in the past gone to enormous lengths in financing notorious hoaxes. The Marquis was also something of an athlete, but his physical capabilities could obviously not be equated with Jack's superhuman stunts. Even the fittest man on earth couldn't leap 25 feet into the air, as Jack was alleged to have done many times.

In 1859, the Marquis met his death after falling from a horse. But the reports of the "Jumping Man" continued to pour into the police stations of London and the newspaper offices. Spring-heeled Jack was apparently still at large.

In August 1877, 40 years after making his debut on Barnes Common, Jumping Jack turned up unexpectedly one moonlit night at Aldershot North army camp for what would be the most audacious performance in his infamous career. On that night, Private John Regan was standing in his sentry box, guarding the powder magazine, when he heard what he later described as "the shrill scraping sound of something metallic" being dragged down the nearby road. Regan cocked his rifle and moved stealthily from his box towards the source of the sound, but there was nobody to be seen on the stretch of road. After shrugging his shoulders at his colleague in the other sentry box thirty feet away, Reagan turned and walked back to his box. As he reached the sentry box, he felt the clammy ice-cold touch of a hand on his cheek. As he screamed with fright, the other sentry left his box and came charging over, toting his rifle. As the sentries met, Spring-heeled Jack suddenly appeared. His helmet glinting in the moonlight, he jumped into the air, clearing the heads of the soldiers by ten feet. He landed behind them and stood there, sneering, waiting for the soldiers to make the next move. Reagan's rifle was still cocked, so he raised it at the creature and challenged it in a nervous voice, saying, "Who goes there?" After a nerve-wracking silence, the Batman of the nineteenth century hurtled towards the soldiers. Reagan opened fire, but his rifle was only loaded with blank ammunition, and instead of scaring Jack off, it angered him instead. Jack vomited a blast of blue flames, bedazzling Reagan, then sprang 20 feet into the air, cackling. The two sentries deserted their posts.

Soon after that episode, Spring-heeled Jack went on a terrorizing trek across the country. A month after the Aldershot incident, Jack turned up in Lincolnshire one evening, where he shattered the rustic calm by leaping over several thatched cottages wearing a sheepskin. A mob of yokels confronted the laughing leaper and blasted him with shotguns at point-blank range, to no effect whatsoever. When the buckshot hit Jack, it sounded as if it was hitting a metal bucket.

In January 1879, a man was driving his cart home from Woodcote, Shropshire, at 10 p.m. As he crossed a bridge on the Birmingham and Liverpool Junction Canal, a black, hideous-looking creature with large luminous eyes leapt out of a tree and landed on the horse's back. The man tried to knock the oddity off with his whip, but the creature managed to hold on to the frightened animal, which broke into a wild gallop. When the man got the cart back under control the black bug-eyed "thing" darted into the air and disappeared into the trees.

By the end of the nineteenth century, the geographical pattern of sightings of Spring-heeled Jack indicated that he was moving in a westerly direction across England, towards Lancashire. In September 1904, the bouncing blackguard turned up in the south of Liverpool, where he was seen hurtling down from the roof of a reservoir. However, it was in the Everton district of the city that Jack gave a typical performance. One night he was seen clinging to the steeple of St Francis Xaviers in Salisbury Street. Before the awe-struck crowds filling the streets below, Jacko jumped suicidally from the steeple and landed somewhere behind a row of houses. The mob stampeded to see where he had landed, and a rumour spread that he had killed himself. The Evertonians were subsequently startled when a helmeted "egg-headed" figure in white suddenly ran down the street towards them, and as several women in the crowd screamed, Jack lifted his arms and flew over William Henry Street. After that memorable night, Jack made himself scarce for 16 years.

Late one evening in 1920, a man dressed in a "radiant-white costume" was seen by scores of witnesses in War-rington's Horsemarket Street, jumping back and forth from the pavements to the rooftops. He finally cleared the town's Central Railway Station in one mighty leap and was never seen in the north of England again. In 1948, the last recorded sighting of a sinister, leaping figure took place at Monmouth in the south of Wales. Locals who saw a "strange-looking man" leaping over a stream near Watery Lane surmised that he was the spectre of a man who had drowned in the stream, but the few Welsh folk who were later unfortunate enough to encounter the leaper at close quarters swore he was too solid to be a phantom.

Who or what was Spring-heeled Jack? Many bizarre theories have been advanced to answer this question. Some said he was an insane acrobatic fire-eater, while others believed him to be a dressed-up kangaroo, or a mad inventor who had built an anti-gravity device. But one theory that does fit the facts is the alien hypothesis. If we suppose that Jack was from another planet, this would explain his alien appearance, behavior, jumping ability, and longevity. When the American astronauts first landed on the moon, they discovered that the easiest way to move around the lunar surface was by hopping, because their legs were too powerful to walk in the moon's weak gravity-field. In fact, the astronauts could have jumped over 30 feet in height had they wanted to. Perhaps Spring-heeled Jack had found himself at a similar advantage. His home planet may have been much larger than Earth, and possessed a greater gravitational pull. After being reared in this high-gravity environment, Jack would experience the Earth as a low-gravity world, just as the moon is to earthlings.

Returning to the first lunar astronauts, during their stay on the moon, many of these well-trained men became over-excited and would often sing and talk gibberish. And it wasn't solely because of their momentous achievement. Psychologists have noted how astronauts and cosmonauts exhibit symptoms of "Solipsism Syndrome" — a mental condition where the space-travellers just cannot believe they are off the Earth and report feeling unreal and lightheaded. Jack may have reacted in an identical way in his new environment, as he was often heard screaming and laughing hysterically.

This strange behaviour may also have resulted from the inhalation of our terrestrial atmosphere. It's a well-known fact that any inhibition of a creature's respiratory system directly affects its brain activity. In the early days of aviation before the employment of the oxygen mask, many pilots climbing to high altitudes found their mental faculties severely impaired. Their brains were starved of oxygen to such an extent that they could not remember what the altimeter dial signified. Similarly, Jack's brain might have found our atmosphere of 78 percent nitrogen and 21 percent oxygen deficient in certain gases vital for its correct functioning.

The descriptions of Spring-heeled Jack's fiery gaze

seem to indicate that he had retro-reflective eyes, similar to a cat's, which would suggest that he was ideally suited to a nocturnal environment. His fire-breathing, however, isn't easily explained. Perhaps what Jack really breathed into his victim's eyes was not real fire (for none of those attacked suffered burns, nor did the "fire" ever singe a single hair), but a type of odorous phosphor. This isn't as far-fetched as it seems. Many species of insect and marine life are endowed with bioluminescence, which means that they can radiate light through the action of certain compounds in their metabolism. One example that comes to mind is the glow worm. Furthermore, Jack's alien body may have been capable of generating bioelectricity. If this was so, his exhalations could have been electrically charged, which would account for the stunning effect his victims experienced after he breathed the shimmering blue gas into their faces. Again, here on Earth we have examples of bioelectricity in the electric ray fish and the electric eel, which can generate a paralyzing shock of up to 300 volts.

Another unanswered riddle is the fate of Jack. If he was a misunderstood alien, marooned on our world, was he finally rescued, or did he die a lonely death here? We will probably never know.

WAS POE A MURDERER?

In July 1841, the body of Mary Rogers, a 21-year-old brunette, was found in the Hudson River at New Jersey. She had been sexually assaulted, and her hands had been tied behind her back. She had also been strangled with a piece of lace.

Mary Rogers had been the only daughter of a respectable widow who ran a boarding-house for clerks in New York. In her teens, she was known as the "cigar girl" at John Anderson's tobacconist shop on Broadway. Her beauty and soft, almost child-like voice made her very popular with the clientele, and she was asked out by customers almost every day. And yet, Mary was unaffected by her good looks, and had an irreproachable character for chastity and veracity.

In October 1838, she went missing for a week. When she reappeared, she told her boss Mr Anderson that she had been "tired" and had been staying with her Aunt during the missing period. However, it was later discovered that the girl had been seduced by an officer of the US Navy, and kept at Hoboken for a week. And while she was at Hoboken, people had reported seeing her with another man who was described as a tall individual with a dark complexion. Mary never revealed who this man was.

About a week after she returned to Anderson's store, Mary Rogers decided to leave her job. She returned to her mother's boarding-house and took up a job there. One of the lodgers at the house, Daniel Payne, found Mary irresistible, and she found him quite attractive, so they became engaged.

Mary tapped on Daniel's door on the morning of July 25th, 1841. When Daniel answered, his fiancée told him she was going to spend the day with Mrs Downing, her aunt, and she asked Daniel to collect her later in the evening. But Daniel forgot to pick her up. The next day, Daniel called on Mrs Downing but she said her niece hadn't visited her.

On Wednesday, Mary Rogers was found floating in the Hudson Bay. She had been mutilated and a piece of lace torn from her dress had been used to strangle her. The length of lace still hung about her neck. A post-mortem revealed that the girl had been raped repeatedly - possibly by up to six men, according to the coroner. Mary's battered face was barely recognizable, and her shoulders and loins were black and yellow with severe bruising.

When Daniel Payne was informed of his fiancée's death, he went into a state of shock and committed suicide a few weeks later. The police had considered Payne as a suspect, but they also suspected two other people: Joseph Morse, a wood engraver who had always been eyeing Mary in an lustful way, and William Kucuck, a sailor who had once lodged at the boardinghouse. Morse was cleared when a young woman came forward who said he had been with her on the day that Mary Rogers had been missing. Kucuck had no alibi, but the police decided that he had no motive for the murder and released him. John Anderson, Mary's former employer, was also grilled by the police, but he too had a concrete alibi.

The murder investigation seemed to have reached a dead end, when the coroner on the case received a letter from an anonymous man. The writer of the missive claimed that he had seen Mary arrive by boat at Bull's Ferry, Hoboken on the fateful Sunday. She was in the company of six rough-looking men, and seemed to be flirting with them in a sexually provocative manner. She entered the nearby woods with the men, laughing and singing. Another boat arrived minutes later carrying a trio of distinguished, well-dressed gentlemen. These three men got off the boat, approached two bystanders, and asked them what the woman was doing in the company of so many uncouth louts. The anonymous letter-writer didn't hear what the bystanders said in reply.

The New York and New Jersey police worked long and hard on the evidence contained in the letter without any success, but the course of the investigation took a dramatic turn when the two bystanders came forward to corroborate the details of the anonymous letter. More witnesses then came forward. A driver who had been in the area of Hoboken that Sunday said he had seen Mary Rogers with a tall, well-dressed gentleman going into a road-house near the Elysian Fields summer resort. The road-house was called Nick Mullen's.

The police lost no time in taking up this new lead. They interviewed the road-house keeper, a Mrs Loss, and she confirmed the driver's story. She said Mary and the mysterious tall dark stranger had eaten a meal, then left the road-house and were seen entering the local woods. Mrs Loss and several people present later heard a scream coming from the woods. Around this time, two watchmen said they also heard the sounds of a woman moaning somewhere in the woodland. Days later, Mrs Loss's children were playing in the woods when they found Mary's petticoat, parasol, silk scarf and handkerchief in a thicket. Again, the case reached a cul-de-sac, and the police finally admitted defeat.

Eighteen months later, the case became immortalized in a detective story by one of the world's most famous writers - Edgar Allan Poe, master of the macabre. He called his story *The Mystery of Marie Roget* - and he set his version of the Mary Rogers murder case in Paris. In the tale, Poe's brilliant, wry detective Dupin quickly reconstructs the events that led to the brutal murder of the young woman. He discredits the coroner's findings of gang-rape and asserts that the killer was in fact a lone assassin. He easily deduces this fact by pointing out that there were signs of a struggle at the scene of the crime in the woods, but if six men had been involved as the police had said, then they would have easily overpowered the girl, and there would be no indications of any struggle whatsoever. Dupin eventually gets to a point in the story where he is about to name the murderer, when Poe irritatingly uses a literary diversion to end the story by pretending he is the editor of the magazine, thus censoring the climactic denouement.

However, it now looks as if Edgar Allan Poe was not using the false censorship gimmick as a literary trick at all. He may well have used it to avoid implicating himself in the murder of Mary Rogers. In the light of recent evidence, it seems that Poe's amazingly realistic story detailing Marie Roget's demise is based on facts that could have only been known to the murderer of Mary Rogers. And Poe may have been that man.

In the summer of 1841, the imaginative 32-year-old writer was in an alcoholic limbo, drinking continually to ease the stress he was experiencing over the slow death of his wife Virginia, who had consumption. According to Poe himself he was insane during this traumatic period and "suffered long fits of absolute unconsciousness". He would often seek refuge from his trouble by going into the local woods.

According to several reliable reports, Poe, who was a frequent visitor to New York, actually visited Anderson's tobacconists on October 3rd, 1838, and became infatuated with the ravishing, porecelain-skinned cigar girl. Was Poe the tall dark-complexioned man Mary was seen talking to at Hoboken when she went missing for the first time in October 1838? And was he the man of the same description who left the road-house with Mary Rogers for the woods on the day she was mercilessly battered to death after a repeated, unusually brutal rape? The horror writer certainly fits the bill. He was tall - about 5 feet 9 inches, and he was olive-skinned.

If Poe did kill Mary Rogers, why did he feel the need to write about his vile deed? Did he get some perverted pleasure out of it? Poe's books are populated by sick, egocentric sadists, and the writer often told acquaintances that the death of the desirable women in his stories never failed to give him "a poetic thrill".

At the age of 40, Poe - now a drunk and a drug addict - lay dying on his deathbed whispering, "Lord help my poor soul" over and over again until he died.

A VICTORIAN SORCERER

Daniel Dunglas Home was born near Edinburgh on March 20th, 1833. His father, William Home, was the illegitimate son of Alexander, tenth Earl of Home, who died in 1841. Little is known of Daniel's early life, but when he was four, the eighth child of the Home family started to "see" pictures of future events of which he could not possibly have had any knowledge. The family showed little suprise at Daniel's gift of "second sight," for his mother was herself a clairvoyant descended from a clan of Highland seers. Mr and Mrs Home, who could not afford to feed and clothe their latest child, left him in the care of an aunt, who reared young Daniel until he was nine; at that age Daniel's aunt took him to America to be reunited with his family at Connecticut.

In 1850, 17-year-old Daniel became a convert to the new doctrine of spiritualism at a time when the United States was in the grip of a psychic "contagion". Three years earlier at Arcadia, New York, two girls - the infamously fraudulent Fox sisters, had sparked a psychical mania after convincing the gullible that spirits of the departed were communicating from the "other side" by rapping on the walls and furniture of their home. The Fox rappings incident was but the first of a series of widely-reported accounts of supernatural goings-on in New York which inaugurated the movement of "Modern Spiritualism".

The conversion to this controversial movement came about when Daniel Home realized that he possessed a psychic talent which manifested itself by the onset of strange knocking sounds which echoed about his Connecticut home. This naturally frightened his family, but the last straw came when the furniture of the house began to glide about. Daniel's aunt was terrified by the animated chairs and dancing table, and several ministers of religion were called in, but they could not halt the manifestations; the holy men would merely leave after blaming diabolical forces. The finger of suspicion finally pointed at Daniel. The Home family realized that he was always in the house when the strange phenomenon occurred, and on several occasions his father caught him smirking at the sight of distraught family members being chased by a dining room chair. Enough was enough. The mischievous cynosure was turned out into the street to fend for himself. He wandered aimlessly for years, staying with friends here and there, but never settling down. Wherever the teenager went, so did the supernatural disturbances, but far from being a nuisance, these psychical commotions proved to be the roaming youth's bread and butter. He gave seances and developed a repertoire that was similar to the stock in trade of contemporary spirit mediums: Home would arrange for the guests to sit round a table, he would go into a trance, and soon rappings and spirit voices would pierce the deadly silence. The table would often simultaneously tilt and rise from the floor. But there were several curious aspects to these seances: they were always staged in well-lit rooms (often in the daytime), and they were never held in Home's own house, in contrast to most spiritualists of the day who insisted on holding seances in total darkness or on their own premises, usually for fraudulent reasons.

When Home returned to Britain in March 1855, he put up at Cox's Hotel in Jermyn Street, London. Home's overt London seances put him in a different league from most of the psychics of his day, but he did have his detractors, the most notable of them being the poet Robert Browning, who loathed the medium. Still, Home had no shortage of eminent admirers, including Queen Victoria, Charles Dickens, Lord Lytton, William Makepeace Thackeray, John Ruskin and Elizabeth Barrett Browning.

By this stage in his career, Home had added levitation, apports (disembodied hands that dissolve after materialization), and bodily elongation to his routine. An early account of his gravity-defying ability reads:

I had hold of his hand at the time, and I felt his feet - they were lifted a foot from the floor! Again and again he was taken from the floor; and the third time he was carried to the lofty ceiling of the apartment, with which his hand and head came into gentle contact.

On another occasion, Home flew into the house of a Mr. S.C. Hall (at No. 15 Ashley Place) via an open window on the third floor. Mr Hall recoiled in terror at the sight, then watched in disbelief as Home floated around the room like a soap bubble, before skimming through the open window again. He came to earth with a slight jolt a few yards away from Hall's home. Mr Hall excitedly told the first caller to the house, a Mrs Henrietta Ward, about Home's flight, and he declared, "I don't doubt the day when he will float around St Paul's!"

Between the years 1855 and 1864 Home travelled around Europe, performing at the courts of Holland, France, Russia and Prussia. His series of séances in the Tuileries in Paris greatly impressed Napoleon III and the Empress Eugenie and he even received an audience with the Pope. In 1859, he married a goddaughter of the Tsar, a beautiful young lady, charming and possessed of means, but she died four years later.

In 1871, the multi-talented physicist and chemist Sir William Crookes investigated Home. Crookes subjected the famed medium to a number of tests, beginning with a simple experiment designed to measure Home's alleged ability to move objects at a distance (telekinesis). Crookes asked the psychic to move a spring balance at the end of the room. Home easily achieved this, which shocked and intrigued Crookes. The scientist then instructed Home to sit at a table under which a closed copper cage was situated. The cage contained an accordion, which Crookes asked Home to play using his telekinetic powers. Home obliged. The accordion played by itself, even though it was untouched by human hands. It continued to play even when Home moved away from the table.

Home also gave a startling demonstration of his

immunity to fire. He reached into an open fire in front of Crookes and stirred the burning coals with his hand. He then picked up a piece of red-hot coal - "as big as an orange" according to Crookes - and proceeded to blow on it until it became white-hot. He later put the incandescent lump of coal back onto the fire and when Crookes examined Home's hand, he was baffled to see that the medium had suffered no burns whatsoever. Crookes carried out more tests, and later made a list of the strange phenomena he'd experienced while investigating Home. He catalogued the following:

Unaccountable movement of heavy bodies with contact, but without physical pressure. Currents of air.

Changes of temperature (registered on a thermometer). Percussive noises - sometimes raps, but sometimes faint scratchings, sometimes detonations.

Alteration in the weight of objects.

Movement of furniture with no contact.

Levitation of furniture with no contact.

Levitation of Home himself.

Movements of articles at a distance.

Tunes on musical instruments while nobody was playing.

Luminescences.

Materializations - I have retained one of these hands in my own. I firmly resolved not to let it escape. There was no struggle or effort made to get loose, but the hand gradually seemed to resolve itself into vapour and faded in that manner from my grasp.

'Direct writing" - hands, visible or invisible, taking up pens to write messages.

Phantoms.

Demonstrations of intelligence that could not be attributed to the medium: the provision of information, say, about relations of sitters who were no longer alive, and whom Home could have never known.

Translocations — "apports."

Points of light darting about and settling on the heads of different persons.

Crookes evidently forgot to add Home's fire-immunity to the list.

Other scientists of the Victorian age were unwilling to be seen in the same street as Home, let alone in a laboratory with the prodigy. These myopic "men of science" reasoned that the things Home allegedly did were simply contrary to the laws of nature, and were therefore quite impossible. But the laws that the sceptical scientists referred to were the old imperial laws of the pre-Einstein, pre-Quantum Theory days of physics, when an atom was thought to be an indivisible billiard ball. Crookes bravely put his reputation on the line when he published his findings and his paranormal theory of Home, and was forced to endure the howls of laughter from his colleagues. Crookes recorded that Home's psychic power was:

> . . . *connected with the human organization, which for convenience may be called the Psychic Force.*

At the age of 40, Daniel Dunglas Home went to live in the Mediterranean because of a recurrent tubercular condition, a move which effectively terminated his psychic career. When Home died in 1886, Sir William Crookes, the only scientist who had been bold enough to look into the medium's powers, said, "He was one of the most lovable of men, whose perfect genuineness and uprightness were beyond suspicion."

Over the years, many researchers have tried to find evidence that detracts from Home's legendary reputation, but it seems as if the lowly-born born psychic's claims to fame are faultless. Perhaps researchers should be looking in the opposite, positive direction; instead of concentrating on the demolition of a man who died over a century ago, it would perhaps be more profitable if they opened their minds as Crookes did in an age when freethinking was sadly equated with lunacy. In our era of continual technological progress, they should know better; yet there are still scientists who think like their Victorian ancestors.

AN 18TH CENTURY SPACEMAN

There have been many reports of visitors from other planets dropping in on Earth. In 1954, the Japanese authorities detained a man trying to enter the country with a passport that revealed he was from an unheard country named "Taured". A thorough check was made by the customs officials to see if there was such a place anywhere on Earth, but they drew a blank. The stranger refused to throw light on the whereabouts of the mysterious nation of Taured and quickly left Japan. A similar incident occurred in 1851 when a man calling himself Joseph Vorin was found wandering in the German village of Frankfurt-an-der-Oder. When the German authorities asked the man where he was from, Vorin told them that he was from Laxaria, a country on the continent of Sakria. This baffled the authorities because neither of the places existed anywhere on their map of the world!

In 1905, a young man who was arrested in Paris for stealing a loaf was found to speak an unknown language, and after a lengthy interrogation session, the man managed to convey that he was from a place called Lizbia. Thinking he meant Lisbon, the man was shown a map of Portugal, and a Portugese interpreter was brought in to talk to him, but it was soon established that the young offender was not from Lisbon. The language the youth spoke was not an invented babble either; it had all the consistent syntactical rules of a language similar to Esperanto. Eventually, the strange-speaking man was released - never to be seen again.

The great student of the unexplained, Charles Fort, once commented on the subject of visitors from other planets: "If there have ever been instances of teleportations of human beings from somewhere else to this Earth, an examination of infirmaries and workhouses and asylums might lead to some marvellous disclosures. Early in the year 1928, a man did appear in a town in New Jersey, and did tell that he had come from the planet Mars. Wherever he came from, everybody knows where he went after telling that."

One of the best documented reports of a possible visitant from another world landing on Earth came from the little French town of Alencon, which is situated about 30 miles north of Le Mans. The town is nowadays famous solely for its fine lace, but over two hundred years ago, Alencon became renowned for something far less mundane.

At around 5 a.m. on June 12th, 1790, peasants watched in awe as a huge metal sphere descended from the sky, moving with a strange undulating motion. The globe crash-landed onto a hilltop, and the violent impact threw up soil and vegetation which showered the hillside.

The hull of the globe was so hot (possibly from a rocket motor or because of the rapid descent through the atmosphere) that it ignited the surrounding dry flora, and a grass fire quickly broke out. The peasants rushed up the hill carrying pails of water, and within a short time, the fires were extinguished. A large crowd encircled the crashed globe, and some of the more adventurous stepped forward to touch the hull of the unearthly craft to discover that it was quite warm. A physician, two mayors from nearby towns and a number of officials also turned up to see what had descended from the morning sky, and these important witnesses arrived just in time to see something sensational.

A hatch of some sort slid open in the lower hemisphere of the globe, and a man in an outlandish, tight-fitting costume emerged through the hatchway and surveyed the observers with an apprehensive look. He started mumbling something in a strange language and gestured for the crowd to get away from him and his vehicle. A few people stepped back, at which point the man ran through the break in the circle of spectators and fled into the local woods. Some of the peasants also ran away, sensing that something dangerous was about to happen and the remainder of the crowd decided to follow suit. Seconds after the last members of the crowd had retreated from the sphere, it exploded with a peculiar muffled sound, creating a miniature mushroom-shaped cloud. The debris from the craft "sizzled" in the grass, and gradually turned to powder.

A police inspector named Liabeuf travelled over a hundred miles from Paris to investigate the crash, and he quizzed many of the witnesses, including the mayors and physician who had been present at the strange spectacle. The inspector organized a thorough search of the woods where the oddly-dressed man had taken refuge, but the hunt resulted in nothing. The stranger seemed to have vanished as mysteriously as he had arrived.

In the report to his superiors, Inspector Liabeuf put forward the suggestion that the man who had landed in the globe could have been "a being from another world" - but the higher authorities in Paris dismissed the intimation as "a ludicrous idea".

PHANTOM WRITERS

The earliest mention of mysterious writing is in the Old Testament. In Daniel 5: 31, there is an account of strange handwriting that appeared on the wall of Belshazzar's palace on the night of the feast. The mysterious message is interpreted by the prophet Daniel as an omen foretelling the loss of Belshazzar's kingdom. Since those remote times, there have been many more reports of mysterious scrawlings. Some baffling messages have been in the form of graffiti, such as the message left on the wall by Jack the Ripper, which is as incomprehensible today as it was over a century ago when Jack chalked it after killing two women in the early hours of Sunday, September 30th, 1888 (but see my groundbreaking interpretation of the message in my book *Jack the Ripper - Secret Service*). The Whitechapel Murderer's cryptic five-liner declared:

The Juwes are
The men That
Will not
be Blamed
for nothing

Another piece of puzzling graffiti greeted the citizens of Owensville, Indiana, on the morning of December 7th, 1939. In huge letters on the sidewalk of the public grade school, someone had painted a sentence in huge white letters that read: "Remember Pearl Harbor!"

A policeman in the town scratched his head as he read the words and said, "Crazy kids. Where is Pearl Harbour, anyway?"

No one in the town seemed to know, until two years later, to the day, when an armada of 350 Japanese carrier-launched warplanes attacked the US Pacific Fleet at Pearl Harbour, Hawaii. The Japanese killed 2,330 military personnel and wounded 1,145 in the attack, as well as destroying 247 aircraft, sinking three battleships and eleven warships. But who was the mysterious graffiti writer who had warned the United States of this horrific military assault two years before it happened? No one knows.

Mysterious writing in the form of letters is less common than strange writings on walls, but from time to time there have been reports in the newspapers of malicious chain letters circulating through our cities. These anonymous epistles often instruct the person who opens them to send exact copies of the chain letter to at least three friends, and the abominable letter often says that any failure to duplicate the original missive will result in bad luck or death to the person who has opened the letter. Many of these letters are no doubt sent by people with a warped sense of humour, but some of the senders may be fully-fledged sadists who delight in propagating a wave of dread via the postal system. And nowadays of course, the computerized version of the chain letter routinely traverses the internet along with scam emails and other internet junk-mail.

In 1956, the paranormal researcher Andrew Green was pleasantly surprised to receive a letter from a poltergeist! The letter began, "Mr Green, Do you remember me? I am Donald ... I took leave to write ... I spoke to you by the glass."

The address at the top of the letter was: 63 Wycliffe Road, Battersea. Green had investigated an alleged poltergeist at that address weeks before, and believed that the writer of the spook letter was a 15-year-old girl who seemed to be at the epicentre of the supernatural goings-on. But Green couldn't prove his theory, and so may be in possession of the only letter written by a poltergeist.

What must surely rank as one of the most bizarre cases of eerie correspondence is the case of the phantom postcard sender which hit the headlines in Britain in 1977. A former councillor and parliamentary candidate Trevor Silverwood started receiving postcards at his home in Bridlington, Yorkshire in 1967 - from an irritating nosy parker who told Mr Silverwood about the most trivial details of his private life: what he had eaten for breakfast, what programmes he watched on television, even the colour of his socks. Naturally, Mr Silverwood was a little unnerved by the postcards - which were stamped with postmarks from all over the world, but this soon turned to irritation with the snooper, who continued to plague him for years on end. The writing was always in shorthand, and the anonymous correspondent signed the postcards with a little matchstick figure of the Saint - the Leslie Charteris creation. Mr Silverwood, who passed away a few years ago, was truly baffled by the writer - who posted his annoying messages in India, America, Canada, the Middle East, and from cities as near to home as Rotherham and Sheffield.

Shortly before Christmas in 1977, a postcard from Australia arrived at Silverwood's home. One sentence on it read: "Just for you."

Silverwood told the press: "I would dearly like to get my hands on the Big Brother or Sister who is watching me. It was amusing at first, but now no longer."

As a last resort, Mr Silverwood placed an advertisement in the personal column of his local newspaper, begging the postcard writer to identify himself. A few days later, a postcard arrived from Tenerife that read: "Don't be naughty. What a nice picture of you the newspaper published!" The anonymous writer was referring to the photograph of Mr Silverwood printed in a national newspaper that included an article on the postcard mystery.

After being questioned by police over a minor driving matter, Mr Silverwood received a postcard from another exotic overseas place that gave a blow-by-blow account of the police questioning, as if the writer was trying to create the impression that he was omniscient.

The identity of the unknown correspondent is still a mystery, as is the identity of a similar correspondent who changed the course of British politics in the eighteenth century. This correspondent wrote under several pseudonyms, penning his first satirical letter in 1767, but from January 1769 to January 1772, he wrote 70 vicious but brilliant letters under the pen-name "Junius"; even the mere mention of the name induced feelings of terror and dread in the corrupt circles of the British elite.

All of the letters appeared in Henry Woodfall's *Public Advertiser* in London. The first one, printed in the popular readers' letters column on 21 January 1769, accused the Prime Minister of being a gambler. The libelous sentence in the scathing letter read: "The finances of a nation, sinking under its debts and expenses, are committed to a young nobleman already ruined by play."

In December 1769, Junius criticized King George III. In the seditious letter, Junius warned the monarch of the dire repercussions that could result from the oppression of the Irish and the Americans, and audaciously reminded the king of the execution of Charles I. Junius ended the caustic criticism with a sentence about the king that shocked every reader: "While he plumes himself upon the security of his title to the crown, he should remember that, as it was acquired by one revolution, it may be lost by another."

The printer of the *Public Advertiser*, Henry Woodfall, was promptly arrested on a charge of seditious libel, but the jury refused to convict him, and he was soon released.

The letters from Junius ended in early 1772. Junius, whoever he was, had single-handedly exposed the corruption that was rife in the upper echelons of eighteenth century London. His razor-sharp pen cut down the corrupt king himself, his fawning hypocritical bigwigs, and the mercenary Members of Parliament whose only incentive for entering the House of Commons was to make a killing for themselves. Junius opened the eyes of the common man to the rotten hierarchy of the king and his Government, and because of him, newspapers were allowed to report Parliamentary debates, and those in power remained under the close scrutiny of the press. For over two centuries, historians have argued over the identity of Junius. All that is known is that he was obviously an ardent Whig partisan of the Grenville faction and a fierce opponent of the administrations of the Duke of Grafton and Lord North. Over a hundred people have been suspected of writing the Junius letters, the most likely candidates being Edmund Burke, the Irish philosopher, politician and orator, and Sir Philip Francis, a politician and pamphleteer, who was a clerk in the War Office in 1762. Of these two suspects, Francis emerged as the prime one in 1963, when Alvar Ellegard, a Swedish linguistics expert, put copies of the Junius letters and handwriting samples of Sir Philip Francis through a mainframe computer. The results of the computerized text analysis apparently convinced Ellegard that Junius was Sir Philip. But many historians disagreed with the results, so we'll probably never know the true identity of the most feared social critic in the history of British politics. This is precisely what Junius smugly predicted shortly before the letters ceased. He wrote, "I am the sole depository of my secret, and it shall die with me."

HE FLEW BEFORE
THE WRIGHT BROTHERS

In the early years of the twentieth century, one of man's oldest dreams was finally realized: the dream of manned flight. History records that Orville and Wilbur Wright made the first powered and controlled flights on December 17th, 1903, at Kitty Hawk, North Carolina. Their first flight was ground-breaking enough, but the second one lasted 59 seconds before their propellor-driven glider came to earth 250 metres from the take-off point - quite an achievement in those times. The two aviation pioneers were subsequently hailed as heroes, and were able to abandon their cycle business for more lucrative enterprises. Wilbur shipped the aircraft to France, where it was passionately received as a modern wonder of the world, and in 1909, Orville secured a contract to supply the US Army with his planes. It was a real American success story. But unknown to the Wright brothers, a humble

Welsh carpenter named Bill Frost had already taken to the skies in a powered, heavier-than-air flying machine, some eight years before the historical flights at Kitty Hawk.

It all began around 1868 when 20-year-old Bill Frost was working on Hean Castle - an absurd Victorian folly. As the youth was carrying a 12-foot-long pine plank along scaffolding, a sudden fierce gust of wind rushed up under him and propelled the plank - and Frost - into the air. The carpenter landed gently, still clinging to the plank - and that aeolian incident fired his imagination. From that moment on he was continually preoccupied with finding a way to invade the domain of the birds and clouds. The people of Saundersfoot, the village in the west of Wales, where Frost lived, laughed at his dream, just as the dullards of long ago had laughed at the futile flight attempts of Leonardo da Vinci and the dangerous balloon escapades of the Montgolfier brothers. Even the men that were to go down in the official history of flight - the Wright brothers - were initially regarded as fools. For hours, the brothers would watch gannets gliding through the sky and imitate the birds by stretching out and tilting their arms. This provided ample amusement for the coastguards who used to watch the seemingly crazy, would-be aeronauts. So Bill Frost was in good company when he ran down Stammers Hill, entrapped within hopelessly inadequate aerofoil designs, while onlookers smiled and laughed scornfully. It was always the same outcome - the nineteenth century Icarus demoralized and breathless at the bottom of Stammers Hill, as those content to remain on terra firma gloated at the "Bird Man".

But Bill Frost learned from his mistakes, and possessed a vision that was decades ahead of its time - a flying machine that could be driven by two propellers revolving horizontally, which would provide lift in a way similar to the Harrier jump jet. But because the poor carpenter had no one to approach for advice in his isolated village, and had no books to help him, most of the blueprints for his wonder machine stayed in his head, until he eventually managed to borrow and save enough money to patent the aeroplane in 1894. In September of the following year, the Bird Man of Stammer Hill took off in his prototype plane from the field of his father-in-law, Fred Watkins. The strange-looking contraption buzzed through the warm evening air over Stammers Hill, and soared over the heads of the people who had previously laughed at Bill Frost's gravity-defying attempts. None of them laughed now. They surveyed the 48-year-old flying man slanting across the coppery-coloured clouds. The children below squealed with delight at the acrobat, but a storm suddenly roared in from Cardigan Bay which shook the plane violently. Frost started to lose altitude. The plane nosedived, then levelled off, but continued to lose height. It scudded low over the fields until its undercarriage smashed into the top branches of an ash tree. Frost was incredibly lucky to survive the first ever air crash, as the plane was wrecked beyond repair. The people who had observed the stomach-turning descent came running to the crash-site to take a look at the strange machine's remains. Some still scoffed at the fallen pilot.

With no money to rebuild his plane, Frost decided to offer his patent to the War Office. He expected a substantial financial return, but instead, he received a letter from the Under Secretary of State, William St John Broderick, which declared, "This Nation does not intend to adopt aerial navigation as a means of warfare." For years, Bill Frost told anyone who would listen that manned flight would soon change the face of war, travel and commerce - but few took his predictions seriously. In his last years he realized he was becoming blind, and became a familiar, pathetic-looking character in the village, led about by two goats. With tears in his dying eyes, the Welsh visionary smiled and pointed skywards in the early days of World War One, when he saw three German airships looming in the clouds, high over Pembrokeshire. "Look!" he shouted, "I *said* they could do it. Look!"

THE TEENAGER WHO
DIVIDED A NATION

On the night of January 1st, 1753, 18-year-old Elizabeth Canning went missing. Earlier on that New Year's Day she had left her employer, Mr Lyon, who ran a carpentry business in the City of London, telling him she was going to visit her mother. Elizabeth did see her mother, and she also paid a visit to her Uncle Tom Colley who lived near the London Docks, and he made such a fuss of his favorite niece that she didn't get away from his home until 10 p.m., and even then, he insisted he would have to accompany her on her homeward journey to Aldermanbury Street in the City. Her uncle and aunt escorted the teenager as far as Houndsditch, a mere ten-minute walk from her home, when Elizabeth said she would be alright from there on, and after kissing her, Uncle Tom Colley reluctantly turned and headed home with his wife.

Over an hour later, Elizabeth's mother, Bet, a widower with five children, stood on her doorstep, waiting anxiously to catch sight of her overdue daughter. As midnight came and went, Mrs Canning began to fear her eldest daughter had been murdered or abducted. The people of Aldermanbury Street quickly came to Bet Canning's aid. The neighbours made a collection to finance a reward for anyone who could provide information about the girl's whereabouts. Some of the collected money paid for a "missing" advert that was printed in the local paper. The advert gave a description of Elizabeth and offered a two-guinea reward for information leading to her discovery. But four weeks passed without any news of the teenager. Then, out of the blue, on January 29th, Elizabeth Canning turned up at Aldermanbury Street, limping and half-naked. A bloodstained piece of torn cloth was tied around her head, and she sported a nasty gash on her left ear.

She hobbled into her house, where her mother threw her arms around her battered and bruised daughter and sat her at the table.

"Oh dear! What happened to you? Who did this? Who did it?" cried Bet.

Elizabeth explained how, soon after leaving her Uncle Tom, she had been brutally set upon by a couple of burly rogues. One of the scoundrels hit her on the head with a cosh, knocking her unconscious, then they ripped off her dress and apron and stole her half-guinea. When Elizabeth came around, she was being dragged along the ground, but was too weak to resist. She was taken into a house and thrown at the feet of an old woman. Two younger women were present, and looked down at Elizabeth, grinning.

"Why don't you go our way, m'dear?" the old woman asked Elizabeth and the kidnapped girl suddenly realized that the old woman was asking her to become a prostitute. The place was a brothel.

Elizabeth felt her bloody head wound and said, "No. Let me go!"

The old woman produced a knife and cut the laces

of Elizabeth's corset, then slapped her face. She grabbed hold of the frightened girl and took her upstairs to a dismal-looking room where she remained a prisoner for four weeks, living on a moldy loaf of bread and a pitcher of water that had been left for her. Almost freezing to death in front of the empty fire grate, the teenager finally decided to make an escape attempt. She pulled down the hard wooden boards that were nailed across the window, climbed out onto the penthouse roof and dropped into the secluded street. She then made the arduous ten-mile journey home.

"Where was this place?" Bet asked, shaking with anger.

"Hertford Road, mother," replied Elizabeth, enjoying the warmth of the fire.

When Mrs Canning told her neighbour Robert Scarratt about Elizabeth's ordeal, he said he knew the road well. He said, "I'll lay a guinea to a farthing that the house where Liz was kept was the brothel that Mother Wells runs. Aye, she's a gypsy."

Elizabeth said she had heard the surname Wells or Wills mentioned at the house.

The news of the girl's terrible ordeal traveled the length of Aldermanbury Street, and a mob immediately set out for the house of Mother Wells.

Later that day, the crowd arrived at the house and several members hammered on the door. Mother Wells herself answered and was pushed aside as the vengeful multitude poured into the alleged house of ill-repute. They found a dark room upstairs which seemed to be the one described by poor Elizabeth. There was hay on the floor, a water pitcher, a cask, and a saddle. But there was no sign of the fire grate that Elizabeth had mentioned, and no penthouse roof outside the window which Elizabeth claimed to have climbed on during her escape.

Elizabeth was taken to the house, where she identified the room where she had been kept a prisoner. Downstairs, Mother Wells and Mary Squire, another old gypsy, were spat on by the mob, even though the two women professed to be baffled by the invasion of their home. Elizabeth came downstairs and pointed to Mary Squires. She said, "That's the old woman that robbed me."

"Eh?" Mary Squires was shocked at the girl's accusation. "When did I rob you?"

"On New Year's Day!" screamed Elizabeth.

"Impossible. On that day I was 120 miles away," Mary Squires replied. The other inhabitants of the house stood by, frightened by the hubbub of the irate mob. Mary Squire's daughter Lucy and her young friend, a beautiful blonde prostitute named Virtue Hall, were naturally suspected of being the two young women that Elizabeth had mentioned in her story, and Mary's thick-set son George was assumed to be one of the despicable brutes who had attacked and abducted young Liz. The five suspects were taken to the house of the local magistrate. Mother Wells and Mary Squires were charged and taken to jail, screaming they were innocent. Four days later, Virtue Hall was brought before Henry Fielding, the novelist and playwright, who was also London's first police magistrate. Fielding interrogated Hall in such a severe manner that she was reduced to tears, and she finally agreed to tell Fielding all she knew about the Canning incident. The prostitute told Fielding that Elizabeth Canning had been brought to Mother Wells's house by two gypsies, but before Hall could provide further details, Fielding was accused of bullying the prostitute just to extract the statement he wanted.

When Mother Wells and Mary Squires went on trial a fortnight later, the latter called three witnesses to prove that she had been in Abbotsbury, Dorset on the day the alleged abduction took place. But the jury simply refused to believe her and the two gypsy women were later found guilty. Squires was sentenced to death by hanging, but Mother Wells was given part of her punishment immediately, before the court. An incandescent branding iron was brought in and she was held still by two men as the branding iron was pressed against her hand. She let out a terrible scream which was swamped by the cheering of the court spectators, then she fainted and was taken away to Newgate prison to begin a six-month sentence. British justice had been done - or had it? Sir Crispe Gascoyne, London's Lord Mayor, didn't think so. He thought the trial had been a totally biased travesty of justice and wrote to the vicar of Abbotsbury, asking him to question the three witnesses who had been produced at the court for the defence. The vicar replied that the men in question were honest and trustworthy citizens who still maintained that the condemned Mary Squires had been with them on New Year's Day.

Virtue Hall was also questioned by Gascoyne, and she nervously admitted that she had given false evidence to avoid going to prison. Gascoyne immediately visited Mother Wells in her cell, and after questioning the old woman about the events of that fateful New Year's Day, he was satisfied that Wells and Squires were victims of a gross miscarriage of justice. Thanks to his diligent efforts, Squires was pardoned just one day before the execution date, and Mother Wells was also released.

By now, the nation was divided by the Canning affair. The "Canningites" believed that Wells and Squires had kept Elizabeth Canning imprisoned, whilst the "Egyptians" (thus called because it was commonly held that gypsies were descended from the Egyptians) maintained that Elizabeth Canning was an evil liar. In May 1754, the Egyptian campaigners managed to convince the authorities that Elizabeth Canning had been somewhat economical with the truth, and the teenager was indicted for perjury. She was found guilty and transported on July 31st, 1754. What became of her is a mystery, and just what happened on that New Year's Day in 1753 has never been explained. Was she abducted, or did she invent the incident? If she did, how can we account for her injuries, and where did she stay for four weeks? The Canning affair remains a perplexing case.

THE AMERICAN LEVITATOR

Dream researchers - or oneirologists, as they are officially known — say that the most commonly reported dream in every culture is the dream of unaided flight. In this sleep fantasy, the dreamer takes to the air and soars above trees and buildings in a state of ecstasy. But unaided flight is just a dream, surely?

For centuries there have been tales of Eastern gurus and other holy and mystical men of the world who have allegedly been capable of levitation, but scientists are very skeptical about reports of people overcoming the laws of gravity, although the late scientist and science-fiction writer Isaac Asimov claimed that one day in the not-too-distant future men would be able to fly under their own power on the moon - under pressurized domes. An Earth-dweller on the moon would only weigh one-sixth of his terrestrial weight, thus allowing anyone with even rudimentary strap-on wings to fly through the air - although Asimov stresses that if the common lunar gas Argon was mixed with the dome's atmosphere, the resulting denser air would make flying even easier. But here in this world, in the state of Missouri in June 1884, there was a report of one man who could resist the gravitational pull that makes us all prisoners of the Earth.

In the pastoral town of Dexter, near the Mississippi River, there lived a 27-year-old farm-worker named Reynard Beck. Reynard and his elder brother Samuel worked the small farm for their widowed mother. After the death of Sam Beck senior in 1879, the Beck family had a rough time trying to make enough money to live decently. The family had the utmost respect from their neighbours, who admired the way the proud Becks refused help from anybody, but their integrity meant that the Becks had virtually no social life at all. Sam and Reynard couldn't even afford the most basic pleasures in life like good clothes or the occasional drink. In fact, both boys were unable to court girls because of their financial position, but they plodded on, content with what little they had.

One morning, before the sun was up, Mrs Beck called her sons to breakfast. Reynard awoke to the aroma of eggs and bacon, yawned, rubbed the sleep from his eyes, then suddenly experienced an intense feeling of delight - and a sensation of weightlessness. He threw back his blankets and was about to get out of bed when he started to float up towards the ceiling. He wasn't frightened - just amazed. He felt light as a feather, and assumed he must be dreaming. The farmer reached out and grabbed hold of the headboard of his bed and pulled himself down onto the mattress in a state of disbelief.

Mrs Beck shouted to her son again and told him his breakfast was going cold. Reynard reacted by letting go of the headboard, hoping that the weightlessness had subsided - but it hadn't - and he found himself floating slowly upward like a soap bubble. He ended up spread-eagled against the ceiling, where he remained wondering at the incredible thing that had happened to him. But what was it? He knew he was about 200 pounds in weight, so how could he just float? Naturally, he was baffled. He pressed the soles of his bare feet against the ceiling and pushed them hard, propelling himself down to the bed. Before he could rise again, he grabbed the bed's headboard and pulled himself down onto the mattress again. He then took hold of a chair and clutched it against his chest. The weight of the chair was just sufficient to keep him grounded. Reynard ignored his mother's impatient cries for him to come down to breakfast and slowly moved toward the chest where his clothes were kept. He opened a drawer and took out an old leather belt that he wore for fishing. Attached to this belt were various lead weights he used on his fishing rod. Reynard wedged his feet under the chest, put the belt on, and was relieved to find that the weighted belt kept his feet firmly on the floor.

Reynard was a God-fearing, superstitious individual, and feared telling anyone about his experience in case they said he had made a pact with the Devil. So he went down to have breakfast with the belt covered by a loose shirt and worked in the fields without breathing a word to anyone about his strange secret.

Before he went to bed, Reynard took off his belt and instantly started to levitate again. At that moment, his brother came into the room and saw him with his hands on the headboard and his feet in the air. He naturally assumed Reynard was performing a handstand.

"What are you doin'?" Sam asked, bemused.

Reynard suddenly lost his grip on the headboard and started rising through the air to the ceiling. Sam stood there, completely shocked as he watched his brother bump the ceiling with his head.

"The belt! Hand me the belt, Sam!" shouted Reynard, and Sam picked the weighted belt from the bed and handed it up to his airborne brother.

"How did you do that? That's one neat trick. How on earth did you do it?" Sam said, suspecting the amazing feat was performed by wires. But he could see that there was none and this truly perplexed him.

As soon as Reynard put the belt back on, he descended again. After he'd told his brother how he had woken up to discover his new talent, they both decided to tell their mother, but she seemed more concerned with what people would say about her levitating son than the mysterious ability he possessed.

Sam convinced his brother that there was money to be made out of his paranormal ability, and the two men decided to go on the road, exhibiting Reynard as "The Floating Wonder".

The act proved to be very popular. When the crowds crushed into the booth to see the show, Reynard simply undid his belt and rose steadily through the air to the canvas roof, where he held onto a metal frame.

When news spread of the astounding "stunt", thousands of people flocked to see the show, and the takings mounted considerably each day.

When the Floating Wonder displayed his anti-gravitational antics at a town in Oklahoma, a few skeptics employed a gang of hooligans to wreck the booth in order to "expose" the fraudulent goings-on. But the vandals were shocked to see that no wires or trickery were involved at all. This revelation only served to bolster the reputation of the Floating Wonder.

Scientists and doctors turned up at the shows, determined to disprove the myth of the flying farmer, but they saw Reynard Beck was no hoaxer - he really could levitate, but as that went against accepted science, the men of learning refused to comment on the inexplicable gravity-resistant man.

In April 1887, a reporter from *The Kansas Star* was assigned to get to the bottom of the Floating Wonder. He later wrote of his attempts to discredit the brothers from Dexter: "Before the exhibition, I thoroughly searched the room, looking for wires, hydraulic ramps, hidden supports - any device that might provide a clue to the mystery, but I found absolutely nothing. While Mr Beck sat in a reclining position three feet from the floor, I beat the air above and below him with a cane, but met no resistance. With the utmost reluctance, I came to the conclusion that he was floating in mid-air."

The Floating Wonder was continually quizzed about the method he employed to leave terra firma, but was unable to offer an explanation. He was as puzzled as everyone else by his unearthly capability.

After six years on the road the Beck brothers had netted over one million dollars from their Floating Wonder sideshows. But in the spring of 1890 the brothers suddenly announced that they were closing down their booth and returning to the farm in Dexter. There were rumours that this had come about because Reynard had lost his strange power. Crowds of curious sightseers swarmed over the Beck farm, hoping to catch sight of Reynard, but he sternly refused to make any more public appearances and became a recluse. After publishing an account of his bizarre condition, Reynard begged for privacy. His last statement to the press in August 1890 was enigmatic: "Once a man has flown in the air, he can never be quite the same man again."

In September of that year, a rumour spread from Dexter and circulated around Middle America. It was said that the Floating Wonder had deliberately taken his belt off outdoors and had flown up into the sky to certain death by asphyxiation. The newshounds responded to the gossip by invading the Beck farm in droves, where they found a tearful Mrs Beck being comforted by her son Sam. They admitted that Reynard had been missing for three days - and revealed that his weighted belt had been found in a field near the Tennessee border.

Reynard Beck was never seen again. Was the Flying Wonder a mammoth hoax perpetrated by the penurious Beck family - or did the young farmer really levitate?

VISIONS OF DEATH

The French eighteenth-century writer Jacques Cazotte was a man of exceptional imagination and foresight, and these talents are evident in his books. In *Le Diable Amour ex* (1772), Cazotte tells the weird tale of a man who falls for a beautiful, voluptuous woman — who is really the Devil in disguise. Monsieur Cazotte also explored the sci-fi and fantasy genres long before the birth of Edgar Allan Poe. In his continuation of the Arabian Nights tales, the Frenchman wrote a series of astounding submarine adventures set in the Mediterranean. Some contemporaries credited Cazotte's literary talent to his infamous dabbling in the occult, which probably involved a ouija board and crystal-ball scrying.

Cazotte was also something of a prophet who scored more hits than misses, and because of his psychic ability, he was frequently invited to the salons of the rich and famous. At one such salon, on a pleasant summer evening in 1788, an assembly of notabilities settled down to a Parisian dinner party and talked of the approaching shadow of the Revolution, and the changes that were in store. Cazotte was invited to speak on the matter, and what he had to say caused a mixed reaction. Some laughed, but others shivered and protested when Cazotte told the gathering of writers, poets and courtiers that King Louis XVI, as well as several of the distinguished ladies sitting at the table, would be executed in the coming upheaval. During the subsequent commotion, Cazotte stared at Nicholas Sebastian Chamfort, a writer and critic. Cazotte seemed to be focusing his powers of second sight. When the writer smiled at the seer's gaze, Cazotte started to speak in a low, disturbing voice. He told Chamfort, "You will meet a long, suffering death after trying unsuccessfully to slash your wrists 22 times."

The writer shook his head and smiled, but seemed uneasy.

Cazotte then turned his attention to the Marquis de Condorcet, a prominent mathematician and philosopher whose progressive ideas helped to shape nineteenth-century sociology. Cazotte told him, "You sir, will die on the floor of a prison cell after taking poison to cheat the executioner."

"Nonsense!" said a lady seated next to the Marquis, and she added, "How could someone as distinguished as the Marquis de Condorcet end up in a prison cell? Charlatan!"

The final prediction of Jacques Cazotte concerned Jean de la Harpe, a critic and bitter atheist. Cazotte told the non-believer that the Revolution would change him into a God-fearing Christian. Upon hearing this prophecy, one of the guests exploded with laughter and shouted, "All my fears are now gone, for if we have to wait until La Harpe becomes a Christian we shall live forever!"

In 1789, the dreaded upheaval finally arrived in the

form of the French Revolution, and with it came the abolition of the old order through mass executions on the guillotine. In the midst of this epic turmoil most men of learning either joined the revolutionaries or fled the country.

Nicholas Chamfort decided to support the Revolution in its early stages, but later becamed sickened by the indiscriminate beheadings. In 1793, the year of the "Reign of Terror", Chamfort was confronted by the Jacobin leaders and threatened with arrest. He knew he too would go to the guillotine sooner or later, so he cut his wrists to end it all - but committing suicide was more difficult than he had imagined. He slashed his wrists 22 times, and suffered an agonizing death several days later, just as Cazotte had predicted.

As for the Marquis de Condorcet, he was actively involved in championing the revolutionary cause and was soon elected to represent the French capital in the Legislative Assembly. He went on to become its Secretary, and proposed a scheme for state education. He also agreed that the ex-king of France should be indefinitely suspended from his duties. The Marquis seemed to be a level-headed man of the people and went from strength to strength with the revolutionaries - until he voted against the execution of Louis XVI. The Marquis quickly fell out of favor with the rebels, and when he also opposed the arrest of the Girondins, he was branded an enemy of the masses. The Marquis went into hiding and became quite paranoid, convinced that the house he was hiding in was being watched. He went on the run for three exhausting days and under the cover of nightfall sought sanctuary in the village of Clamart. But somebody recognized him and he was taken to Bourg-la-Reine and imprisoned. The following morning he was found dead on the floor of the prison cell. He had poisoned himself to escape the guillotine - just as Cazotte had prophesied six years previously.

Like Chamfort and Condorcet, Jean de la Harpe, the final subject of Cazotte's prophecy, was also an advocate of the Revolution in its early days, but being a natural critic, he started to find faults with the new order and was soon classed as a dissenter and thrown into prison for five months. Within days of losing his freedom, the renowned atheist became a reformed man and ended up as an ardent supporter of Christianity, thus fulfilling Cazotte's prediction. Jacques Cazotte's own fate is a sad one. In the superstitious age in which he lived, no rational attempt was made to investigate his strange powers of precognition, and so in 1792, he too became a suspected enemy of the people and was guillotined in Paris for being a "Royalist". One wonders whether this man of incredible foresight actually saw his own fate years before in the Parisian salon.

THE REAL FRANKENSTEIN

According to the scientists, life on earth began around four thousand million years ago when the world was a young, but forbidding planet. The turbulent atmosphere in those times was a mixture of steam, nitrogen, methane, ammonia, carbon and many other gases. But one gas was absent: oxygen. This gas is produced by plant life and did not exist in a free state before the arrival of life, but how exactly, did life on earth begin? Well, established science holds that life came into being in an entirely accidental way. The dead matter floating about in the oceans of the early earth supposedly consisted of various random molecules that collided with one another, and one day, a specific molecule was formed in this random way which could reproduce copies of itself. But there are problems with this theory.

Protein chains - organic compounds containing the elements carbon, hydrogen, oxygen and nitrogen - consist of sub-units called amino acids, and there are 20 possibilities for each link in the protein chain. The

French biophysicist Lecomte de Nouy has calculated that if a new combination were tried every millionth of a second, it would take a period longer than the life of the earth to form the right type of protein chain! Nevertheless, scientists are adamant about the theory of life beginning in the world's primeval ocean-soup. In 1952 it occurred to an American graduate student - Stanley Lloyd Miller - that an experiment to reproduce the environment conducive to life in primordial times could be set up in the laboratory. He put methane, ammonia, hydrogen and water in a flask and boiled the contents for days, occasionally discharging some artificial lightning (via two electrodes) through the mixture to simulate the ultraviolet radiation of the sun. Miller observed that the mixture in the flask quickly darkened. After a week, he analyzed the solution that had formed in the flask and found that, in addition to rudimentary substances lacking in nitrogen atoms, he had glycine and alanine, two simple amino acids. There were also minute traces of more complicated amino acids.

Miller was surprised at the compounds forming so quickly in such large quantities. In the mere space of a week, one-sixth of the methane in the flask had produced such startling compounds.

The fact that Miller had created the building blocks of life in a laboratory generated shockwaves that elated the scientific community and naturally upset the religious authorities, but 115 years before Miller's experiment, a 53-year-old Englishman named Andrew Crosse carried out a similar experiment. Crosse's experiment allegedly produced no mere amino acids, but the formation of a totally new type of insect.

Andrew Crosse was born into a wealthy family on June 17th, 1784. He was a child prodigy who mastered Ancient Greek at the age of eight. When Crosse was nine he was sent to Dr Seyer's School at Bristol, where he was captivated by the subject of science. Around the age of twelve, Crosse became obsessed with the new science of electricity. Young Crosse was a notorious joker, and often wired up the metal doorknobs of the classroom doors to a huge accumulator in order to give the teachers at the school an electric shock whenever they entered the class. Electricity was to become a lifetime obsession, and when Crosse inherited the family estates and fortune upon the death of his mother in 1805, the young science buff used a substantial sum of his newly-acquired wealth to set up a well-equipped laboratory at Fyne Court, his family seat, where he was to perform a series of bizarre experiments.

The isolated country mansion of Fyne Court in the Quantock Hills of Somerset gained an eerie reputation, thanks to Crosse. The locals were sure he was an evil wizard, because of the way Crosse captured the powers of lightning by conducting the bolts through a network of copper cables (over a mile in length) that radiated from the Fyne Court laboratory like a gigantic web. Whenever a storm raged over the Quantock Hills, the superstitious locals would watch the forks of lightning dancing about on the copper cables. To the Somerset yokels, Squire Crosse had to be in league with the Devil to be capable of attracting the lightning, but unknown to them, Crosse was tapping the huge voltages from the lightning flashes to power his electrical experiments. The scientist was intrigued by the various types of crystals that are formed when an electrical current is passed through certain mineral solutions. The outcomes of this pioneering experimental work were written in a notebook. In 1837, this notebook recorded a dramatic incident that has never been explained. The entry reads:

In the course of my endeavours to form artificial minerals by a long continued electric action on fluids holding solution such substances as were necessary to my purpose, I had recourse to every variety of contrivance that I could think of; amongst others I constructed a wooden frame, which supported a Wedgewood funnel, within which rested a quart basin on a circular piece of mahogany. When this basin was filled with a fluid, a strip of flannel wetted with the same was suspended over the side of the basin and inside the funnel, which, acting as a syphon, conveyed the fluid out of the basin through the funnel in successive drops: these drops fell into a smaller funnel of glass placed beneath the other, and which contained a piece of somewhat porous red oxide from Vesuvius. This stone was kept constantly electrified.

On the fourteenth day from the commencement of this experiment, I observed through the lens a few small whitish excrescences or nipples, projecting from about the middle of the electrified stone. On the eighteenth day these projections enlarged, and stuck out seven or eight filaments, each of them longer than the hemisphere on which they grew. On the twenty-sixth day these appearances assumed the form of a perfect insect, standing erect on a few bristles which formed its tail.

On the twenty-eighth day these little creatures moved their legs...

After a few days they detached themselves from the stone, and moved about at pleasure.

Crosse was obviously amazed at the incredible outcome of his experiment, and he tried in vain to find a rational explanation that would account for the strange insect. He immediately repeated the experiment and recorded the outcome in his notebook again:

After many months' action and consequent formation of certain crystalline matters, I observed similar excrescences with those before described at the edge of the fluid in every one of the cylinders except two which contained the carbonate of potassa and the metallic arsenic; and in due time the whitish appearances were developed into insects. In my first experiment I had made use of flannel, wood, and a volcanic stone. In the last, none of these substances were present.

But Crosse could still not accept what he was seeing. The existence of the new mites - or acari, as they are called - seemed to run contrary to the laws of biology. Crosse was determined to get to the bottom of the mite mystery, so he carried out the experiment yet again, and later wrote:

I had omitted to insert within the bulb of the retort a resting place for these *acari* (they are always destroyed if they fall back into the fluid from which they have emerged). It is strange that, in a solution eminently caustic and under an atmosphere of oxihydrogen gas, one single *acarus* should have made its appearance.

Crosse wrote a detailed report of his bizarre discovery and sent it to the Electrical Society in London. Although the report was sceptically received, W. H, Weeks, a respected experimenter was chosen by the

Electrical Society to repeat the Crosse experiment. Weeks was much more careful than Crosse at setting up the experiment. He thoroughly sterilized all of the lab equipment and worked under stringent quarantine-like conditions. News of the Crosse experiment broke as Weeks worked. A newspaper in the west of England published an account of the Crosse experiment, and soon the news agencies of Britain and the rest of Europe were running the story. Then the results of the Weeks experiment were announced; Weeks too had produced the strange insects. The reclusive Crosse suddenly found himself in the eye of a hurricane of unwanted publicity. The mites he had created were named *Acarus Crossii* in his honour, and the creator-scientist was hailed as a genius by many of his colleagues. But the religious authorities and the ignorant hoi polloi were outraged by the 'blaspheming' Crosse. They saw him as a meddling devil who had set himself up as a rival of God. When Crosse returned to Fyne Court, the locals threw stones at him and killed his livestock. On several occasions the dullards even set fire to his crops, and the local Reverend Philip Smith, who incited much of the trouble, even conducted a service of exorcism on Crosse's country estate!

On July 6th, 1855, the controversial scientist died after suffering a paralytic seizure. His last words were, "The utmost extent of human knowledge is but comparative ignorance."

Even today, scientists cannot explain away the acari that were apparently created by Crosse, and what's more, no scientist is even willing to reproduce the fascinating 19th century experiment.

THE ELUSIVE MONARCH

In medieval times the European map of the world was surrounded on all sides by the mists of terra incognita and strange, seemingly endless seas. According to the map makers of those times, the mysterious Atlantic ocean was speckled with strange islands peopled by fairies and the dead, and terrifying gigantic serpents roamed the waters. The imaginative cartographers filled in the blank parts of the map representing unexplored regions with drawings of the exotic beasts of fable: unicorns, dragons, griffins and one-eyed giants. Factual knowledge of Africa and Asia was particularly scant - the Romans had known more of the "Dark Continent" and the Far East centuries before in the days of Pliny; and Africa and the East remained as unknown to most medieval Europeans as the Moon is to the average person today. What hindered European expansion into the mysterious East was the vast Islamic empire that stretched from southern Spain to the peripheries of China. The "Christian" crusaders had, of course, gained some footholds in Syria and Palestine, but the "menace" of Islam would not go away. So imagine how pleased the outnumbered Europeans in the Holy Land were when they heard tales of an unknown Christian monarch who ruled an immense kingdom near India (a generic term at the time for the unexplored lands beyond the River Tigris). No one knows where the stories of the mysterious ruler originated, but the first definite record of an enigmatic priest-king known as "Prester John" (his first name was derived from "Presbyter" - Greek for "priest") was made in 1145 when the French bishop Hugh de Gebal (now Lebanon) told the Pope of "a certain John, a king and a priest who dwells beyond Persia and Armenia in the uttermost East, and with all his people, is a Christian. It is said that he is a lineal descendant of the Magi of whom mention is made in the gospel and that ruling over the same peoples which they governed, he enjoys such great glory and wealth that he uses no sceptre save one of entire emerald. Inspired by the example of his forefathers who came to adore Christ in his manger, he had planned to go to the aid of Jerusalem, but was prevented from crossing the Tigris because the river was frozen."

This was sweet music to the ears of the Pope. For centuries there had been persistent rumours that Christian colonies existed in India, founded by the apostle Thomas. Now the Pope was certain that India was Christianised. The news of the good "King of the Indies" flew across Europe. Prester John would be the ally who would help the Christian world to crush the Saracen hordes.

But nothing more was heard of the remote ruler until 1165, when three letters were sent to Pope Alexander III, the Byzantine Emperor Manuel, and the Holy Roman Emperor Frederick. The letters, written in Latin, read:

From Prester John, by the grace of God, most poweful king over all Christian kings.

Let it be known to you that we have the highest crown on earth as well as gold, silver, precious stones, and strong fortresses, cities, towns, castles, and boroughs. We have under our sway forty-two kings who are all mighty and good Christians.

Our land is divided into four parts, for there are so many Indias. In Greater India lies the body of the Apostle Saint Thomas, and this India is towards the east, for it is near the deserted Babylon and also near the tower called Babel.

Written in our holy palace in the land of Prester John.

The contents of this letter - which was quickly translated into all the principal European languages, and even Hebrew — surpassed all previous expectations of the priest-King's glory. Another grandiose letter from Prester John began:

We have been told that you would very much like to know about us and our country and our nation and our animals, and the nature of our country.

The writer of the royal epistle then goes on to paint an incredible picture of an incredible kingdom. In the sprawling country of the Four Indias existed marvels such as the fabled race of beautiful blonde giantesses known as the Amazons, wild hares as large as sheep, the overgrown vestiges of the Garden of Eden, two bellicose races of cannibals known as Gog and Magog (imprisoned behind a chain of mountains in the far north of the country), a pepper forest infested by enormous snakes, strange cannabis-like plants that gave psychic powers to those who ate them, and the descendants of the ten lost tribes of Israel. As for the way of life in the kingdom of Prester John, there were no thieves or adulterers, and poverty was unknown. The ruler had seven ravishing wives, but he only slept with them four nights a year. The court of the priest-king consisted of 30,000 people - and they enjoyed a royal banquet every day. At the right of Prester John, twelve archbishops sat, and at his left twenty-three bishops, including the Patriarch of St Thomas, the Bishop of Samarkand, and the Archbishop of Susa.

The claims of these letters will seem absurd to the modern-day reader, but to the Europeans of the twelfth century, anything could exist in the Orient and the lands beyond, because no one had visited those realms to debunk the fabulous tales. So when the Greek and Roman emperors asked their scholars if the letters from Prester John were genuine, they judged them to be authentic. A Mecca for the adventurers of Europe was now sketched on the incomplete maps of the Orient and Asia: the Wondrous Kingdom of Prester John.

In 1177 Pope Alexander III became excited at the news brought back from travellers in the East about Prester John's desire to be instructed in the Catholic faith. The Pope's private physician, a Dr Philippus, had recently returned from an Eastern expedition with the news, and he also informed the Pope of Prester John's wish to build a church in Rome and his yearning to construct a fabulous altar in the Church of the Holy Sepulchre in Jerusalem.

The Pope was ecstatic, and he wrote a letter to the legendary monarch which he gave Dr Philippus to deliver. The physician set off on his mission - but was never heard from again. There were no further letters from Prester John, but in 1221, rumours of the priest-king began to circulate again. It was said that a "great Christian warlord was on the move in the East" - trouncing the Muslims with military manoeuvres reminiscent of the Romans. It was said that the holy warrior's path of conquest would soon bring him to Western Europe, where he would join up with his Christian brethren and launch a final attack to eradicate the Saracens from the face of the earth forever. But this conquistador, according to the rumours, was not Prester John at all, for he had died. The man who was to save Europe and Jerusalem from the adherents of Islam was Prester John's grandson, David.

No one took the rumours seriously, but a year later an army did arrive in Europe, and the leader of the hordes of strange-featured soldiers had a name that sounded like Prester John: his name was Genghis Khan - but he was anything but Christian. The Mongol armies of Genghis had recently plundered the citadel of Bukhara where they slaughtered around 30,000 men and enslaved their wives and children. After the slaughter, the Great Khan climbed into the pulpit of the sacked city's mosque and delivered his chilling sermon: "Oh people! Know that you have committed great sins! If you ask me what proof I have for these words, I say it is because I am the punishment of God! If you had not committed great sins, God would not have sent a punishment like me upon you!"

The Mongolian warrior who today ranks in notoriety with Alexander the Great, Napoleon and Hitler, was backed by an army of a size that hadn't been witnessed in Europe since the days of the Roman invasions. A Persian civil servant of the time wrote of the Mongol swarm:

The troops of the Great Khan were more numerous than ants or locusts, being in their multitude beyond estimation or computation. Detachment after detachment arrived, each like a billowing sea.

Russia, Poland and Hungary were ravaged by the Tartar armies, but fortunately, Genghis Khan had to return to Asia to settle a squabble in the Mongolian royal dynasty, and his forces left Europe badly bruised, but unbeaten. The empire of Khan, which stretched from the Pacific to the Danube, made the old Islamic threat now seem microscopic in comparison. Fears of a new Mongol menace proved to be unfounded. The Mongol empire made it clear that it had no intention of absorbing the West, and trade routes, policed by the Tartar horsemen, soon opened up, providing Europeans with safe highways to the lands of the beckoning East. At last, the search for Prester John could soon begin in earnest.

As the Mongols were pagans, it was hoped in the West that they could be converted to Christianity and then join in the Holy War against the Muslims. So the first travellers who ventured into Asia were monks and friars, such as John of Piano Carpini and William of Ruysbruck. These holy men managed to convert some of the Tartars and returned to give encouraging news of an Asia inhabited by a largely peaceful population. Many European merchants were captivated by the promising tales of Asia and Cathay and hit the roads to the East, hoping to buy spices, furs, precious stones, and perhaps to form alliances with the powerful khans of Mongolia. The best known of these travellers was a Venetian by the name of Marco Polo, who first visited Peking in 1275. Polo actually claimed to have located the long-sought kingdom of Prester John. According to Polo, Prester John's kingdom was Tenduk, a large domain in the north of Mongolia, and he was murdered by his own vassal - Genghis Khan. At the time of Polo's visit to Tenduk, the ruler was a Christian God-fearing man who still held the title of Prester John. What's more, a majority of the inhabitants of Tenduk were also Christian. Of all the travellers to the East, Marco Polo was the least likely to invent fanciful tales, so did he find the Kingdom of Prester John? No one is sure, even today. Many historians believe that the kingdom was probably simply an embroidered description of the Abyssinian Church. Shortly after the death of Christ, the African church was founded in Abyssinia (now known as Ethiopia), a region ringed by almost impenetrable mountains, and until the sixteenth century, this remote outpost of the Christian faith survived behind the Islamic barrier of Egypt. The Abyssinian church was never attacked by the Muslims because it was said that when the prophet Mohammed announced his mission to all the kings of the world, it was only the ruler of Abyssinia who was courteous enough to send a punctilious reply.

The holy Abyssinian king ruled over a vast territory that certainly bears some resemblance to the strange land of Prester John. Abyssinia was exceedingly rich in mineral resources, and on the outskirts of the country there lived a tribe of pygmies and an exceptionally tall race, both now extinct. The Abyssinian monarch was said to be a direct descendant of King Solomon, a claim that was upheld by Haile Selassie, the twentieth-century emperor of Ethiopia.

So, is that it? Was Prester John just an inflated yarn based on an Ethiopian king? Not quite. When the ambassador of Abyssinia arrived in Rome in 1441, he strenuously denied that his sovereign was named "John". He said, "No! His true and only name is Zareiacob, meaning 'Descendant of the prophet Jacob'." Our file on Prester John, then, must remain open.

THE MAN IN THE VELVET MASK

In the sixtieth year of King Louis XIV's reign, an enigmatic individual known as the "ancient prisoner" died in the Bastille. The reason for the man's 34-year incarceration was never divulged but today, thanks to the romantic novelist Alexandre Dumas and his book *The Man in the Iron Mask*, we all know the bizarre aspects of his imprisonment. Dumas popularized the notion that the Bastille's most famous prisoner was either the Sun King himself or his twin brother, and that the prisoner wore an iron mask, but the real facts concerning the masked prisoner are much more mysterious. All that is known for certain is that in July 1669, a man was arrested in Dunkirk (which was then in English hands); whether this man was entering or leaving the country has never been established. He was taken to the prison fortress at Pignerol (near Turin) in Piedmont, north-west Italy. Monsieur Saint-Mars, the governor of the prison had received a letter from the French Minister of War, the Marquis de Louvois, telling him to take extraordinary security precautions with the prisoner:

The king has commanded that I am to have the man [the prisoner] named Eustache Dauger sent to Pignerol. It is of the most importance to His service that he should be most securely guarded and that he should in no way give information about himself nor send letters to anyone at all.

I am informing you of this in advance so that you can have a cell prepared in which you will place him securely, taking care that the windows of the place in which he is put do not give on to any place that can be approached by anyone, and that there are double doors to be shut, for your guards must not hear anything. You must yourself take to him, once a day, the day's necessities and you must never listen, under any pretext whatever, to what he may want to reveal to you, always threatening to kill him if he ever opens his mouth to speak of anything but his day-to-day needs.

Shortly after Dauger arrived at Pignerol, the prison governor wrote back to the Marquis de Louvois, confirming the prisoner's arrival:

Monsieur de Vauroy [the military governor of Dunkirk] has handed over to me the man named Eustache d'Auger [sic]. As soon as I had put him in a very secure place, while waiting for the cell I am having prepared for him to be completed, I told him in the presence of Monsieur de Vauroy that if he should speak to me or anyone else of anything other than his day-today needs, I would run him through with my sword. On my life, I shall not fail to observe, very punctiliously, your commands.

This obviously suggests that Dauger was no ordinary prisoner, and that he had information that posed some sort of dire threat to the security of the realm. In March 1698, Saint-Mars was given the post of governor at the Bastille and Dauger was transferred with him to Paris, now wearing a black velvet mask with metal clasps.

The arrival of the masked prisoner naturally made everyone in the Bastille curious. The gossipers at the prison had a field day. Some said that the strange prisoner was the illegitimate offspring of the Queen Mother and her Chief Minister Cardinal Mazarin, while others believed that the prisoner was the real Louis XIV and that the king of France was an illegitimate son. Voltaire, one of the greatest intellects of his age (and the man who invented the myth of the "iron" mask), proposed that the prisoner in the mask was an illegitimate half-brother of Louis XIV, the result of an act of infidelity by the queen of Louis XIII. There was no shortage of theories, but the only person who ever saw the face of the prisoner was Saint-Mars, and he never revealed what he knew. A doctor who once examined the man in the mask never actually got to see his face; he inspected only the man's tongue and his naked body, noting that the prisoner had dark skin, and was "admirably made". He also said that the enigmatic captive had an "interesting voice", but never elaborated further on this curious remark.

In 1703, the man in the mask died at the Bastille. All the furniture and personal belongings in his cell were burned, and the surfaces of the cell's walls scraped and whitewashed in case the prisoner had engraved a message. Even the tiles on the floor were replaced.

The faceless "ancient prisoner" who had lived his prison life in such anonymity was buried in an unmarked grave. The name on his burial certificate names him Marchioly, which only deepens the mystery surrounding his identity. The most important clue to his identity must lie in the mask. Why was it so important for his face to remain concealed for so long? Did he bear a striking resemblance to some prominent person in France? The fact that a special governor was appointed to the masked prisoner for all of his life means he must have been someone of note. Why wasn't he simply executed after his arrest at Dunkirk? Was he allowed to live because he meant too much to someone in power? Several historical revisionists have come to the conclusion that Voltaire may have hit the nail on the head when he suggested that the prisoner was the half-brother of Louis XIV.

Another unusual theory that has been put forward in recent years is that the prisoner was the real father of Louis XIV. It is known that for 13 of their 22 years of marriage Louis XIII and his queen, Anne of Austria, had no children, because the king was impotent. Cardinal Richelieu - who was at the time the effective ruler of France - knew it was in the interests of the monarch to produce an heir (who could also become the puppet king of the Richelieu faction). The couple had separated, but Richelieu used his diplomatic skills to get them back together for a reconciliation, and the result of this rapprochement was the birth of a boy in 1638. The news of the birth shocked the French nation, as it was widely known that the royal couple detested one another, and many thought it strange that the king and queen - who had never had a child before - were suddenly able to produce an heir. It has been suggested that the unprincipled Richelieu persuaded the queen to have sexual intercourse with a young nobleman in order to produce an heir to the throne. This nobleman would probably have been one of the bastard sons of the promiscuous Henry of Navarre - all half-brothers of King Louis XIII - which would have meant that the queen's lover had royal Bourbon blood in his veins. This theory would certainly explain why Louis XIV was so unlike his royal "father".

Perhaps the masked prisoner had to have his face concealed because of the tell-tale resemblance he bore to his son. This would also explain why the "Sun King" never had the most famous prisoner of the Bastille secretly murdered; that would have been patricide.

THE VANISHED LORD

At 9.45 on the evening of Thursday, November 7th, 1974, a petite brunette in a bloodstained nightdress ran into the bar of the Plumbers Arms public house in London's exclusive Belgravia district. To a handful of startled drinkers, the woman shouted, "Help me! Help me! I've just escaped from being murdered! My children! He's in the house! He's just murdered my nanny!"

The woman, who had sustained seven bloody head wounds, was 37-year-old Lady Lucan, wife of Richard Bingham, Lord Lucan, and the murderer she spoke of was her estranged husband.

Arthur Whitehouse, the barman of the Plumbers Arms, dialled 999 while his wife treated Lady Lucan's head injuries until an ambulance arrived. Ten minutes later a police van pulled up outside the pub. After being quizzed by detectives, Lady Lucan was taken to the casualty ward at St George's Hospital, Hyde Park Corner.

Meanwhile, Sergeant Baker and Police Constable Beddick arrived at the alleged scene of the crime - Lady Lucan's terraced house at Number 46 Belgrave Street, a mere stone's throw from Buckingham Palace.

The two policemen saw that the house was in darkness and tried to peer into the living room of the raised ground floor, but net curtains prevented them from seeing anything. They descended the outside stairs that led to the basement, and through a window saw the faint glow of a red lamp on an electric kettle beyond the Venetian blinds. The officers then returned to the front door of the house and finding it locked, decided to force it open.

Inside, they found that the hall light wasn't working. Thinking the murderer could still be lurking in the dark hall, Sergeant Baker told PC Beddick to fetch a torch from the patrol car. Baker produced a small pocket torch and went into the house. By the faint light of his torch Sergeant Baker noticed streaks of wet blood on the wallpaper at the end of the hall.

Beddick re-entered the house with a powerful torch and rejoined the Sergeant. Together, they slowly descended the stairs to the basement, following the trail of blood. At the foot of the stairs was a large pool of blood within which the faint outlines of a number of footprints could be discerned. The basement was quickly checked, but finding no intruder present the two policemen proceeded to search the rest of the six-story house.

Upon entering a bedroom on the second floor, they found a bloodstained towel draped across a pillow. The two policemen then heard sounds emanating from the floor above. They went upstairs and discovered that the sounds were from a colour television set that had been left on in the nursery. For some inexplicable reason, the volume control had been fully turned up.

On the top floor, Baker and Beddick found Lady

Lucan's children. Two of them were sleeping soundly, but the third, ten-year-old Frances, was wide-awake and standing by her bed. "Where are Mummy and Sandra?" she asked. The Sandra she referred to was 29-year-old Sandra Rivett, the nanny of Lady Lucan's children.

As soon as the children had been put safely in the care of a summoned police officer, Baker and Beddick resumed their inspection of the basement. They discovered a canvas United States mail bag near the foot of the basement steps next to the door of the kitchen. An arm was protruding from it. Inside the mail bag was the body of the nanny, Mrs Rivett. She had been bludgeoned to death. The body was still warm, but no pulse was present. Shortly afterwards, detectives found the murder weapon in the ante room off the hall. It was a nine-inch-long piece of lead piping bound in surgical tape.

Detectives made routine inquiries and started piecing events together. Later that eventful night, Detective Sergeant Graham Forsyth called at Lucan's flat at 72a Elizabeth Street. Lucan wasn't there.

At 10.45 p.m., Lucan telephoned his 75-year-old mother, the Dowager Countess of Lucan. He told her that there had been a "terrible catastrophe at Number 46" and that his wife and her nanny had been badly hurt. Lucan went on to tell his mother how he had been driving past his wife's house when he saw a fight in progress through the blinds of the basement window. He went in and saw "something terrible in the basement. I couldn't bring myself to look."

Lucan's mother asked her son where he was going. Before he hung up, Lucan said, "I don't know."

In his dark blue Ford Corsair, Lucan travelled 42 miles south to the village of Uckfield in Sussex. At 11.30 p.m., he called at the home of Susan Maxwell-Scott, a long-standing friend. When she answered the door, the shocked and dishevelled-looking peer asked Susan if her husband Ian (another close associate of Lucan) was around. Mrs Maxwell-Scott said he wasn't at home, and asked Lucan what was wrong.

Lucan said, "I have been through a nightmarish experience. It's so incredible, I don't think you or anyone else could possibly believe it."

Lucan then reiterated the same story he had told his mother. Mrs Maxwell-Scott urged Lucan to visit the police with her first thing in the morning, but Lucan said that was out of the question. At 1.15 a.m. he drove off into the night, never to be seen again. Later that morning, around eight o'clock, his abandoned car was found parked outside a house in the south coast port of Newhaven. Inside the vehicle on the front seats, dashboard and steering wheel, were smears of dry blood. In the boot, the police found a second length of lead piping wrapped in sticking plaster.

Detectives took a statement from Lady Lucan in hospital. According to her version of events, shortly before nine o'clock on the night of the murder, she and Sandra Rivett had been watching television with the three children in the nursery on the third floor. After putting the two younger children to bed, Mrs Rivett went downstairs to the basement kitchen to make a cup of tea. When she had failed to return after 20 minutes, Lady Lucan became suspicious and went down to see what was wrong. As she reached the dark hallway, she called out the nanny's name, but received no reply. Lady Lucan walked down the steps to the basement, when suddenly, Lord Lucan leaned over the banister and started beating her over the head with a length of lead pipe. He landed seven blows to her skull, but incredibly Lady Lucan remained conscious and fought her attacker. Her husband thrust his gloved hand down her throat and attempted to throttle her. Lady Lucan grabbed his testicles and squeezed them. This did the trick. Lucan quickly let go of her.

The exhausted couple then decided to talk things over.

Lucan helped his wife upstairs, then went to the bathroom to fetch a towel. Lady Lucan took the opportunity to flee from the house, heading straight for the Plumbers Arms, a mere 30 yards away.

Scotland Yard launched a nationwide manhunt, and Interpol later joined in the search. Unconfirmed sightings of the aristocratic fugitive started coming in from places as remote as New Delhi and Paraguay, but subsequent investigations established that most of the sightings were cases of mistaken identity.

A month after the murder, the suspicions of the Australian police were aroused when a distinguished-looking Englishman turned up in Melbourne. He was promptly arrested and grilled. It turned out not to be Lucan, but the former Labour government minister John Stonehouse, wanted by police in Britain after faking his suicide in Florida in order to escape from business problems.

Because Lucan had relatives in South Africa, many believed that the various sightings of the peer in Johannesburg were genuine. Detective Chief Superintendent Roy Ranson, who was assigned to the

Lucan case from day one, firmly believes that Richard Bingham is hiding out in South Africa. In 1994, shortly after his retirement, Ranson published *Looking For Lucan*, an intriguing account of his ongoing search for the peer. The book is laced with controversial hints and allegations. Ranson draws attention to some startling and previously-unknown facts and links that add a new dimension to the renowned murder case, such as Lucan's frequent use of a private plane, and his friendship with racing driver Graham Hill - a seasoned pilot who died in 1976 when his twin-engined Piper Aztec crashed near his home at Elstree. Did Hill fly Lucan out of Britain? According to Ranson, Hill regularly flew all over Europe (often with a total disregard for European aviation laws) and had once transported Lucan's Mercedes car from Britain to the peer's Estoril villa in Portugal — but Ranson admits that we will probably never know if Hill performed an even greater and controversial favor for Bingham in November 1974.

Britain's Channel Four Television commissioned a documentary team to follow the retired Ranson in his quest for the shadowy aristocrat, but despite a number of interviews with people who had allegedly encountered Lucan, the programme ended on a disappointingly inconclusive note.

The book makers Ladbroke's once offered 1000-1 against Lucan being found. But the odds were recently withdrawn. Did Lucan commit suicide, or is he still hiding from justice? If the latter is true, he is presumably being sheltered, but by whom?

THE INCREDIBLE HEALER

Being born on February 14th, 1629, it was decided that the baby boy would be called Valentine, but none of the Irish Greatrakes family could have suspected that the babe would one day become a famous and controversial healer whose fame would travel across Europe.

The young Valentine Greatrakes was as normal as any other child, and he exhibited no out-of-the-ordinary talents in the early stages of his life in Affane, County Waterford, where he was brought up in the Protestant tradition of Ireland. At the age of 20, Greatrakes began his seven-year military career as an officer in the Parliamentary army during the English Civil War. He was a loyal cavalry lieutenant for Cromwell, and when he was discharged in 1656, he was rewarded by the Lord Protector with a number of high-powered appointments, including that of Justice of the Peace. With the Restoration of 1660 - the reinstatement of the English monarchy under Charles II - Greatrakes lost his civil appointments, but he was later made High Sheriff of Waterford.

In 1663, at the age of 34, Greatrakes had a series of strange recurrent dreams in which he received the gift of healing from a God-like being. He told his wife about the strange repetitive dream, and she told him not to worry about it, but shortly afterwards he experienced, while awake this time, what he described as "an impulse or strange persuasion" to heal. Again, Valentine told his wife about "preternatural forces" that were inwardly urging him to cure people, and she told him he should try to put his thoughts into practice by attempting to heal the poor disfigured people to whose medical treatment she charitably contributed. Greatrakes followed his wife's suggestion, and later wrote of the first unfortunate individual he encountered:

There was one at hand that had the Evil grievously in the eyes, throat and cheeks, whereupon I laid my hands upon the places affected, and prayed to God for Jesus' sake to heal him. In a few days afterwards, the father brought the son with the eye so much changed that it was almost quite whole, and to be brief (to God's glory I speak it) within a month he was perfectly healed and so continues.

Being a rather squeamish man, Greatrakes felt quite nauseous at the sight of the victims of Scrofula - a tuberculosis of the lymphatic glands that was also known as "king's evil" after Edward the Confessor (c. 1042-66), who is recorded to have healed victims by "royal touch". In England, Scotland and France, it had long been thought that the touch of a royal hand was a sure remedy for Scrofula and similar disfiguring diseases. Scarcely was Charles I on the throne when he too began to demonstrate his curative powers, and scores of scrofulous people flocked from far and near to benefit from his touch. When he became Lord

Protector, even Oliver Cromwell attempted to continue the tradition of the royal touch, but failed.

Greatrakes treated another victim of Scrofula, a woman named Margaret MacShane, who had been unsuccessfully treated by a certain Dr Anthony, a well-known physician of the day. Greatrakes visited the woman and later described how his healing hands:

. . . suppurated the nodes and drew and healed the sores which formerly I could not have endured the sight of, nor touched, nor smelt without vomiting, so great an aversion had I naturally to all wounds and sores.

Amazingly, Margaret MacShane made a miraculous recovery over a period of six weeks, and was completely cured.

Scrofula was just one of a host of diseases rife in the seventeen century. Greatrakes decided to test his healing powers on a victim of the ague, a feverish, convulsive condition that was as widespread as Scrofula. Again he met with success, and by 1665 - the year the Great (bubonic) Plague killed 68,000 Londoners - the news of Greatrake's healing ability had spread like wildfire. The Irishman was soon healing the sick from six in the morning till six in the evening, three days a week, and so many people people visited his home he had to build out-houses to accommodate them. But Greatrakes's fame also reached the ears of the ecclesiastical authorities, and the "Irish Mesmerist" - as some called him - was summoned by the Dean of Lismore to appear before a bishop's court. The result of this was that Greatrakes was forbidden to practice, but he angrily ignored the injunction, and such was his popularity (and his social standing), that the religious authorities were powerless to take further action against him.

The Leonardo da Vinci of his day, a brilliant Irish physicist named Robert Boyle, John Evelyn, the diarist and founder of the Royal Society, the poet Andrew Marvell, and the journalist Roger L'Estrange paid a visit to Valentine Greatrakes when he visited plague-stricken London, and the latter was surprised to learn first-hand that the famous healer was not taking money for his cures. The journalist also interviewed a woman who had been cured of deafness, blindness, cancer, sciatica, and palsy. By this time, Greatrakes had earned the nickname of "the Stroker" because of the way he moved his hands with a stroking motion above the affected part of the patient's body without actually touching them. Robert Boyle subjected the Stroker to a thorough investigation and declared him to be a genuine healer, although John Evelyn believed that Greatrakes's health-restoring talents were only effective against certain ailments. The diarist wrote:

To my observation, the cures he commonly pretended to were most effectively on tumours, aches, rheumatisms and other wandering distempers; but did not extend to fevers, agues, pleurisies, etc., where the habit is vitiated. However, I say the history is by no means to be slighted.

Andrew Marvell was greatly impressed by the Stroker's successful treatment of plague victims, and many of London's prominent academics and physicians also spoke in favor of Greatrakes.

In 1683, Valentine Greatrakes died at the age of 54.

No one has ever given an adequate explanation for the Irishman's gift. It is said that as Greatrakes got older, the strange faculty began to fade, but many who were close to him said that his healing power had not diminished; he had merely withdrawn from public view because certain dogmatic clergymen, fearing obsolescence, had hounded him with baseless accusations of witchcraft.

THE MEN IN BLACK

In January 1952, Albert K. Bender, a dedicated American UFO investigator, founded the International Flying Saucer Bureau in Connecticut. Bender spent an intensive year studying the UFO phenomenon from every conceivable angle, and then, one night, the "solution" hit him. Bender later stated, "I went into the fantastic and came up with the answer."

But no one ever got to know just what this answer was, for according to Bender, he was silenced by three sinister men who appeared in his bedroom. The UFO investigator had typed an article about his findings for his own non-profit-making journal *Space Review*, when he experienced a sudden dizzy spell. He went to lie down, and was terrified at the sight of three black silhouettes materializing in his bedroom. When the shadows became solid, Bender saw that they were three men dressed in black clothes, their faces partly shaded by the Homburg style hats that they wore. Bender said he felt the strangers probing his mind, and one of them told him that his speculation about the UFOs was correct. Then Bender suddenly noticed that this man in black was holding the typescript of the article he had written for the UFO journal.

A strong voice in Bender's head told him, "You are *not* to tell anyone the truth; it is your duty as an American citizen. We have a special assignment down here and must not be disturbed by your people. We are among you and know your every move."

Moments later, the odd trio were nowhere to be seen - they'd vanished into thin air. Naturally, Bender was ridiculed when he told his colleagues about the strange visitors but, unknown to most UFO researchers at the time, Bender's encounter with mysterious men in black was by no means a unique occurrence - reports of identically-dressed visitors have been cropping up since the flying saucer era began in 1947. In the early days it was assumed that the strangers were CIA or FBI personnel because of their clandestine behaviour. In all the early reports, the men in black were said to wear outdated black suits and trilbies, and were always seen to arrive in a black Cadillac bearing number plates that turned out to be bogus. The visitors' faces, invariably described as oriental-looking, were often said to be crudely daubed with makeup. The victim who was harassed by the men in black was always a person who had encountered a UFO, and this person was always alone at the time of the visitation, like Albert Bender.

In November 1961, office-worker Paul Miller and three companions were on a homeward journey to Minot, North Dakota after a hunting trip, when they noticed a 50-foot-long cylinder hovering in a field. The cylinder was glowing with a whitish-green light. Two figures descended from the underside of the strange object. From his stationary car, Paul Miller watched them advance, and panic seized him. He grabbed his rifle, got out the car, and fired at the creatures, wounding one of them. He then jumped into the car with his friends and tore away from the area, but when they arrived at Minot, they felt strange, and learned that they had somehow lost three hours. Then they started to recall how they had all simultaneously suffered a strange blackout while travelling down a secluded road, but the four men agreed to keep their experience of the UFO encounter a secret.

The next morning, three men arrived at the office where Miller worked. They said they were government officials, but never showed their credentials. They quizzed Miller in private about the UFO encounter, but for some reason did not mention the shooting incident. The men - described as dark-skinned and dressed in black - took Miller to his home and asked to see the clothes he had worn on the previous night. One of the men kept examining the soles of the shoes Miller had worn on the hunting trip. Miller asked the men how they had found out about the UFO sighting, but he received no reply. After probing the house for an hour the men suddenly left, and the Air Force later told Miller they too were in the dark regarding the identity of the visitors.

In August 1965, a Californian highway inspector named Rex Heflin saw a metallic disc-shaped object floating across the sky over the Santa Ana Freeway. Heflin had a Polaroid camera at hand which he used for his job, and took four photographs of the UFO. The fourth picture was of a doughnut-shaped ring of smoke that the UFO left behind when it manoeuvred off into the heavens. The sighting attracted widespread media attention, and Heflin got a call from a man who said he was from the North American Air Defence Command (NORAD). An individual in typical "men in black" attire turned up at Heflin's home and persuaded him to hand over the Polaroid snaps of the UFO. Luckily, Heflin had taken the trouble of copying the photographs, because the man in black never returned the original snapshots. NORAD denied any knowledge of the "representative" who had visited Heflin's home. Two years later, another suspicious-looking official turned up on Heflin's doorstep one night, and mindful of his last encounter with a dubious visitor, Heflin asked the stranger to show him some form of ID. The stranger presented his credentials: a number of cards and documents that suggested that the caller was a Captain C.H. Edmonds of the Space Systems Division.

"What's your business?" Heflin asked Edmonds.

"It's about the photographs you took of the UFO. Are you going to try to get the originals of them back?" Edmonds asked.

"No," replied Heflin, and he noticed how his answer seemed to make the visitor smile slightly. Heflin suddenly saw a black Cadillac parked in the street nearby. A silhouetted figure in the back of the vehicle was pointing a small device at Heflin and the visitor. This device was not unlike a modern camcorder, and Heflin felt he was being filmed with it.

The "Captain" then started to ask Heflin if he had heard about the so-called Bermuda Triangle. Heflin nodded, but the stranger then digressed into mundane talk, before saying goodnight.

A subsequent investigation proved that there were four Captain C.H. Edmonds on the Air Force's list of officers, but none of them resembled the man who had visited Heflin, and none of the captains had any connection with the Santa Ana UFO case.

Some time later, Heflin returned home to be told by two of his neighbours that they had seen men in military uniform sneaking around the back of Heflin's house. One of the mystery men seemed annoyed and resorted to knocking heavily on the front door of the house — before storming off in a Cadillac. On several occasions, Heflin found that the envelopes containing his mail had been tampered with, and whenever he used his telephone, he heard strange clicks which convinced him that he was being bugged.

While driving at night in July 1967, Robert Richardson of Toledo, Ohio was negotiating a bend in a road when he found himself confronted with a strange circular craft that was blocking the road ahead. Unable to stop in time, he rammed the unearthly-looking object, which somehow "faded away" seconds after the impact. Richardson told the police about the strange collision, but when they accompanied the driver to the scene of the crash, the officers could only make out the skid-marks of Richardson's car. Richardson returned to the crash-scene the next day, and was surprised to find a small irregular-shaped lump of metal that looked as if it had come from the UFO. Richardson informed the Aerial Phenomena Research Organization (APRO) and told them what had happened. A member of APRO recorded the time and date of the alleged incident and filed it, and Richardson later took the strange piece of metal to them for analysis.

Three days later, at 11 p.m., two men in their late

twenties confronted Richardson at his home and, without identifying themselves, asked a series of questions relating to the UFO encounter. For some unexplained reason, Richardson felt peculiar, and had no desire to ask the visitors for their credentials. The strangers were very pleasant, and when they'd finished with their inquiries, they left the house and climbed into a black 1953 Cadillac. Richardson scribbled down the car's number, but when the registration was checked it was found that no such number had ever been issued in the United States.

A week later, two different men visited Richardson. They were dark-complexioned, and one spoke in a perfect English accent, while the other had a similar accent with a slight indeterminable foreign intonation. The men tried to persuade Richardson that he had imagined the UFO, but they later demanded Richardson to hand over the lump of metal. When Richardson said that APRO had the metal, one of the men in black warned, "If you want your wife to stay as pretty as she is, then you'd better get the metal back."

APRO concluded that the metal contained an unusually pure proportion of magnesium and iron, and handed the sample back to Richardson. He waited for the men in black to return for the metal lump, but they never did.

Another classic men in black incident took place at Maine, USA, in September 1976 at the home of Herbert Hopkins, a 58-year-old doctor and hypnotist who was acting as a consultant on an alleged UFO abduction case. Early in the evening, a man phoned Hopkins and identified himself as the vice-president of the New Jersey UFO Research Organization. The caller asked Hopkins if he could come to his home to discuss the abduction case, as it was of immense interest to him. Dr Hopkins said he was welcome to come over. After putting the phone down, Dr Hopkins walked to the porch of his house - and there was the caller, walking up the porch steps. There was no car to be seen, and even if the man had travelled by car, Hopkins knew that the stranger couldn't possibly have got to the house that fast from any phone (in 1976, personal mobile phones were not in widespread use).

Hopkins later said that the caller looked like an undertaker. The hat, suit, tie and shoes he wore were a funereal black. His shirt was white, and his suede gloves were grey.

The visitant was admitted to the house, and he and Dr Hopkins had been discussing the abduction case for about 20 minutes when the visitor suddenly suggested something that made the doctor suspicious. The man in black told Hopkins, "Erase the tapes you have made of the hypnotic sessions with the UFO witnesses. Have nothing further to do with the case."

The suggestion made the doctor uneasy. The man in black put his gloved hand to his mouth and wiped what appeared to be a thick layer of lipstick. Upon seeing the red smear on his glove, the stranger quickly took off his gloves and put them in his inside jacket pocket. Hopkins watched in fear as the visitor stood up and approached menacingly. He said, "You have two coins in your pocket. Give me one of them."

The doctor reached into his pockets and discovered that the visitor was right - he did indeed have two coins. Hopkins placed one of them on the visitor's outstretched hand. Seconds later, the coin on the man's palm seemed to go out of focus - and then vanished before the doctor's unbelieving eyes.

"Neither you nor anyone else on this planet will ever see that coin again," the man in black said.

A few minutes later, the caller became unsteady on his feet, and his speech faltered. He enigmatically commented, "My energy is running low . . . must go now . . . goodbye."

The visitor staggered out of the house and descended the porch steps with great difficulty. Dr Hopkins saw a bluish-white light flashing in the driveway, but was too afraid to see what it was.

Later that night, when the doctor's family had returned from visiting relatives, someone noticed strange markings on the driveway. The black streaky markings ran along the centre of the driveway - where no wheels could have been. On the following morning, the markings had vanished, yet there had been no rain to wash them away.

Dr Hopkins was naturally reluctant to tell anyone of the man in black episode, but three days later, on September 24th, the mystery deepened when his daughter-in-law Maureen was also involved in a men in black incident.

Maureen received a telephone call from a man who said he was a friend of her husband, and he asked if he and his girlfriend could come to visit. Maureen asked her husband John who the caller was, and he explained that he had met an odd man a couple of days back at a fast-food restaurant. Maureen told the caller he was welcome to come over with his companion.

When the couple arrived, Maureen saw that they both appeared to be in their mid-thirties, but wore curiously old-fashioned clothes. The woman's breasts were set very low, and she walked in a peculiar way which seemed to be due to a hip problem. Both visitors took slow, short steps, as if they were frightened of falling. John and Maureen offered them two bottles of cola. The couple accepted the drinks with enthusiastic nods but never even bothered to taste them.

John and Maureen surveyed the way the couple sat awkwardly on the sofa - there was something artificial and robotic about their movements. The man started to rub his partner's breasts with his hands, looking at John as he did so, and asked, "Is this the way it is done?"

John and Maureen were flabbergasted at the man's behaviour.

"Do you and Maureen watch television much?" the man suddenly asked, and stopped fondling his partner.

"Yes, I suppose so. Why?" John answered, now intrigued by the couple.

The man continued to quiz them. He asked if they read books. What did they read? What did they talk about? He then put two audacious questions to Maureen: "Do you have any nude pictures of yourself? How were you made?"

Enough was enough. Maureen ordered the couple to leave immediately.

The man and woman stood, but the former seemed unable to walk. This seemed to frighten the woman, who turned to John and said, "Please move him; I can't move him myself."

The man suddenly became animated, and walked

directly to the door in a straight line, followed by his female companion. They both left without saying goodbye.

One sunny Saturday afternoon in Liverpool, England, in November 1978, a 27-year-old woman named June was gazing idly out the window of her flat on the thirteenth floor of Crosbie Heights, off Everton's William Henry Street, when she noticed something odd, high up in the blue sky – a little white triangle with rounded corners – and it was hovering there, stationary. She shouted to her husband George – who was watching a Rugby League match on the television – to come and look at the strange craft. George saw the UFO too and rummaged about in a sideboard for his old bird-watching binoculars. The craft had vanished by the time George had taken the binoculars out the case, but June used them to survey the skies for a while – and she spotted not one, but three of white triangular craft, flying in a row as they descended from the blue.

George had gone for cigarettes and a sports newspaper by now, and June wished he'd hurry back so she could show him the strange objects that were descending onto the waterfront. Then she had a funny turn. June felt dizzy and then nauseous, and she ran to the toilet to be sick. George then returned and when June said she'd been sick all of a sudden, he told her to lie down. At this time, June noticed that the binoculars had gone missing. She and George looked high and low for them but never found them or their leather case and lens caps. On the following day, George was on his way to work on his motorbike when he had a serious crash which left him in hospital. Something unexplained took place at this well-known Liverpool hospital shortly after the crash. George was laying in the hospital bed in traction, with weights hanging from frames, pins in his legs, and a plaster-cast on his arm. When June went to visit him, she discovered that George's bed was empty and no one knew where he was. The patient obviously hadn't been discharged nor could he have discharged himself, for he was dosed with morphine and unable to move anyway with pins in the bones of his legs. The traction weights rested on pulleys around the empty bed, but George was nowhere to be seen. That evening at 9pm, George was found tucked into his hospital bed and unable to say where he had been. He recalled nothing to explain his whereabouts. June then began to recall what had happened that Saturday when she had become ill after watching the triangular UFOs. She had heard a cough to her left as she was looking through the binoculars at the strange craft, and she had turned to see a tall black man, dressed all in black, and was naturally startled by his presence. In a low voice devoid of any accent, the stranger told June to say nothing about the UFOs she had just seen – 'Or we'll take you away and no one will ever see you again,' he had threatened. That's all June could remember. Had this man taken her binoculars? Years later June read about the mysterious 'men in black' who often turn up to harass witnesses who have seen UFOs. Had the man who appeared in her living room been one of these, and had he something to do with George's inexplicable disappearance and reappearance at the hospital?

The reports of these strange individuals who pop up at the home and workplace of UFO witnesses are still being reported. The FBI has shown an interest in the men in black phenomenon, and has frequently attempted to track down the "impostors" - but to date no one has been arrested. The men in black are always one step ahead of the authorities, and they now seem to be changing their mode of transport. The reports of black Cadillacs have now been almost entirely superseded by accounts of black unmarked helicopters buzzing the neighbourhood of UFO witnesses. In early 1994, George and Shirley Coyne, directors of the American UFO investigation organization MUFORA actually presented the FBI with a videotape that clearly shows a black helicopter tailing their car. The couple have allegedly received threats from the men in black, but Shirley Coyne says, "We're not afraid. They haven't done anything to us yet."

Since the collapse of communism in the former Soviet Union, the Russians have released many top secret reports of men in black incidents which have occurred in their country. In April 1992, one female witness who observed a UFO at close range near Moscow was later harassed by three mysterious men in black. One of the men actually paralyzed the woman simply by touching her. Throughout the intense paralysis, the woman felt as if her mind was being ransacked by the "oriental-looking" man. For months after the traumatic incident, the woman also exhibited a strange bio-magnetism: pots and pans, anything metal, would stick to her as if she were a magnet, and people who touched her hands often experienced a severe electric shock.

Who are the sinister black-clad stalkers? Suggestions that they are secret service men sowing the seeds of disinformation - a typical CIA practice - just don't stand up when we realize that these unearthly thugs have been reported in countries as far afield as Russia and China, where Western intelligence agents cannot operate. This leaves us with only one other possibility: that the men in black are from another planet - perhaps even another dimension. But what is their purpose here on Earth? Only time will tell.

HOLY MAN OF
THE HIMALAYAS

In the early 1890s Sundar Singh, a young Indian boy from a wealthy Sikh family accompanied his mother, a deeply religious woman, on a visit to a sadhu — a mystic who has opted for a nomadic life in his search for truth. The encounter with the old holy man had a profound effect on young Sundar, and he was soon embarking on his own search for God. When Sundar's mother and brother died when he was 14, his grief turned into hatred directed against the Christian missionaries who were visiting India. Sundar detested the Western religion, and he started to demonstrate his hatred by stoning the local Christian preachers. On one occasion, he held a Bible in the air, waved it at the missionaries, then set fire to it. Three days after this act of denouncement, the embittered teenager prayed all night for "a sign from the true God". Suddenly, in the middle of the long prayer session, a vision of Jesus Christ materialized in front of the Indian boy, who almost fainted with fear. The vision said to him, "How long will you persecute me? I have come to save you. You pray to know the right way. Take it."

The apparition vanished, leaving Sundar elated, but surprised that he had been visited by a Christian God.

He looked at the spot where the figure had appeared, shaking his head in disbelief until it dawned on him that his search was over - he must preach the Gospel he had once despised.

In 1905, Sundar was baptized into the Christian Church and took an Anglican ordination course, but he later decided that Anglicanism was too conventional. His new-found faith remained as strong as ever, but he thought the rituals of Anglicanism were not compatible with his Indian traditions and culture, and he was sure he could spread the word of God without the need for a white dog-collar. He regarded himself as a spiritual hybrid! a Christian sadhu, in fact.

Sundar visited Tibet by crossing the Himalayas on foot. He knew it was dangerous to preach Christianity in a Buddhist country, and on his third trip across the mountains, he was arrested and condemned to death for trying to convert the Buddhists to his faith.

Buddhist law prohibits a true disciple to kill, so malefactors are executed in ways that exonerate adherents of Buddhism from direct responsibility. Sundar was beaten, his clothes ripped from him, and pushed down a deep dry well. When he hit the bottom, he landed on a layer of decomposing bodies: the carcasses of previous victims. There was a resounding clang, then darkness. The Buddhists had closed the well's heavy iron lid above him. Now it was only a matter of time: he would surely either starve to death or be asphyxiated when the air ran out.

Sundar lay there, almost suffocated by the stench of rotten flesh. Many would have resigned themselves to certain death in such a gruesome predicament, but the sadhu only had to recall the vision of Jesus to allay his fear. Sundar started to pray again, and on the third night the sound of a key rattling in the lock of the iron lid above interrupted his prayers. The metal cover lifted, and a voice boomed down the well: "Seize the rope!"

A rope with a loop at its end was lowered down to Sundar, who grabbed the rope, placed his foot in the loop, and found himself being hauled out of the well. He wondered who had saved him, but when he was back above ground, Sundar saw that there was no one at the other end of the rope. He staggered from the area, taking deep breaths of fresh air, and realized he had been plucked from death by something unearthly. The sadhu rested in bushes until dawn, then returned to the local caravansenai (a type of inn where travellers rested), where his inexplicable reappearance caused a sensation. Sundar was promptly arrested and taken to the head Lama, who asked him how he had managed to escape from the well. Sundar's account of the paranormal "rope trick" enraged the Lama. He suspected that someone had stolen his key, but on examining the bunch of keys on his girdle, he saw that the key to the well-cover was still there; it had never left him, and this so frightened the Lama that he ordered Sundar to leave Tibet immediately.

Sundar continued to have mystical encounters. He claimed to have made contact with a secret Indian Christian sect, whom he urged to declare themselves publicly. He also maintained that he had met a rishi (hermit) who was incredibly old, living in a cave 13,000 feet above sea-level. The old man was an advanced mystic, and was able to impart a series of apocalyptic visions to Sundar, but the sadhu refused to divulge what he had seen.

In the 1920s, Sundar made many trips to Burma, Ceylon, China, Malaysia, America, Japan and Europe. He continued to preach all over the globe, but in 1929, he disappeared without trace in the Himalayas.

WAS RICHARD III REALLY BAD?

In 1674, workmen demolishing a staircase in the Tower of London's White Tower discovered a wooden chest buried ten feet deep. It contained the skeletons of two children, the taller one lying on its back and the other lying across it face down. King Charles II ordered an investigation, and the official examiners concluded that the skeletons were the remains of 12-year-old Edward V and his 10-year-old brother Richard, Duke of York - the two Princes who had disappeared in suspicious circumstances at the Tower of London in July 1483. King Charles had the remains interred in Westminster Abbey in a marble tomb designed by Christopher Wren. In 1933, a pathologist and a dental surgeon were given permission to examine the alleged remains of the Princess, and the bones were exhumed. Pathologist William Wright and dental surgeon George Northcroft were able to determine that the skeletons were of two children, aged 10 and 12. The investigators could not tell what sex the children were as they had died before reaching puberty, and the bones were hard to date, but they seemed to belong to a time period near to the fifteenth century.

The disappearance of the Princes in the Tower has been the subject of much debate for hundreds of years. The consensus is that the Princes were murdered by their uncle, Richard III, popularly portrayed (thanks to Shakespeare and Sir Thomas More) as a sadistic hunchbacked schemer with a twisted mind.

Upon the death of Edward IV in 1483, his brother Richard was appointed Protector of the Realm and guardian of Edward's sons, the boy king Edward V and his younger brother Richard, Duke of York. As soon as the preparations for Edward's coronation were under way in London, Richard rode to Stony Stratford, near Northampton, and escorted Edward to the Tower of London. Edward's younger brother Richard was taken by his mother, Queen Elizabeth Woodville to Westminster Abbey for sanctuary, but the Queen was later persuaded to let her son join his brother in the Tower.

In June of that year, cleric Ralph Shaw proclaimed that the Princes were bastards because Edward IV's marriage to Elizabeth Woodville had been invalid, and so, in the following month, Richard of Gloucester had himself proclaimed as king and was crowned on July 6th. Meanwhile, the Princes were still in the Tower. Many were angered at Richard's speedy path to the throne, and most people doubted that the Princes were illegitimate. The Duke of Buckingham, who wanted Henry Tudor to be king, led a revolt against Richard, but the rebellion was unsuccessful and the Duke was beheaded. Around the time of the failed insurgency, England was rife with rumours about the Princes in the Tower. It was said that they had been murdered by the usurper king.

Thirty years after the sinister disappearance of the Princes, Sir Thomas More, in his biography of Richard III, claimed that, shortly after his coronation, the king sent a messenger to the Keeper of the Tower, ordering him to kill the Princes, but the Keeper, Sir Robert Brackenbury, refused. The king then ordered his protégé Sir James Tyrell to do the despicable deed, and after persuading Brackenbury to hand over the keys to the rooms where the Princes were staying, Tyrell put his murder plan into action. He instructed his burly horsekeeper John Dighton and Miles Forest, who had been minding the Princes, to kill the boys as they slept. Dighton and Forest came into the chamber at midnight and quickly wrapped the Princes up in their bedclothes. Dighton pressed their featherbed on them and lay on it until all the violent wriggling and kicking had ceased.

According to More, Tyrell then instructed the murderers to bury the suffocated Princes at the foot of the stairs in the Tower under a heap of stones. But how true is More's account? He based his story on an alleged confession to the crime made by Tyrell before his execution in 1502. More was an upholder of the Tudor state, and as such was probably using his biography of Richard III to defame him. It was More who claimed that Richard III was "crooked-backed" and "ill-featured" - despite the fact that no contemporary portrait of Richard III exists which shows him as ugly or deformed in any way.

Today, historians are still uncertain about the actual fate of the Princes. Some believe they were not murdered at all, but smuggled out of the Tower, probably to spend the rest of their lives in obscurity under assumed names. For years, a rumour has persisted that one of the fully-grown Princes, Richard of York, is actually depicted as an adult in a Hans Holbein painting of Sir Thomas More and his family.

But if the Princes were murdered, is Richard III the only suspect? Someone else who had a strong motive for the double murder was Henry Tudor, who defeated Richard at the Battle of Bosworth Field in 1485 and became Henry VII. Being the great-grandson of Edward III's illegitimate son, Henry was excluded from the succession. His claim to the throne was based only upon the right of conquest, and so to strengthen his claim, he married Elizabeth of York, sister of the Princes in the Tower. He then had his wife declared illegitimate, which meant that her brothers in the Tower were the same, a state of affairs which meant that Henry would have to dispose of the Princes if he was to become king. Furthermore, Henry did not claim that Richard III had murdered his nephews until almost a year after Richard's death. When Richard III gained the throne, Henry accused him of tyranny and cruelty - but we'll never know why he didn't accuse Richard of murder at that time..

SWIFT'S MARTIAN MOONS

The English satirist Jonathan Swift was born in Dublin, to English parents, in 1667. He was educated at Kilkenny Grammar School and Trinity College, Cambridge, and in 1726, at the age of 59, wrote the book for which he is best remembered: *Gulliver's Travels* — a satirical sci-fi and fantasy allegory about Anglo-Spanish relations. In the middle of this world-famous classic, Swift writes of the Martian satellites, describing "two lesser stars or satellites, which revolve about Mars. The innermost is distant from the centre of the primary planet exactly three of its diameters, and the outermost five; the former revolves in the space of ten hours, and the latter in twenty-one and a half."

This is a quite remarkable statement, for the moons of Mars - Phobos and Deimos - were not discovered until 150 years after Gulliver's Travels was first published. Furthermore, when the astronomer Asaph Hall discovered the Martian satellites with a 26-inch refracting telescope in 1877, he saw that the moons were precisely in the orbits that Swift had described in his book.

The mystery deepens when we take a closer look at the moons of Mars. Phobos, the innermost moon, is remarkably close to the planet, and may approach within 3,600 miles of the Martian surface. It is the only known natural satellite that has a revolution period shorter than its primary, in this case Mars. Phobos circles the Red Planet every 7 hours and 39 minutes, and Mars only turns on its axis once every 24 hours and 37 minutes. To an observer on Mars, Phobos would be seen to rise in a westerly direction and set towards the east, and it would only be visible for four and a half hours at a time. Deimos, on the other hand, orbits at a distance of 14,600 miles, and takes 30 hours and 14 minutes to circle Mars once.

Since the discovery of Phobos and Deimos, their orbital nature has been the subject of much debate. Are they ex-asteroids captured from the minor planet zone by the gravitational pull of Mars, or are they something more sinister? The eminent Soviet astronomer Joseph Shklovsky studied the Martian system for years, and concluded that Phobos was either a hollow asteroid — or a hollowed-out asteroid, intimating that it was perhaps a space station for Martians, but predictably, Shklovsky's suggestion was not taken seriously by the scientific community.

So, how does Phobos manage to whizz around a planet at a velocity greater than the planet's rotational speed? Well, no space probe has yet answered the question. Mariner 9 approached Mars in late 1971, took several photographs of the moons, and discovered another mystery - that the origin of the craters on Phobos cannot be determined. Meteoric impact was suggested, but the Japanese astronomer S. Miyamoto pointed out that the craters on Phobos were of the blowhole variety, and blowhole craters form only when molten rock cools.

The Viking Orbiter 2 then came within 545 miles of Phobos in September 1976 and beamed back pictures that indicated that the Martian moon was made of solid rock - which doesn't make sense, considering its rapid orbit. As a homage to Jonathan Swift, who knew about the moons and their peculiar orbits before NASA, a crater was named after him on Phobos.

But this takes us back to the original mystery: where did Swift get his knowledge of Mars from? The late American astronomer Carl Sagan was of the opinion that Swift most probably got his knowledge from Johannes Kepler, the mathematician who discovered the laws of planetary motion, but if this was so, why didn't Kepler himself, or any astronomers who were aware of Kepler's Laws predict the moons of Mars and their exact orbits? In any case, Kepler's Laws cannot explain the unique motion of Phobos, and even today, despite the computerized tools that astrophysicists have at their disposal, the Phobos mystery remains unsolved.

In an effort to solve the Phobos enigma — and to look into many other Martian anomalies — NASA sent a $1.5 billion probe named Mars Orbiter to the Red Planet in 1992. On August 21st, 1993, just three days before the probe was due to secure an orbit around the planet, the probe switched off its transmitter, as programmed, as it prepared its orbital manoeuvre. For some inexplicable reason, the spacecraft never switched its transmitter on again. The one hundred-strong staff in the control room at NASA's Jet Propulsion Laboratory in Pasadena were shocked into silence by the probe's behavior. Some of those who watched the blank monitors had worked on the probe for over a decade, and everyone was at a loss to explain what had gone wrong. Everything had been checked and re-checked, and many of the engineers who worked on it were experienced NASA veterans who had also participated in the construction of the Viking spacecraft.

Two rumours gathered momentum in the US. Some thought that the probe — which was to have taken highly detailed pictures of Mars and its moons - had been deliberately switched off by high-ranking NASA officials because it had photographed evidence of a Martian civilization, while another rumour had it that the Martians themselves had sabotaged the billion-dollar probe.

Other probes have been to the red planet and the Martian moons since that disaster, but these later probes have uncovered more mysteries which warrant a manned mission to Mars. A 'monolith' the size of a building has been photographed on the surface of Mars, and it has even attracted the attention of the legendary Apollo 11 veteran astronaut Buzz Aldrin, who thinks it needs to be investigated further. Another suspicious-looking monolith has also been found in recent years on the surface of Phobos, and scientists and astrophysicists still believe Phobos is still a mysterious object that doesn't seem to display the usual behaviour of a moon regarding its size and orbital speed about Mars. Phobos is still thought to be partly hollow and unusually porous.

MOTHER SHIPTON'S PROPHECIES

In July 1488, the midwife tending to Agatha Southiel as she gave birth was in for a nasty shock. As the nurse cut the umbilical chord and tied up the loose ends, the newborn babe started to chuckle. Simultaneously, the raging thunderstorm outside came to an abrupt end, and the inky skies over the North Yorkshire town of Knaresborough in Northern England turned to a delightful azure as the sun reappeared. The neighbours of Agatha Southiel who had watched also the strange birth exchanged frightened glances. Everyone present, including the midwife, made a mad dash out of the cottage, leaving Agatha and her freakish baby daughter to look after themselves.

Rampant rumours of "the Devil's child" and "Lucifer's daughter" circulated through Knaresborough, and Agatha Southiel was soon shunned by everyone who knew of the "laughing baby". Backs were turned on the woman who had apparently copulated with Satan, and in the end, the malicious gossipers drove Agatha into a convent. The baby that had been the talk of the town - Janet Ursula Southiel - was given to a nurse, who decided to delete the baby's first name.

When little Ursula Southiel began school, she was taunted by classmates for having no parents, but she didn't allow the cruel remarks to upset her; she simply set her invisible "demon friend" on her classmates, and he, or it, would bite, punch and pinch them. The unseen companion - naturally presumed to be Old Nick himself - didn't exactly make the schoolmaster feel comfortable, and he quickly made it clear that Ursula was no longer welcome at the school. Snubbed by every school she was sent to, the witch-girl spent most of her days alone with only the company of her supernatural playmate. But her lonely days ended in her early teens when she met a young carpenter named Tobias Shipton. It was love at first sight, and the two lovers were soon married. The newly-weds moved to the town of Skipton, about 35 miles west of York.

At Skipton, Ursula discovered that she had the ability to look into the future. She accurately foresaw Henry VIII's invasion of France in 1513, and correctly predicted that the "English Lion" (Henry again) would defeat the "Lillies" (the French), and that the "Princely Eagle" (Maximillian of Habsburg) would join the Lion in the battle. She also predicted that the English Cavalry would "cause great shame unto" the French, and was correct in this prediction, for the French retreated so fast from the English cavalry that the short-lived military encounter was later known as the Battle of the Spurs.

In the year 1530, Ursula predicted that "The Mitred Peacock" (Cardinal Wolsey) would hide out from trouble with Henry VIII by trying to escape to York, but would never live to enter the city. News of this prophecy spread through most of the villages of England until it reached the ears of Wolsey himself. The Cardinal was intrigued; his relationship with the king was shaky to say the least, and so keen to see if the "Yorkshire Witch" could gain knowledge about the king's court, he sent three spies to Ursula Shipton's home. They were the Duke of Suffolk, Lord Darcy, and Lord Percy, and they wore disguises for the assignment. A Yorkshire man named Beasley accompanied the noblemen as a guide.

When the four men arrived at Ursula's cottage, Beasley knocked on the door and the prophetess answered.

"Come in Mr Beasley, and the three noble Lords with you," said Ursula. Beasley and the three noblemen were stunned at Ursula's knowledge of their identities. The four men entered the house and Ursula treated them to delicious oatcakes and ale. The Duke of Suffolk asked Ursula if she had really said that Cardinal Wolsey would never see York.

"No, I said he might see the city but never enter it," Ursula replied, as she sat studying the flames of the blazing fire.

"When he comes to York he will surely burn thee," The Duke of Suffolk warned her.

Ursula suddenly threw a linen handkerchief onto the fire and said, "If this burns, so shall I."

The four visitors watched the piece of linen intensely. It rested on the incandescent log, and the flames licked at it, but 15 minutes later, Ursula cackled to herself and lifted the piece of linen out of the fire with a poker. The cloth hadn't been touched by the flames.

This impressed the noblemen, and one of them asked Ursula to tell them their fortunes.

She pointed to the Duke of Suffolk and said, "My

love, the time will come when you will be as low as I am, and I am a low one indeed."

The Duke was puzzled at the witch's words, but years later, in 1554, the Duke of Suffolk was beheaded for treason, and was thus made a low one when his severed head lay on the ground.

To Lord Percy, Ursula said, "Show your horse in the quick, and you do well, but your body will be buried in York pavement and your head shall be stolen from the bar and carried into France."

Lord Percy was beheaded in 1572 and, as Ursula predicted, his head was impaled on a pole over the Michelgate Bar Gate at York, and later stolen by a Catholic fanatic and taken to France.

Finally, to Lord Darcy, the seeress said, "You have made a great gun! Go and shoot it off, for it will do you no good. You are going to war, and you will pain many a man, but you will kill none."

Being a soldier as well as a statesman Darcy was concerned with artillery, but all the guns he commanded could not save him when he participated in the Pilgrimage of Grace - a revolt in northern England against the severe economic and religious hardline reforms of Henry VIIFs government. Darcy was one of the 230 men who were beheaded because of their part in the 1536 uprising.

As for Cardinal Wolsey, Ursula was correct yet again. He did travel towards York, but only got as far as Cawood, eight miles from his intended destination. There, Lord Northampton apprehended him and presented him with an arrest warrant. Wolsey was charged with high treason and taken to London to be incarcerated in the Tower until execution, but died on the road to the capital.

Ursula - known in her later years as Mother Shipton -died peacefully in her bed at the age of 73 in 1561. It is alleged that she often quoted the following rhyme, which is said to prophesy the arrival of the automobile, radio, submarine, train, aeroplane, steamship, the World-Wide Web . . . and the end of the World:

Carriages without horses shall go,
And accidents fill the world with woe.
Around the Earth thoughts shall fly,
In the twinkling of an eye;
The world upside down shall be
And gold found at the root of a tree.
Through the hills man shall ride,
And no horse shall be at his side.
Under water men shall walk,
Shall ride, Shall Sleep, Shall even talk.
In the air men shall be seen,
In white, in black, in green;
Iron in the water shall float,
As easily as a wooden boat.
To an end the world shall come,
In the year two thousand and sixty-one.

THE LONG MAN OF WILMINGTON

There are approximately 50 giant carved figures of men and animals to be seen on the hill-slopes of Britain. Many of these epic etchings of the past were created by cutting away the top surface of the ground in order to expose the ivory-white chalk layer below. In Dorset the naked, club-wielding figure of the Cerne Abbas Giant can be seen, and over in Wiltshire on the edge of Salisbury Plain, the elegantly-carved Westbury White Horse still exerts its magic. But none of the chalk figures compares to the Long Man of Wilmington on Windover Hill in East Sussex. The athletic-looking Long Man holds a 240-foot-long staff in each hand, but unlike the vulgar-looking Cerne Abbas Giant, the man on Windover Hill has a blank face and looks quite sexless. At 231 feet in length, the Long Man is probably the largest representation of a human figure in the world, but we have virtually no information on his identity.

The 7,000 bricks that form the Long Man's outline were put there in 1874 in an attempt to restore the ancient image. The earliest record of the Long Man - a sketch of 1799 - depicts the right staff as the handle of a rake and the other staff as the handle of a scythe, and he is wearing a feather on his head. The sketch has proved to be a fairly accurate depiction; an archaeological examination of the Long Man carving in 1979 uncovered the faint outlines of implements that might well be a rake and scythe. The archaeologists also found traces of a plume or feather around the outline of the giant's head which seems to be part of some sort of ceremonial head-dress. But there is still no evidence of the giant's identity. Rock-carvings of similar figures holding poles have been found in Scandinavia, but the poles in the carvings usually have Sun discs at the top, which suggest that the figures were made by solar worshippers.

Over the years, the Long Man has been "identified" as being Julius Caesar, St Paul, King Arthur, King Harold, and many other historical personages, while others have sought clues to the chalk figure's identity at the medieval priory which stands in close proximity to the giant. Wilmington Priory is situated at the southern end of Wilmington village, and although the restored building is but a shadow of the original medieval priory, the crypt, which dates from 1300, is still steeped in mystery. There is an intriguing recess at the southern end where the wall is strangely thin, and it is thought to be the walled-up entrance to a secret underground passage. On the west side of the priory, a 120-foot-deep well shaft sinks into solid chalk, and even today there is still fresh water in the well. After the Norman Conquest, the manor of Wilmington was given to the son of Heluin de Contaville, Robert de Mortain, and he in turn gave it to a Norman Abbot from the Abbey of Grestain, near Hornfleur in France. The Abbot of Grestain, William Husband, was immensely grateful for the English manor, and the first priory was built at Wilmington in the twelfth century.

In 1180 William Husband left his Abbey at Grestain for a lengthy sabbatical in England. The Bishop of Lisieux had been outraged at Husband's un-Christian behaviour and had threatened to excommunicate him from the church if he did not mend his ways. What Husband had done to upset the Bishop is not known, but there were rumours of orgies and dabbling in the occult. William Husband spent some of his time at Wilmington Priory, and seems to have liked the place. There were around 20 monks there at the time, and the priory was beginning to exert a powerful influence over the local village. A considerable amount of the area's agricultural yield was regularly siphoned off which enabled the deputy head of Wilmington Priory to build one of the largest tithe barns in England.

In 1315, the Prior of Wilmington approached the resident of the nearby Milton Manor House and requested money to build a chapel on the wooded mound that is today known as The Rookery. The chapel was built, and soon became the subject of controversy when it was claimed that magical rituals were performed there. The rampant rumours of witchcraft never died down, and when the Prior of Wilmington fell into debt in 1337, the ruthless Sheriff of Middlesex declined to take any action against the "holy" man because he feared repercussions from the Wilmington cult.

No one is sure today what went on in the chapel at the Rookery, but there were unconfirmed stories at the time that members of an heretical cult met there, and for some reason this cult seems to have revered the

Long Man. Many researchers have noted the similarities between the Long Man and seventeenth-century depictions of Mercurius, a naked figure who holds two staffs in an identical way, but the staffs held by Mercurius - a mythical character in early books on alchemy - have serpents wound around them. Mercurius is, in turn, another version of the man depicted in the esoteric diagram of the "Sacred Tree of the Sephiroth" - which is found in the Kabbalah, an ancient book of Hebrew theosophy — but again, the similarity with the Long Man of Wilmington throws little light on his identity. Another figure that resembles the Long Man of Wilmington is often overlooked because it is up in the Andes on the other side of the world. On a plateau 13,000 feet above sea level in Bolivia, there stands an incredible monument that the locals call the Puerta del Sol, which means the "Gate of the Sun." It is an archway hewn out from a single 10-ton block of andesite (an extremely hard volcanic rock) and it measures 12 feet in length and 10 feet in height. Forty-eight carvings on the block surround the central carving of a sexless figure holding a staff in each hand in the exact same stance as the Long Man of Wilmington. Furthermore, the Bolivian carving wears a feathered head-dress. Is this mere coincidence, or is the frieze on the Gate of the Sun somehow connected with the Long Man carving in Britain?

The Gate of the Sun is but a small part of the mysterious ruined city of Tiahuanaco. When the Spaniards reached the long-deserted city in 1549, they asked the elders of the Incan society about the builders of Tiahuanaco, but the old men told the conquerors from Europe that they did not know, because the ancient city had already been deserted when the Incas came to the area. The Spaniards then quizzed the Aymaras, the oldest people of the Andes, about the inhabitants of Tiahuanaco, but the Aymaras could only tell the conquistadors of the legend of Tiahuanaco that had been passed down through countless generations. According to the elders, the city of Tiahuanaco was the place where the first men on earth came to live, and no one knew what became of these men.

Even today, no one has interpreted the frieze on the Gate of the Sun. The central carving of the figure holding the staffs remains as enigmatic as its English cousin thousands of miles away.

WAS TCHAIKOVSKY MURDERED?

Pyotr Ilyich Tchaikovsky was born on May 7th, 1840 at Kamsko-Votinsk (about 100 miles north-east of Izhevsk), where his father was an inspector of the government mines. From an early age it was evident that Tchaikovsky was musically talented, and he was encouraged to develop his gift, but after the family moved to St Petersburg, young Tchaikovsky entered the school of jurisprudence and became a civil servant. He finally enrolled at the recently-opened conservatoire of music in St Petersburg in 1862, and after three years he was employed by Nicholas Rubinstein, his previous orchestration tutor, to teach music at a conservatoire in Moscow. He became a professor there in 1866.

Tchaikovsky was constantly prone to long bouts of debilitating depression, and was forever "recognizing" his weak points. He once said, "I cannot complain of lack of inventive power, but I have always suffered from want of skill in the management of form."

At the age of 37, the self-tormented homosexual was confronted with the heterosexual advances of his pupil, Antonina Ivanovna Miliukova, a 28-year-old nymphomaniac and borderline psychopath. The composer despised his own sexuality at the time, and dreaded being "found out,' but he was forced to tell Antonina that he was unsuitable for her because he was only interested in his own sex. But Antonina pleaded for his love, and threatened to commit suicide if he turned his back on her. The unconsummated marriage lasted for just one month, after which Tchaikovsky left his bride and suffered a nervous breakdown. In an attempt to end his life he walked into an icy river one night and stood waist deep in the waters, praying for pneumonia. He sought refuge from Antonina in the home of his brother, Anatol, where his health deteriorated rapidly, and he subsequently slipped into a coma that lasted two days. In the end, Antonina accepted the abandonment and tried to find solace with a string of lovers. She bore at least five children by various men and ended up in a lunatic asylum, where she died, in 1917.

Tchaikovsky had told close friends that the only woman he had ever loved was his mother, who had died when the composer was 14. Her death had such a profound effect on him that many surmised, rather unreasonably, that the demise of his mother had been a contributing factor to his homosexuality. After a recuperative period abroad, Tchaikovsky resigned from the conservatoire and retired into the country to devote himself entirely to composition. He made occasional trips abroad, and was made an honorary Mus. D of Cambridge University in 1893. Shortly after returning from England in the October of that year, Tchaikovsky conducted his first performance of his Symphony No. 6 in B Minor at St Petersburg. The "Pathetique" Symphony, so called because of its melancholic mien, was not received well by the critics. Tchaikovsky's depression deepened but two days after the Pathetique premiere, Tchaikovsky's grand opera, Eugene Onegin was greeted with a standing ovation. The composer was on top of the world again. He enjoyed meals out with friends and visited the theatre. But a week later, a Reuters telegram from St Petersburg stunned the musical world. It read:

M. Tschaikowsky [sic], the famous composer, died here at 3 o'clock this morning from the effects of cholera. On Saturday evening he dined at a restaurant in the city, and drank some water which had not previously been boiled. Symptoms of cholera showed themselves on Sunday, and although every effort was made by the doctors in attendance to stay the progress of the disease, M. Tschaikowsky's condition became rapidly worse. He lost consciousness yesterday afternoon.

The musical genius who had composed the 1812 Overture and the music for *Swan Lake*, *The Sleeping Beauty* and *The Nutcracker* had allegedly died of Asiatic cholera at the age of 53. He passed away after four days of acute vomiting, diarrhoea and convulsions at his brother's apartment at Number 13 Dzerzhinsky Street, St Petersburg.

The great writer Leo Tolstoy and Tchaikovsky's composer-friend Rimsky-Korsakov were very sceptical of the cholera story. In his memoirs, Korsakov states that Tchaikovsky's death "occasioned all kinds of gossip" and an article in a newspaper of the day reported: "Contradictory rumours are afloat with regard to the causes of Tchaikovsky's illness." The article goes on in a tantalizing manner, skirting around the murmurs of murder and tales of a cover-up surrounding the composer's untimely death.

The body of Tchaikovsky lay in state in an open coffin for two days. Those who came to pay their last respects saw the serene face of the composer, and some thought that his features were too tranquil-looking for a man who had died of cholera; it was more usual for the face of a cholera victim to be contorted and twisted from an agonizing death. Official regulations adamantly stated that all cholera victims were to be kept in a closed coffin and buried immediately, so Korsakov thought it strange that the corpse of a man who had died of such an infectious disease was laid out in an open coffin, in clear breach of Russian health regulations.

Tolstoy wrote of the composer's mysterious death. "I am very sorry for Tchaikovsky - as a man about whom something is not quite clear, even more than as a musician. It's too neat and tidy; it's natural, yet not natural."

Was Tolstoy intimating that Tchaikovsky was murdered? Although the composer was sneeringly regarded by his countrymen as something of a renegade cosmopolitan, lacking in nationalistic pride, Tchaikovsky had no real enemies to contend with in the musical sphere. So how do we explain the following? Thirty years after Tchaikovsky's death, Dr Lev Bertenson - the man who had been the personal physician to Tsar Alexander III - was on his deathbed when he summoned his son, Nikolay, and told him a dark secret. Dr Bertenson told Nikolay that he had been the senior doctor attending Tchaikovsky as he lay dying. Dr Bertenson told his son that the great composer had not died from cholera at all - but had actually poisoned himself with an arsenical preparation. According to the dying doctor, Tchaikovsky had been pressurized into "doing the decent thing" to avoid disgrace. Bertenson's deathbed revelation was backed up by Nikolay Jacobi - the lawyer to the Tsar. According to Jacobi, Tchaikovsky was infatuated with the handsome nephew of Count Stenbok Fermor. The Count was outraged by the homosexual composer's interest in his nephew and wrote to the Tsar, who feared the matter would prove to be an embarrassment to his court. So Tsar Alexander III put the composer before a kangaroo court. Tchaikovsky was found guilty of having a homosexual lust for Count Stenbok-Femor's nephew, and was ordered to take arsenic. What are we to make of the suspicions of Tolstoy and Korsakov, and the apocryphal tales posthumously credited to Dr Bertenson and Nikolay Jacobi? Did Tchaikovsky commit suicide or was he murdered? Perhaps the composer anticipated the ceaseless delving into his suspicious death when he wrote, "The notion that some day people will try to probe into the private world of my thoughts and feelings, into everything that I have so carefully hidden throughout my life, is very sad and unpleasant."

THE CHESHIRE PROPHET

The word prophet usually conjures up visions of bearded biblical characters from the Old Testament, but in more recent times there have been more secular-minded individuals who have had the talent (some might say handicap) of seeing into the future. One such seer was the Cheshire Prophet, an uneducated ploughboy of the fifteenth century named Robert Nixon. Robert was born in 1467, the only son of a virtually destitute Cheshire farmer. Farmer Nixon thought his mentally retarded son would never amount to anything in life, so he put him to use in the field as a ploughboy. Robert was frequently scoffed at and called "the village idiot" because of the apparent slowness of his mind. The boy's head was unusually large and he had protuberant eyes, which also made him an object of ridicule. And yet, despite the spiteful jibes he was subjected to, the ploughboy was very inoffensive and said very little to anyone beyond "yes" or "no." One day Robert suddenly surprised everyone by predicting that an ox belonging to a neighbouring farmer would die. Not long after he had uttered the prediction, Robert and a group of curious villagers watched the healthy-looking ox in the next field collapse. When the beast was examined minutes later, it was found to be dead from no apparent cause.

News of the uncanny prophecy reached the ears of Lord Cholmondeley, and he sent for Nixon and kept him at his estate for a short while. The county squire tried to encourage the boy to read and write, but Nixon resisted all attempts to be educated and ended up back at the handles of his father's plow.

A couple of days after leaving Lord Cholmondeley's estate, Nixon was ploughing a field when he suddenly stopped in his tracks and looked skyward with a gaping mouth. The farm overseer told Nixon to get on with his work, but the ploughboy remained rooted to the spot, engrossed in something he could see in the clear blue sky. The overseer struck Nixon with a strap and told him to stop dreaming, but the boy didn't even react. For an hour he stood gazing up at something in the heavens, until he finally broke out of his trance-like condition and continued ploughing as if nothing had happened. The overseer was burning with curiosity, and urged Nixon to tell him what he had been staring at.

Nixon replied enigmatically, "I have seen things that I cannot tell you, and which man never saw before."

This esoteric answer shook the overseer, as the ploughboy's voice now seemed very clear and unlike his usual muffled speech. It was almost as if something was using the boy as a mouthpiece.

There were further strange remarks from the farmer's son. One day, before a group of startled drinkers in a tavern, Nixon spoke for two hours in the accentless voice of his mysterious, educated alter ego about "the history of the future" - which included the rise of an individual named Oliver Cromwell, the Civil War, the subsequent beheading of Charles I, the

Restoration of the Monarchy, the reign of William of Orange, and the French Revolution. Towards the end of his epic discourse, Nixon predicted the abdication of James II in 1688: "When a raven shall build its nest in a stone lion's mouth on top of a church in Cheshire, a King of England shall be driven out of his kingdom to return nevermore. As token of the truth of this, a wall of Mr Cholmondeley's shall fall!"

Lord Cholmondeley heard of the prediction and laughed. He examined the wall mentioned in the plowboy's prediction and finding it secure, told his bailiff that young Nixon would be wrong on this occasion. The bailiff laughed and nodded in agreement, but the next day the structurally-sound wall inexplicably crumbled to the ground. The remainder of Nixon's predictions came true centuries later, when a raven did build its nest in the mouth of a stone lion gargoyle atop of a Cheshire church in 1688 - a mere day before King James II was deposed. The dethroned monarch later died in exile at Saint-Germain in France.

On August 22nd, 1485, the Cheshire Prophet (as Nixon was now known) was ploughing a field, when once again he angered his overseer by stopping in his tracks. Before the overseer could urge the ploughboy to resume his work with a swipe from the strap, Nixon suddenly lifted his whip and started brandishing it as if it were a sword, shouting, "There Richard! There! Now! Up, Henry! Up with all arms! Over the ditch, Henry! Over the ditch and the battle is won!"

A gaggle of farmworkers came across the field and gathered around Nixon, who was now standing inert with a smile on his face. He suddenly raised his whip in the air and declared, "The battle is over! Henry has won!"

The farmworkers fell about laughing at the ploughboy's amateur dramatics. But these same peasants became curious two days later, when two travel-weary messengers rode into the county of Cheshire with important news: King Richard III had died at Bosworth while fighting the Earl of Richmond - now King Henry VII of England. When one of the villagers asked the messengers what date King Richard had died upon, he was told that the king had met his death on August 22nd - the date the Cheshire Prophet gave his "live" report of the remote battle at Bosworth.

On the day that the messengers came with the news of the King Henry's victory, the ploughboy became extremely anxious, and he asked several villagers if he could hide in their homes.

"Why? Who are you hiding from, Robert?" asked one bemused villager.

"The king's men!" Nixon replied, "They are coming for me. They want to take me to the royal palace, and if I go there I'll die of thirst and starvation!"

The villagers could make no sense of the ploughboy's words.

"Why would the king want the village idiot? And for that matter, how would a guest starve in a royal palace?" the village blacksmith asked.

A few days later, several men rode to the Nixon farmstead looking for the famous Cheshire Prophet. When they caught up with Nixon, they took him to King Henry, who was fascinated by the tales of "the idiot-genius who could for see the future".

The King assigned a scribe to accompany the ploughboy at all times to record any predictions he should enunciate. One of the first prophecies to be recorded by the scribe concerned a future event that apparently hasn't happened - Nixon prophesied that soldiers with white-dust on their helmets would invade the country through a tunnel. One wonders if Nixon was referring to the Channel Tunnel, which links England with France.

Before setting out for a fortnight-long hunting trip, the King left instructions with his cooks telling them to give the Cheshire Prophet all the food he desired. The cooks did this initially, but after a few days they tired of the ploughboy's incessant greed and decided to lock him up in a heavy oaken chest until he was really hungry. In the hustle and bustle of palace life, the cooks forgot all about the ploughboy and two weeks later when the king returned, he asked if the Cheshire Prophet had made any more predictions. Only then did the cooks recall that they had locked him up. With great trepidation they rushed to the thick-timbered chest and opened it to find that Robert Nixon had died from thirst and starvation. The Cheshire Prophet's prediction of his own tragic death had come to pass.

ROBIN HOOD

Way back in the thirteenth century when England was a land of sprawling wild forests where deer, wolves, bears and wild boars roamed, there lived a curious individual named Robin Hood, who was said to be an outlaw. In those times the word "outlaw" didn't just mean a criminal living outside of the law, but someone who had become an outcast of society for a wrong committed against the King.

The earliest record of the Robin Hood legend is a tome printed in 1420 by Wynkyn de Worde entitled, A Lytell Geste of Robyn Hode. According to this early book, Little John is not the giant outlaw we are familiar with, but merely a medium-sized Lytell John, meaning his family name was Lytell. The merry men mentioned in de Worde's text aren't merry, either. In those days "merry" simply meant that the story had a happy ending, but down the centuries the word has become confused with the carefree living-off-the-land philosophy of Robin's men.

In the fifteenth-century story, Robin's enemy, the Sheriff of Nottingham is said to be the King's representative, responsible for keeping law and order over an area stretching from Nottinghamshire and southern Yorkshire to the coast, and true to the modern legend, the Sheriff gets steamed up at the mere mention of Robin Hood's name.

By the nineteenth century, most antiquarians regarded Robin Hood as a mere invention of the medieval storytellers, but the English historian and Shakespearean scholar Joseph Hunter thought otherwise, and decided to appoint himself to the task of unearthing historical evidence to prove that the famous outlaw had existed. Hunter combed the catalogues of the Historic Documents Commission, which covered 800 years of British history, and at the end of his mammoth quest, in 1852, he caused a furore among his fellow historians when he announced that he had found concrete evidence to show beyond a doubt that Robin Hood had been a real flesh and blood individual.

Hunter had found the record of a boy named Robert Hood who was born in the town of Wakefield in Yorkshire between 1285 and 1295. Robert's father was Adam Hood, a forester in the service of the Earl de Warenne, lord of the manor of Wakefield. Robert Hood married a maiden named Matilda, who is recorded as having been brought before a court for taking dry wood from an old oak tree. She was fined two pence. In the year 1316, Robert and Matilda bought a piece of Earl de Warenne's land for the sum of two shillings to build a house on. According to another record, Robert's landlord in the year 1322 was Thomas, Earl of Lancaster. This Earl called upon all his tenants to rebel against King Edward II, and as Robert was a tenant of the nobleman, he went into battle for him, and the record says Robert Hood was very useful in the rebellion because of his amazing skill at archery. Nevertheless, the rebellion failed and the Earl of Lancaster was beheaded for treason. The Earl's estates were then forfeited to the king and Robert Hood and the other survivors of the failed insurrection became outlaws and fled for the cover of Barnsdale Forest in southern Yorkshire. The southern end of this forest adjoined Sherwood Forest.

So was Joseph Hunter right? Had he found positive proof of Robin's existence? No one can be sure, for there are records of other candidates who could be the real Robin Hood. One is Robert Hood of Cirencester, an outlaw who was wanted for murder around the year 1213, and there is another Robin Hood who went to prison in 1354 for offences he committed in Rockingham Forest. Then again there is the record of a Robert Hode, an outlaw of York in 1225. Unlike Robert Hood of Wakefield, none of these candidates lived in close proximity to Sherwood Forest, and none of them was skilled in archery, so there is a strong case for Joseph Hunter's claim.

THE MAN THEY COULDN'T HANG

For ten years, James Berry of Yorkshire was a police constable, and during that time he made many friends and enemies. One acquaintance of the Yorkshireman was William Marwood, an old executioner of the City of London who liked to give Berry a blow by blow account of the techniques he employed to hang criminals. When Marwood died in 1883, 32-year-old Berry decided the police force was not for him, and finding himself desperate for a vocation in life, opted for a macabre career: as a hangman. With all the knowledge of the gallows obtained from Marwood, Berry confidently applied for his deceased friend's job, but was turned down. The ex-policeman persisted with his unusual aspiration, and to his delight, eventually received his first commission of 21 guineas — to hang two men at Calton Prison in Edinburgh. Included in the commission was a second-class return rail ticket from Berry's hometown of Bradford, and money for board and lodgings.

On the night before James Berry was due to hang the men, he had a vivid nightmare about his new occupation. In the dream, Berry found that he could not hang a man because the trapdoor on the gallows refused to open. This same disturbing dream returned to haunt Berry's sleep many times over the years.

However, the following morning everything went smoothly, and the two condemned men were dispatched without any problems.

On the night November 15th, 1884, Miss Emma Whitehead Keyse, a former maid of honour and friend of Queen Victoria was found battered to death with her oil-soaked clothes ablaze at a villa known as "The Glen" in Babbacombe, Devon. Miss Keyse's cook, Elizabeth Harris, discovered the body of her mistress in the dining room after waking in her own smoke-filled room. She said that Miss Keyse's head had been battered in, and her clothes doused in oil from a lamp evidently lit by the murderer. After taking a statement from the cook, the police quizzed the dead woman's other servant, a 19-year-old footman named John Lee, who was the half-brother of Elizabeth Harris.

Lee had a reputation as a petty thief and had only been hired by Miss Keyse out of pity. With such a track record, the footman soon became the prime suspect in the eyes of the police, despite the fact that he had tried to put out the fire on the night of the murder, and had broken down in tears upon hearing that his mistress had been murdered, saying. "I have lost my best friend" to the village constable who was first to arrive at the scene of the crime.

But the police painted a different picture and relied on the body of circumstantial evidence that was building up against the teenager. Lee had bloodstained clothing, and an empty can that had contained lamp oil was found in the pantry where Lee had been seen shortly before the fire broke out. Lee tried to explain. He told the police that the blood on his clothing was his own, from where he had gashed his hand while breaking a window pane to let out the smoke from the fire, although he couldn't explain the empty can of lamp oil.

Lee was arrested and charged with murder, and at his subsequent trial the prosecution made it clear that only John Lee had a motive. Just before her brutal death, Miss Keyse had cut Lee's weekly wages of four shillings in half because he had come under suspicion of theft, so the prosecution alleged; Lee had killed her in fit of anger.

Lee protested, but his words fell on the deaf ears. The jury reached a guilty verdict, and shortly before the sentence was passed, Lee declared from the dock, "I am innocent. The Lord will never permit me to be executed!"

The judge sentenced John Lee to death by hanging.

After the trial, a rumour circulated that Miss Keyse had discovered Lee's half-sister, Elizabeth Harris, making love with a man in bed. Being a rather prim, puritanical individual, Miss Keyse was allegedly outraged and took a swipe at the naked couple, and out of sheer panic, Miss Harris struck back at her frail mistress with her fist, killing her. The rumour went that Miss Harris and her lover then took Miss Keyse's body to the dining room, where they battered the dead woman's skull in order to create the impression that a violent murder perpetrated by an intruder had taken place. Miss Harris then realized the police wouldn't be so easily fooled, so she sprinkled the contents of a can of lamp oil over the corpse and set fire to it, hoping that the flames would make the cause of Miss Keyse's death hard to determine. But the improvised cremation attempt didn't succeed, because John Lee was alerted by the smell of burning and ran into the dining room with a pail of water to douse the flames. As he did so, either Elizabeth or her lover placed the incriminating can of lamp oil in the pantry where Lee had been working.

On the night before the execution, Lee chatted in his cell with the prison governor and the chaplain, and the former told the condemned man that there was no chance of a reprieve. Lee responded by shrugging, then said, "Elizabeth Harris could say the word which could clear me, if she would."

When the governor and the chaplain left the cell, Lee settled down and had no difficulty sleeping. The dream he had was a strange one. Lee dreamed he was standing on the gallows with the noose around his neck, but the trapdoor wouldn't open, despite the hangman's repeated yanks on the lever. When Lee awoke from the dream, he felt that God had assured him that there was nothing to worry about, as he would not die on the gallows.

Shortly before eight o'clock on the morning of Monday, 23rd February, 1885, James Berry led John Lee to the centre of the trap on the gallows, then proceeded to strap Lee's legs together below the knees, before positioning and tightening the rope around his neck. Berry pulled the white hood over the doomed man's head, then walked to the lever. After a short, tense pause Berry threw the lever — and the expected sound of bolts being drawn below the gallows was heard. Death was now only a heartbeat away for Lee, but, to everyone's amazement, the trapdoor on which John Lee was standing refused to open. Berry's recurring nightmare had come true — and Lee's dream also.

Berry trembled. He took the hood and noose off Lee and tested the stubborn trap with a sandbag that weighed exactly the same as Lee. The trapdoor opened this time and the sandbag crashed to the ground under the gallows.

Lee was then pushed onto the trap again with the hood over his head and the noose re-positioned around his neck. This time, all the witnesses to the impending execution were sure that the trap would work.

Berry pulled the lever - but again the trap beneath Lee's feet wouldn't open.

Berry's face started to twitch, and with shaking hands he took the noose and hood off Lee, and guided him off the trap.

A prison engineer and Berry discussed the problem, and a carpenter was summoned. When the edges of the trap had been planed, and the bolts of the hanging apparatus greased, a sandbag was again tested as a substitute for Lee. Everything went like clockwork.

Lee was put on the trap for the third time. The hooded man stood there, waiting for Berry to throw the lever. Berry inhaled the cold morning air, then pulled the lever as hard as he could. The chaplain looked away as the greased bolts slid across as expected. But to his total astonishment, the chaplain saw that Lee was still standing on the unopened trap.

The holy man fainted, but was caught by a warder before he could hit the floor.

It was decided that a messenger should be sent to London to inform the Home Secretary of the botched hanging attempts. While everyone waited for the messenger to return, Lee was asked if he felt like eating a last breakfast, and he later consumed a substantial meal. Ironically, the hangman James Berry had to turn down the meal he was offered because of his nerves. So Lee ate Berry's meal as well!

About nine hours later, the messenger returned from London to inform Lee that he had been granted a reprieve by the Home Secretary - the death sentence would be commuted to life-imprisonment. But Lee was released after serving 20 years. He came out in 1905 and married his childhood sweetheart who had waited patiently for him. The couple went to America, and up until his death in 1933, John Lee, the man who couldn't be hanged, swore he was not a murderer. Whenever people asked him what he thought about being spared from the rope three times in a row, Lee would say it wasn't luck, or freak mechanical failure that saved his neck - but divine intervention.

THE LINCOLN CONSPIRACY

One August night in 1862, US President Abraham Lincoln was riding out to the Retired Soldiers' Home, situated in the woods of northwest Washington, when he heard a gunshot and a bullet whistled past his head. The President's horse, Old Abe, stampeded at the loud report and raced pell-mell all the way to the Retired Soldiers' Home. When Ward Hill Lamon, Lincoln's self-appointed bodyguard, heard of the shooting incident, he told the President that the shot had probably been fired by some Southern extremist, but Lincoln disagreed and denied that anyone had deliberately tried to shoot him. He thought the near fatal shot had come from the gun of a short-sighted hunter in the woods.

In the Spring of 1864, rumours circulated in the press of a rebel plot to assassinate the President, but Lincoln persistently dismissed all the conspiracy stories. "Even if true," Lincoln told the newshounds, "I do not see what the Rebels would gain. If they kill me, the next man in line will be just as bad for them."

Shortly after this statement, Lincoln received a steady stream of hate mail and death threats. The first malevolent missives scared him, but he later became desensitized to the letter menace and routinely filed all the serious threats away in a big envelope marked "Assassination".

"I know I'm in danger," Lincoln told William Seward, the Union Secretary of State, "but I am not going to worry about it."

During the following year, Lincoln's heavy work schedule and insomnia began to wear him down. On the rare occasions that he managed to snatch some sleep, he hardly ever dreamed, but on the night of April 9th, 1865, he experienced the first of a series of disturbing dreams. Lincoln told his wife Mary and Ward Hill Lamon about the first dream: "I could not have been long in bed when I fell into a slumber, for I was weary. I soon began to dream. There seemed to be a death-like stillness about me. Then I heard the subdued sobs, as if a number of people were weeping. I thought I left my bed and wandered downstairs. There the silence was broken by the same pitiful sobbing, but the mourners were invisible. I went from room to room; no living person was in sight, but the same mournful sounds of distress met me as I passed along. It was light in all the rooms; every object was familiar to me; but where were all the people who were grieving as if their hearts would break? I was puzzled and alarmed. What could be the meaning of all this? Determined to find the cause of a state of things so mysterious and so shocking, I kept on until I arrived at the East Room, which I entered. There I met with a sickening surprise. Before me was a catafalque [a coffin stand], on which rested a corpse wrapped in funeral vestments. Around it were stationed soldiers who were acting as guards; and there was a throng of people, some gazing mournfully upon the corpse, whose face was covered, others weeping pitifully. 'Who is dead in the White House?' I demanded of one of the soldiers. 'The President,' was his answer; 'he was killed by an assassin!' Then came a loud burst of grief from the crowd."

Lincoln's wife trembled at the eerie tale. "That is horrid. I wish you had not told it."

"Well, it is only a dream, Mary," Lincoln replied. "Let us say no more about it, and try to forget it."

Similar dreams of death continued to haunt what little sleep Lincoln could enjoy until the fateful date of April 14th. On that day, at 3 p.m., a 26-year-old actor named John Wilkes Booth entered the Kirkwood House bar in Washington D.C., and began drinking heavily. Booth was a handsome raven-haired, olive-skinned man. He sported a heavy walrus moustache which he had grown in an attempt to mature his youthful countenance. He had made his professional debut in 1855 at the Charles Street Theatre in Baltimore as Richmond in Richard III, and had quite a following of female admirers in the midwestern and southern theatrical circuits. His most recent stage appearance had been on March 18th as Pescara in The Apostate at Ford's Theatre in Washington D.C. Booth was a talented, but undisciplined actor who was probably at his best playing melodramatic heroes and villains, but he had once impressed Abraham Lincoln with his performance in The Marble Heart at Ford's Theatre on the night of November 9th, 1863, just a week before Lincoln's famous Gettysburg Address. Although Booth's family supported the Union, the actor secretly sided with the Confederacy.

Several drinkers in the bar recognized Booth, and some noticed that he seemed to be quite anxious. He was spotted an hour later at Derry's Saloon, where he ordered a bottle of brandy. He finished the bottle and moved on to Taltavuls Saloon, which stood next door to Ford's Theatre. In this saloon Booth and George

Atzerodt - another Confederate sympathizer - made the final arrangements for the assassination of Lincoln and Vice-President Andrew Johnson. Booth was to dispose of Lincoln and Atzerodt would slay Johnson. That was the agreed plan.

At the White House, Mary Lincoln had a headache. She said she wasn't keen on the planned trip to Ford's Theatre, but Lincoln coaxed her into changing her mind, saying, "Come, Mary. I need to have a laugh over the country cousin." He was referring to the title of the play he wanted ro see: Our American Cousin by Tom Taylor.

Detective George Crook suddenly begged Lincoln not to go to Ford's Theatre, but the President assured him that everything would be fine.

"Then can I stay on duty sir, and accompany you to the Theatre as an extra guard?" Crook asked.

"No, you've had a long, hard day's work and must go home," Lincoln told his worried friend, and patted him on the back. Lincoln walked with Crook to the portico of the White House and told him to go straight home to get a good night's rest.

Because of last-minute visitors, Lincoln and his wife didn't get away from the White House until 8.15 p.m., when the Presidential carriage finally rolled out into the fogbound street. Inside the coach, Lincoln wore a black overcoat and white kid gloves, and Mary wore a grey silk dress and matching bonnet. Major Henry Rathbone and his fiancée Miss Clara Harris accompanied the Lincolns. The bodyguard for the Theatre visit was John Parker - a strange choice, for he was a lazy oaf with an appalling record of drunkenness, insubordination, and gross inefficiency. Parker had been sent ahead of the Lincolns, and was already at Ford's Theatre. At 8.30 p.m., the Presidential carriage emerged from the swirling mist and pulled up in front of the Theatre. Lincoln and his wife hurried from the carriage to the foyer, as the play had already started, and Rathbone and Miss Harris followed closely behind. Ford's was packed with the top brass of the Union army and assorted Washington socialites. Upon spotting the President in the "state box" which overlooked the stage, the audience gave him a standing ovation, and the orchestra began to play "Hail to the Chief". Lincoln proudly watched his admirers until the music had died and the last ripple of applause had faded. He then sat in a specially-made rocking chair in the state box and turned his attention to the actor Harry Hawk, the male lead of the play, who ad-libbed: "This reminds me of a story, as Mr Lincoln would say." The audience roared with laughter, and Lincoln smiled and chatted to Mary. Major Rathbone and Miss Harris sat in the same box, holding hands. As the play continued, bodyguard John Parker began to pace the hallway that led to the state box, but ten minutes later he left his post and went to the saloon next door. Lincoln was now unprotected.

In Taltavul's Saloon, the alcoholic John Parker stood less than six feet away from John Wilkes Booth and his fellow conspirator George Atzerodt. In the same bar, Lincoln's valet Charles Forbes and Francis Burns, the coachman from the Presidential carriage, were also enjoying a drink. Atzerodt was now so intoxicated and frightened at the potential repercussions of the assassination plot that he decided to abandon the plan.

As Lincoln watched the beginning of the play's third

act, he complained of feeling a strange chill, so Mary slipped her hand into his and hugged him. "What will Miss Harris think of my hanging on to you?" she whispered to her husband.

"She won't think *anything* about it," Lincoln replied, and smiled at the Major's sweetheart.

At 10.15 p.m., the door directly behind Lincoln flew open, and John Wilkes Booth entered the state box brandishing a derringer. He pointed it at the back of the President's head, less than five inches away, and pulled the trigger. A gunshot rang out. The bullet entered Lincoln's head just behind his left ear and tunnelled through his brain until it lodged behind his right eye. The President's right arm jerked up convulsively, and he slumped forward. Mary reached out instinctively and caught her husband while Wilkes stood there - a menacing silhouette almost enveloped in gunsmoke. Every face in the Theatre turned to the state box. Some thought the gunshot had been some theatrical gimmick, especially when John Wilkes Booth emerged from the smoke wearing a ridiculously outsized black felt hat. But when the young actor in the state box produced a dagger and stabbed Major Rathbone, the audience realized that this was not play-acting at all. Booth shouted: "The South is avenged!" and leaped from the state box, intending to land on the stage, but he got one of the spurs in his highboots caught in a regimental flag and crashed down onto the stage, breaking his left shin-bone in the fall. The assassin then left the Theatre via the stage door and at the back of Ford's, leapt onto his horse and rode off into the fog.

Major Rathbone gripped his arm, which had been

gashed to the bone, in an attempt to stop the heavy bleeding. He was in a state of shock and seemed to be speechless. Mary Lincoln let out a terrible scream as she cradled her dying husband, and Clara Harris shouted over Mary's screams, "Stop that man! Stop that man! Won't somebody stop that man! The President is shot!" But Booth had already fled the scene of the crime.

"Is there a doctor in the house?" someone in the audience cried. But there was no answer. Pandemonium broke out, and people were shoved to the ground in the aisles as they stampeded for the exits. The English actress Laura Keene, who had been playing the female lead in the abandoned play, yelled out, "For God's sake, have presence of mind and keep your places, and all will be well!"

But the commotion continued. Charles Leale, a young army doctor, fought through the panicking crowds until he reached the President's box, where Clara Harris was trying to console the now hysterical Mary. Leale laid the President on the floor and quickly removed the blood clot from the wound to relieve the pressure on the brain. The doctor could not feel any pulse, so he listened to the President's breathing, and heard that it was shallow. Leale then opened Lincoln's mouth and attempted artificial respiration. An elderly doctor arrived in the box and instructed Leale to massage the President's left breast. Leale did this as the other doctor raised and lowered Lincoln's arms. The President's heart started beating irregularly, and he started to breathe unaided, but he was still unconscious. The doctors carried Lincoln out into the misty night and across the street to Petersen House, where a War Department clerk had a room. Lincoln was gently laid down on the clerk's four-poster bed and Mary was brought over to see her dying husband.

Meanwhile, the news of Lincoln's shooting spread throughout Washington, and a procession of government officials headed for Petersen House. When Secretary of War Edwin Stanton heard the terrible news, he said, "Now he belongs to the ages." Stanton then took over the government, and he and a federal judge took down testimony from a gaggle of witnesses who identified John Wilkes Booth as the President's assassin. Stanton put the city under martial law and co-ordinated dragnets to capture Booth. A reward of $100,000 was also offered for his capture, but Booth had something of a head start after his despicable deed, because the telegraph lines out of Washington D.C. went mysteriously quiet for several hours after Lincoln was shot, so the rest of America wasn't aware of the President's murder for some time. This sinister fact wasn't made public at the time, and has never been satisfactorily explained.

Abraham Lincoln, the sixteenth President of the United States, died without regaining consciousness at 7.22 a.m. on April 15th. Eleven days later, a man believed to be John Wilkes Booth was tracked down by a Union Army patrol. The time was 2 a.m., and the patrol had cornered the fugitive in a barn on the Richard Garrett property near Port Royal, Virginia. The man refused to come out, so the soldiers set fire to the barn. But the man inside the building never got a chance to flee from the flames, because Union soldier Boston Corbett poked his rifle barrel through a crack in the barn and blasted "Booth" in the back of the neck. The man was dragged outside, but died soon afterwards from his wound. The dead man did not even resemble John Wilkes Booth - Booth's hair was black, while the dead man's hair was red, and his stubby nose was quite unlike Booth's aquiline features. When a physician who had attended Booth set eyes on the corpse, he remarked, "No resemblance whatsoever. Never in a human being has a greater change taken place."

Despite the physician's comments, the red-headed corpse was transported to Washington D.C., and secretly interred under the flagstone floor of Washington Arsenal Prison. It was exhumed two years later and stored in a pine box in a warehouse until 1869, when President Andrew Johnson had the box moved to a funeral home, where Booth's brother Edwin, the famous actor, finally claimed it. Edwin had the coffin reburied in an unmarked grave at Greenmount Cemetery, Baltimore on June 26th, 1869. He was forever haunted by the memory of his brother's evil deed, and it is strange to relate that in 1893, Ford's Theatre - the scene of John Wilkes Booth's atrocious crime - collapsed for no apparent reason during Edwin's funeral.

Lincoln's body was subsequently taken to lie in state in the East Room of the White House, and the widowed Mary Lincoln and Ward Hill Lamon realized that the President's dreams of death had now come true.

On January 13th, 1903 - 38 years after Lincoln's death — an old man lay dying in a lodging house in Baltimore. He said his name was David E. George, a 65-year-old actor, but no one in Baltimore had ever seen him tread the boards, and so most people regarded him as a Walter Mitty-type character. But on his deathbed he made a startling confession to the landlord and a doctor. He said, "I killed one of the greatest men who ever lived."

"He's delirious," the doctor told the landlord.

"No I'm not," retorted Mr George. "I killed Abraham Lincoln."

The doctor shook his head with a defeated look. He could do no more for his patient.

"Do you doubt it?" said Mr George. "I am Booth."

The landlord was intrigued by the old man, and said to him, "How did you escape?"

Mr George slipped into a coma before he could answer the question, and never recovered. He died later that day.

The landlord convinced the doctor that Mr George may have been Booth, so the doctor took out his notepad and wrote down all the identifying marks he could see on Mr George's body. These notes were later analyzed by two doctors who had attended John Wilkes Booth. A scar on Mr George's neck matched the place where an unsightly benign tumor had been removed from Booth's neck, and a deep scar on Mr George's left shin tallied with the site of the shin-bone injury Booth would have received when he fell from the state box onto the stage at Ford's Theatre.

But one injury didn't tie in. The dead man had a scar on his right hand, but no one seemed to recall a similar scar on Booth's hand - until 1904, when Joseph Heidelsen - a man who had been a program-seller at Ford's Theatre in his youth — came forward to fuel the controversy. According to Heidelsen, Booth was rehearsing at Ford's Theatre one afternoon when he accidentally caught his right hand in the curtain-raising mechanism and suffered a deep gash as a result. Was David E. George telling the truth? Was he John Wilkes Booth, or was he just an old dreamer with a fevered mind, trying to make a name for himself before he died? How can we discount the curious comments of the physician who had treated Booth when he examined the red-headed corpse? Or the testimony of the program-seller at Ford's Theatre who was well-acquainted with Booth? All the unanswered questions surrounding the fate of John Wilkes Booth indicate that someone in power not only allowed the actor to escape after he had killed Lincoln, but also arranged for the red-headed fall-guy in the barn to be murdered. If this was so, it would suggest a sinister conspiracy as far-reaching as the intrigue that surrounded the assassination of John F. Kennedy.

THE MURDER OF
AN ENGLISH WARLOCK

In his book, *The Anatomy of Crime*, the celebrated Superintendent Robert Fabian of Scotland Yard, one of the most hard-boiled logical and scientific detectives in the history of criminology, wrote a curious paragraph about one particular murder case that he never solved:

I advise anybody who is tempted at any time to venture into Black Magic, witchcraft, Shamanism - call it what you will - to remember Charles Walton and to think of his death, which was clearly the ghastly climax of a pagan rite. There is no stronger argument for keeping as far away as possible from the villains with their swords, incense and mumbo-jumbo. It is prudence on which your future peace of mind and even your life could depend.

In this warning to the idly curious, Fabian was referring to the baffling case of the "Pitchfork Murder", which occurred in 1945 in the village of Lower Quinton, just a few miles south of Stratford-upon-Avon. But before we look into the murder mystery, we must go back in time to 1662 to understand why the area around the scene of the crime is so steeped in witchcraft.

In the spring of 1662, a Scottish witch named Isobel Gowdie was burned at the stake for using a team of harnessed toads to pull a miniature plough across a field. In Celtic mythology, the toad had always been associated with witchcraft, sorcery, curses and blights, and this myth was carried over into Christianity. In Greek lore, Amerindian legend, and even Chinese mythology, the toad was also regarded as a magical creature identified with the powers of darkness, so nobody in seventeenth-century Scotland thought it was strange to put an old woman to death for employing toads to pull a toy plough. Throughout the rest of Britain, the toad was a much maligned yet respected creature. In the English Fens, for example, a peculiar Roman tradition of using a toad as a compass is still extant. This custom dates back to the days when the occupying Romans would place a dagger on a toad's back, then watch the creature move around slowly until it stopped when the dagger pointed due north.

Over two centuries after the execution of Isobel Gowdie, another old woman who was suspected of being a witch was also killed. She was 75-year-old Ann Tenant of Long Compton in Warwickshire, and the man who slayed her was a mentally retarded youth named John Heywood, referred to locally as the village idiot. Heywood was convinced that Miss Tenant was a member of a coven of witches who held their sabbath rituals in the countryside around the village of Long Compton. Some said the old woman also used toads to blight crops by black magic rituals. At the murder trial, Heywood confessed, "Her was a proper witch. I pinned her to the ground [with a pitchfork] before slashing her throat with a bill-hook to carve a cross."

Local gossip at the time of the trial had it that Long Compton was becoming the epicentre of witchcraft in the region, and an old saying of the day was: "There are enough witches in Long Compton to draw a wagonload of hay up Long Compton Hill." Strangely enough, just south of the village stands a circle of Neolithic or Bronze Age stones known as the Rollright Stones which have been associated with pagan rituals for centuries. Even today, modern witches and occultists still gather within the circle of stones to conduct esoteric rites.

About 15 miles north of the Rollright Stones, the picturesque village of Lower Quinton sits in the shadow of Meon Hill. Even today, Lower Quinton has a spooky aura about it after dark, and is surrounded by eerily-named places such as Devil's Elbow and Upper Slaughter. In a thatched cottage at Lower Quinton in the 1940s, there lived a 74-year-old man named Charles Walton and his unmarried niece, Edith. In his younger days, Walton had worked as a ploughman, but now in old age he was plagued with stabbing rheumatism, and eked out a living putting in a seven-hour day for one shilling and sixpence an hour hedge-cutting for local farmers. He was a familiar figure in the village, with his double-pronged hay-fork over his shoulder and his slash-hook in his hand, hobbling to work up Meon Hill. Outwardly there was nothing to suggest that the old hedger and ditcher was anybody out of the ordinary, but Walton had quite a sinister reputation in the village, where it was common knowledge that he bred huge toads and had once been a legendary horse whisperer. Horse whispering is the ancient and now largely forgotten art of controlling a horse from a distance without any word or command, using a slight gesture of the hand to make the horse stay, run, canter or gallop. Walton's horse whispering ability seemed nothing short of witchcraft, and his power over animals allegedly extended to cattle, toads and birds. What's more, it was said that Walton had been seen on many occasions imitating the songs of the nightingale and chirping to other species of bird. He openly professed to be conversant in the language of his feathered friends, and they seemed to obey his requests to refrain from eating the seeds sown in the fields of his little plot.

On the morning of February 14th, 1945, Charles Walton left home and hobbled up Meon Hill to attend to the hedges that formed the border of Alfred Potter's farm, about a mile from Walton's cottage.

At six o'clock that evening, Edith began to worry about her uncle. He still hadn't returned, and he was usually back before four o'clock. She felt sure that something had happened to him, and suspected that the old man had collapsed as he'd recently been complaining about the unbearable rheumatic pain that was crippling his legs. Edith sought out her neighbour Harry Beasley, and they both hiked up Meon's Hill to Potter's farm - known as "The Firs" - with a growing sense of foreboding.

Farmer Potter told Edith and Harry that he had seen someone in the distance earlier in the day who appeared to be cutting hedges, and had assumed it was Walton. However, Potter thought that Walton had long gone home. He fetched a flashlight and took Walton's niece and her neighbour over the fields to the spot where the old man had last been seen.

The beam of the flashlight revealed the whole horrific scene. Under a willow tree on Meon Hill lay the spread-eagled body of Charles Walton. Potter glanced at the corpse then shielded Edith from the gruesome sight with his arm and took her home. He then summoned the police. Meanwhile, back at the scene of the crime, Harry Beasley stood guard over his murdered neighbour. He saw that Walton had been impaled with his own pitchfork and that the twin prongs of the tool had been driven through his neck with such force, they penetrated the ground to a depth of six inches.

Crosses had been carved on Walton's cheeks, neck and abdomen, and the bill-hook that had been used to cut out the symbols was still wedged between Walton's ribs. Near to the body lay the old man's walking-stick, covered in blood because it had been used to bludgeon his head. The face of Walton was frozen in an expression of sheer terror.

The Warwickshire police force reacted strangely to the crime. They seemed to be reluctant to investigate, and called for a murder squad from Scotland Yard to look into the strange killing. On the following day, Detective Superintendent Robert Fabian and his assistant, Detective Sergeant Albert Webb turned up at the village and were greeted with what appeared to be a conspiracy of silence. The few locals who would speak merely told Fabian that Walton had been a strange, secretive old man who bred large natterjack toads in the damp undergrowth of his garden. Fabian also learned that Walton had never been over-fond of company, buying cider by the gallon from pubs and drinking it alone by his kitchen fireside. Fabian could not allow his reasoning to be clouded by superstition, yet he felt that Walton had been ritually murdered and took the unprecedented step of consulting Dr Margaret Murray, a witchcraft expert. Fabian also delved into the local history of the area and was intrigued to uncover a record of the 1875 murder of Ann Tenant, who had been killed in a very similar manner to Charles Walton. Fabian began to suspect that the person or persons who had killed Walton had carried out the murder in order to purge the village of a man regarded as a practising witch.

The line of inquiry switched to the prisoner of war camp over at Long Marston, where Italian, Germans and Slavonic soldiers were quizzed, but Fabian was confident that the POWs were innocent of Walton's murder.

Then something weird happened. A black dog was found hanged on Meon Hill. There were hushed claims in the village that the hound had been Walton's "familiar" — a demon in disguise. Even the secular-minded Fabian was unnerved by the hanged dog, for on the first day of the murder investigation, he had climbed Meon Hill to examine the crime scene, and been intrigued to notice a large black retriever seated on a nearby wall, watching him. Seconds afterwards, a boy walked past, and Fabian asked him, "Are you looking for your dog?"

The boy returned a blank stare and said "What dog?"

Fabian then noticed that the dog had vanished, and the boy fled down the hill in absolute terror. He later told the villagers that Fabian had seen a ghostly black dog, which was regarded as a portent of death or bad luck.

Shortly after the hanged dog was cut down from the tree, another dog was run over by a police car, and a spate of other inexplicable canine deaths followed during the murder investigation. As if to underline the relevance of the canine coincidences, Fabian's attention was drawn to a curious passage from an old yellowed book entitled Folklore, Old Customs and Superstitions in Shakespeare Land, written in 1930. The text of the passage actually referred to the young Charles Walton:

At Alveston a ploughman named Charles Walton met a dog on his way home nine times in successive evenings. He told both the shepherd and the carter with whom he worked, and was laughed at for his pains. On the ninth encounter a headless lady rushed past him in a silk dress, and on the next day he heard of his sister's death.

Fabian and Webb learned from several of the more talkative villagers that in early spring 1944, crops had been slow in growing, and there had been several fatal accidents with livestock. The harvest was a disaster and even the beer had been unaccountably sour in every local pub. Many thought that Walton was the source of the widespread bad luck, so Fabian easily deduced that the old man had been killed to put an end to his evil magical influences. That killer or killers had probably had an intimate knowledge of the occult and planned the murder months in advance. Fabian knew that the date of Walton's death — February 14th - was Valentine's Day, and occasionally Ash Wednesday also fell on that date, but February 14th also had a special relevance to the ancient Druids - they carried out human sacrifices on that day to procure a good harvest.

Fabian of the Yard finally had to concede. Four thousand statements had been taken and painstakingly cross-referenced, 29 samples of blood, skin, and hair had been analyzed, but to no avail, and the silence in the village remained impenetrable to the London policemen. Fabian and Webb reluctantly retreated to the capital, where more mundane crimes demanded their attention. But for many years afterwards, Robert Fabian returned to Lower Quinton on the anniversary of the Walton killing and hid himself on Meon Hill to keep a watch on the area, perhaps hoping that the murderer would return to the scene of the crime, but they never did. Speaking of the Walton murder to a newspaper in 1976, the then retired Fabian told a reporter: "Detectives deal in facts, but I must admit there was something *uncanny* about that investigation."

ADOLF HITLER – BLACK MAGICIAN?

According to the unfinished manuscript *I Married Hitler's Brother*, which was discovered in the main branch of New York Public Library in the late 1970s, Adolf Hitler had once lodged at a house in the Toxteth district of Liverpool, England, from November 1912 to April 1913. Historians quickly presumed the manuscript was a hoax, but as they read through the work, many of them concluded the claims it contained were not as bizarre as they had initially thought.

The author of the controversial manuscript was one Bridget Hitler, the wife of Adolf's half-brother Alois. Irish-born Bridget's maiden name had been Dowling, and she had met Alois Hitler at the annual Dublin Horse Show of 1909. Dressed in a brown suit and a homburg hat, the debonair Austrian introduced himself to 17-year-old Bridget in broken English, and it was one of those supposedly rare cases of love at first sight. Bridget began to date the foreigner, who claimed to be in the hotel business, but her parents didn't approve of Alois, and they were shocked to discover that Alois's claim to be in the hotel business meant in fact that he was merely a waiter at the nearby Shelbourne Hotel. This was the final straw, and Bridget's parents demanded an end to the relationship. But Bridget was in love and she eloped with her sweetheart and married him in London. A year after the marriage, Bridget bore Alois a son, and he was named William Patrick. Bridget later addressed her son as Pat, while Alois called him Willie.

In their second year of married life, the couple

decided to move to Liverpool, where they opened a small restaurant in the bustling thoroughfare of Dale Street, but it was only a modest success. Alois was a restless person, and he decided to sell the restaurant in order to buy a boarding-house in another part of the city. The boarding-house venture was an utter disaster, and Alois became bankrupt. However, his economic outlook improved shortly afterwards when he won a fortune from backing the winner of the Grand National Steeplechase. Alois used the money to set himself up in the safety-razor business. He decided he needed a partner, so he wrote to his brother-in-law Anton Raubal in Vienna, asking him and his wife to come to Liverpool straightaway, and enclosed the travelling expenses.

On a cold November morning in 1912, Alois and Bridget went to Liverpool's Lime Street Station and waited for the 11.30 train to steam in. When the train arrived, the couple waited with baited breath for Anton and his wife to disembark, but they were disappointed. The outline of a solitary figure descending from the train was barely visible through the cloud of steam drifting across the platform. A pale-faced young man in a worn-out suit approached and offered his hand to Alois. It was Adolf, the younger half-brother of Alois. He explained that he had come in the place of Anton Raubal, who had not been able to make the journey for various reasons.

A heated discussion in German broke out between the brothers, and Bridget was so embarrassed that she left them and went home.

In the evening, Alois brought Adolf to his three-bed-roomed flat at 102 Upper Stanhope Street, and seeing that the brothers were now on friendlier terms, Bridget cooked dinner for them. After the meal, Adolf retired to the drawing room, while Bridget scolded her husband for giving his brother such a rough reception. Alois said that Adolf - who he referred to as "my artist brother" - had deserted from the Austrian army and had been on the run for 18 months. "That's why he came here to me," Alois explained, "When he confessed this at the station he wondered why I didn't welcome him with open arms."

At that time in Vienna, there was a rigid system of registration of domicile, and this system made it easy to locate anyone failing to report for military service. Alois said that Adolf had got round this by using the identity papers of his dead brother Edmund. But when the Viennese police finally tracked him down, Adolf fled to Liverpool after begging Anton Raubal's wife for the travelling expenses that Alois had sent to her husband.

Now that Alois had explained the facts, Bridget understood why her husband had made such a scene at the station.

According to Bridget, her 23-year-old brother-in-law spent most of his time lounging around the house and playing with two-year-old William Patrick. At first, he hardly spoke to her, but gradually, as the weeks went by, Adolf became friendlier and began talking about his interest in painting and his future plans. He told Bridget how disappointed he was when his application to become an artist at the Academy of Art in Vienna was turned down by a Jewish professor who said that he couldn't paint, but had a minor talent for architecture.

Another subject young Adolf discussed - or rather, argued - with his sister-in-law, was Germany's future. It was Adolf's unshakeable belief that Germany would one day take its rightful position in the world, and whenever he talked about the "fatherland", he would unfold a map of the world that belonged to Alois, spread it across the floor, and explain how Germany would first conquer France, and then England. Sometimes Adolf would disrupt Bridget's housework to discuss his political predictions, and on one occasion when Bridget became so irritated by his ranting that she carried on cleaning, Adolf began to scream and shout at her for ignoring him. Bridget retaliated by telling Adolf that he would never live to see England destroyed by Germany, and added that he wasn't even German - just a low-living Austrian deserter. Hitler was so taken aback by Bridget's riposte that he became speechless, and began to shake as he swelled with anger. One day, Alois took Adolf on a daytrip to London, where Adolf became captivated by the various architectural styles of the city's buildings and landmarks. He was enchanted by the dome of St Paul's Cathedral, and the workings of Tower Bridge. On the train back to Liverpool, the future dictator made several sketches of an enormous version of St Paul's, but Alois said that such a construction would be just a pointless folly. Adolf rambled on about his magnificent dream of building a domed temple to outlive the Pyramid of Cheops, but Alois fell asleep.

In her controversial manuscript, Bridget mentions a Mrs Prentice - a neighbour who was into astrology and the occult. Adolf allegedly spent hours in her home having his cards and horoscopes read. He was enthralled by her prediction that a tremendous future lay ahead of him. Mrs Prentice looked at the Austrian's palm and told him he had a prominent line of destiny, which indicated that he would have a phenomenal career. However, Mrs Prentice also noted that Adolf's "heart line" crossed his destiny line, which meant that his life's goal could be thwarted by his own emotions if they got the better of him.

Adolf eventually outstayed his welcome, and Alois told him to go home. So, in May 1913, Adolf left England and returned to Germany. Bridget says in her manuscript that she blamed herself for turning loose a man who plunged the world into its costliest war, and she regretted not teaching him English. Many historians who have analyzed the manuscript believe that Adolf's trip to Liverpool is entirely credible, and furthermore, November 1912 to May 1913 is something of a lost period in the Fuhrer's life. Hitler never mentioned his stay in Liverpool in *Mein Kampf*, but then that could be because he didn't want to publicize his shameful days as a draft-dodging drop-out. Ironically, the last bombs to fall on Liverpool demolished the very house in Upper Stanhope Street where Hitler once lived.

Hitler returned to Vienna, where he lived on his wits and made a precarious living selling below-average postcard sketches, beating carpets and doing any odd jobs that came his way. He lived in a doss-house, infested with lice, and continually wore a long black overcoat given to him by a sympathetic Jewish tailor.

To escape the cold, Adolf would often wander through the corridors of the Hofburg Museum, where one particular exhibit never failed to mesmerize him:

the Holy Lance. This was said to be the very spear which pierced Christ's side when he had given up his ghost on the cross. According to legend, the "Spear of Destiny" as it was called, belonged to the Roman soldier Longinius, who smote Jesus. And in the romance of King Arthur, the merchant Joseph of Arimathea is said to have brought the spear to Britain, where Sir Balim the Savage used it to wound King Pelham. It then went to Austria, and somehow wound up in the Hofburg Museum as part of the Habsburg regalia. Hitler was well-read, and he knew the biblical reference about the spear from John 19: 33-37 by heart:

But when they came to Jesus, and saw that he was dead already, they broke not his legs: But one of the soldiers with a spear pierced his side, and forthwith came there out blood and water. And he saw it bare record, and his record is true: and he knoweth that he saith true, that ye might believe. For these things were done that the scripture should be fulfilled, A bone of him shall not be broken. And again another scripture saith, They shall look on him whom they pierced.

The spear Hitler was obsessed with had been discovered at Antioch in 1098 during the First Crusade. It seems that this same lance had been carried as a talisman in the ninth century by Charlemagne, and it was reputed to have helped him win 47 campaigns.

It was also said that when Charlemagne accidentally dropped the lance one day, he suddenly died.

The lance then passed into the hands of Heinrich the Fowler, the founder of the royal house of the Saxons, who drove the Poles eastward. The lance later came into the possession of five Saxon monarchs, and generations later, it became the coveted property of the succeeding Hohen-stauffens of Swabia. The most prominent of this line, Frederick Barbarossa, conquered Italy and even subdued the Pope, forcing him into exile. Barbarossa made the same fatal mistake as Charlemagne; he dropped the lance while wading in a stream in Sicily on his way to the Third Crusade, and within minutes he was dead.

All these stories of the magical lance fired the imagination of the poverty-stricken Austrian. According to Dr Walter Johannes Stein - a prominent mathematician, economist and occultist who had known Hitler in his youth - the future leader of Nazi Germany had a vast understanding of black magic and saw the lance as the equivalent of a magician's wand or the staff of Moses. In the summer of 1912, Stein visited an occult bookseller in Vienna and bought a worn edition of Parsival, an Arthurian romance about the Holy Grail by the thirteenth-century German poet Wolfram von Eschenbach. The margin of this book was full of scribbled notes by someone who evidently had a deep knowledge of the occult - and a pathological hatred of the Jews. Stein wondered about the book's previous owner, and when he looked at the inside of the flyleaf he found his name: Adolf Hitler. Stein traced him through the bookseller and spent many hours listening to Adolf's strange views on eugenics and politics, which he found repugnant yet somehow alluring. Stein later said that even though Hitler was only in his early twenties, he felt he had some grand mystical destiny to fulfil, and radiated a peculiar evil charisma. One day, the conversation between Stein and Hitler turned to the Holy Lance, and Hitler expressed his belief that the ancient weapon would one day come into his hands, telling Stein of a stirring vision he had witnessed while looking at the lance in its case: "I slowly became aware of a mighty presence around it, the same awesome presence which I had experienced inwardly on those rare occasions in my life when I had sensed that a great destiny awaited me. A window in the future was opened up to me through which I saw in a single flash of illumination a future event by which I knew beyond contradiction that the blood in my veins would one day become the vessel of the Folk-Spirit of my people."

Hitler never divulged the details of his vision, but Stein was convinced that he had probably seen himself 25 years on, in the Heldenplatz outside the Hofburg Museum addressing thousands of his fellow Austrians. At that very place on March 14th, 1938, the Fuhrer announced his annexation of Austria and ordered the removal of the Habsburg regalia to the spiritual home of the Nazi movement - Nuremberg. Many historians were baffled by this, as Hitler had always condemned the house of Habsburg as betrayers of the German race, but they overlooked the legendary reputation of the Spear of Destiny. On October 13th the spear was carefully loaded onto an armoured train with an SS guard and taken over the German border. The relic was then given a new home in the hall of St Catherine's Church, which had been converted into a Nazi war museum. With the lance now in his possession, Hitler seemed drunk with power, yet had a morbid fear of losing the relic, for he knew that those in the past who had let the lance fall from their grasp had soon died.

Many students of twentieth-century history have remarked on Hitler's amazing rise to power from his days as a down-and-out postcard painter. It seems that no two historians can agree on whether Hitler was simply in the right place at the right time, or whether he was merely the puppet of some sinister evil genius who lurked in the shadows of the Nazi Party. How Hitler was able, unchecked for over ten years, to implement policies of unprecedented atrociousness is another question that will continue to plague mankind. Stein believed Hitler's rise to power and his ability to get away with genocide was due to the dictator's involvement with the black arts. But are there any facts to support Stein's claims?

The official insignia of the Nazi Party was the swastika, an old symbol that has been found in many cultures across the world, including those of the American Indians and the ancient Greeks. It was usually a symbol of the sun or good luck, but the Nazi swastika was reversed - to denote evil and paganism. The transposed swastika had first been used as an emblem of a neo-pagan movement by the German occultist Guido von List in the late nineteenth century. List renounced his Catholicism at the age of 14 in 1862 and swore he would one day build a grand temple dedicated to Odin, the Scandinavian god of war. Eight years later, List had attracted a sizeable group of like-minded people who also felt a strong spiritual connection with the old mythological deities of Scandinavia. These followers observed the pagan feasts at the solstices and equinoxes, and worshipped the sun as Baldur, the old Norse god who was slain in battle, but rose from the dead - just as the sun rises to end the funereal night. Their sun-worshipping rite was held on the top of a hill in Vienna, and on one occasion, the heathen liturgy ended with List burying eight wine bottles laid out in the shape of his swastika.

When the National Socialist Party was still in its infancy in the 1920s, Hitler realized that the movement needed a symbol. The Russian communists had the hammer and sickle, and Britain had the easily-identifiable Union flag. An interesting suggestion was put forward by a Sternberg dentist named Friedrich Krohn: a black swastika on a white disc set on a red flag. The red symbolized blood and the social ideal, and the white disc stood for purity of race and nationalism. The swastika at the centre of all this signified "the struggle for victory of the Aryan man".

Krohn immediately captured Hitler's imagination with his proposal. The most infamous symbol in the history of mankind had been conceived. Shortly after the birth of the Nazi "cross", Hitler imposed a baffling directive that has never been understood by modern historians; all occult writings and practices were to be rigorously stamped out. Why did someone like Hitler, who was so preoccupied with the occult himself, wish to eradicate occultism? In 1934, the Berlin police impounded thousands of books on mysticism and the occult. Then came the widespread suppression of all occult groups in Germany - even groups such the German Order (of which Friedrich Krohn was a member) and the Thule Society - which contained many members of the National Socialist Party, including Rudolf Hess. Hitler's directive to wipe out the occultists seems contradictory, but recent evidence has surfaced which indicates that the Nazi leader attacked the occultists because he saw them as rivals. Similarly, Stalin persecuted and disbanded the occultists in Russia because he feared their secret societies; he also tried to wipe out the ultra-secretive Freemasons. As far as the Fuhrer was concerned, only one occult movement was permissible under his Third Reich — all competitors would *have* to be removed.

Among the many accounts we have from people who met the Fuhrer or worked alongside him, there are recurring stories of his strange powers of persuasion and ability to literally bewitch people. In April 1943, the Italian dictator Mussolini visited Hitler in Germany in a state of deep depression and mental and physical exhaustion. An entry in the diary of Josef Goebbels describes how Hitler revitalized Mussolini:

By putting every ounce of nervous energy into the effort, the Fuhrer succeeded in pushing Mussolini back onto the rails. In those four days Mussolini underwent a complete change. When he got out of the train on his arrival the Fuhrer thought he looked like a broken old man. When he left again he was in high fettle, ready for anything.

Hitler's powers of suggestion and motivation were also experienced by Karl Donitz, commander of the U-Boat fleet. Donitz once said of the Fuhrer's uncanny influence: "I purposely went very seldom to his headquarters, for I had the feeling that I would best preserve my power of initiative and also because, after several days at headquarters, I always had the feeling that I had to disengage myself from his powers of suggestion. I was doubtless more fortunate than his staff, who were constantly exposed to his power and personality."

On another occasion, Dr Hjalmar Schacht, the Nazi Party's financial wizard, asked Hermann Goering to discuss a minor point of economic policy with Hitler. Goering promised he would raise the matter but when he came face to face with Hitler, he found that he could not bring himself to speak. Goering later admitted to Schacht: "I often make up my mind to say something to him, but when I meet him face to face my heart sinks."

Many in the higher echelons of the Nazi Party, as well as SS guards, were convinced that Hitler was possessed. Herman Rauschning, the Governor of Danzig and confidant of the German dictator, claimed that Hitler often suffered terrible nightmares, and awoke many times to see a phantom-like being in his room. Rauschning gives an account of the Fuhrer's night-terror in his book Hitler Speaks:

A person close to Hitler told me that he wakes up in the night, screaming and in convulsions. He calls for help, and appears to be half paralyzed. He is seized with a panic that makes him tremble until the bed shakes. He utters confused and unintelligible sounds, gasping, as if on the point of suffocation. The same person described to me one of these fits, with details I would refuse to believe had I not complete confidence in my informant.

Hitler was standing up in his room, swaying and looking all round as if he were lost. "It's he, it's he," he groaned; "he's come for me!" His lips were white; he was sweating profusely . . . suddenly he screamed: "There! There! Over in the corner! He is there!"

But there was nobody in the corner. All the same,

Hitler lived in fear of his nocturnal demon. In the Bible several people possessed by demons are described as falling to the floor and frothing at the mouth - during his screaming rages Hitler did the same. Rauschning believed that the man who caused the deaths of more than 30 million people was but a mouthpiece for some evil force:

One cannot help thinking of Hitler as a medium. For most of the time, mediums are ordinary, insignificant people. Suddenly they are endowed with what seems to be supernatural powers which set them apart from the rest of humanity. These powers are something that is outside their true personality - visitors, as it were, from another planet. The medium is possessed. Once the crisis is past, they fall back again into mediocrity. It was in this way, no doubt, that Hitler was possessed by forces outside himself — almost demonic forces of which the individual named Hitler was only the temporary vehicle.

Curiously enough, many other observers of Hitler's oratorical skills independently reached the same conclusions as Rauschning. "I looked into his eyes - the eyes of a medium in a trance. Sometimes the speaker's body seemed inhabited by something," Bouchez once remarked. "The Devil's children have the Devil's luck" is an old adage that certainly applied to Hitler. In World War One, Corporal Hitler fell asleep in a trench and dreamt that a shell killed him. He awoke in a sweat and ran from the spot. The bemused soldier who took his place was blown to bits by an enemy shell minutes later. Then in 1923, Hitler lead a column of National Socialists through the streets of Munich. The police machine-gunned the column, killing 16 storm troopers. Hermann Goering was badly wounded, but Hitler somehow escaped injury. On another occasion, in 1931, Hitler stepped off a pavement in Munich and into the path of a speeding Fiat motorcar, driven by the multi-millionaire Lord Howard de Walden. Hitler survived the collision without even a bruise, and even shook hands with the speechless de Walden and forgave him. On July 20th, 1944, a bomb planted by Colonel Berthold von Stauffenberg under Hitler's conference table exploded. The Fuhrer survived the assassination attempt and Stauffenberg was shot on the following day. His 150 fellow conspirators were also executed.

But Hitler's luck was dealt a severe blow when he allowed the Spear of Destiny to leave him. Because of heavy allied bombing on Nuremberg in October 1944, Hitler had the spear and the rest of the Habsburg regalia transferred to a specially constructed reinforced vault.

Within six months, the momentous D-Day landings had been a great success, and the Allies were closing in on the Fuhrer in his Berlin bunker. He knew all hope of victory had long gone, and that it would only be a matter of time before the end came. But for some reason, Hitler waited until April 30th, 1945 until he shot himself through the head. It may have been a coincidence, but an ancient occult feast called Walpurgis Night also falls on that day. Hell's demons are said to hold high revelry under their chief - the Devil.

On the day of Hitler's death, Lieutenant William Horn of the American Seventh Army located the Spear of Destiny in its underground bunker. Longinius's famous lance was lying on a bed of red velvet. Horn took possession of the relic on behalf of the United States government.

A MAN OF TWO WORLDS

No book about mysterious personages would be complete without a description of the psychic scientist Emanuel Swedenborg, who was born in Stockholm in 1688, the son of Jesper Svedberg, later Bishop of Skara. From an early age, Swedenborg exhibited a remarkable intellect, and in due course he entered Uppsala University. After graduation, Swedenborg traveled widely across Europe to study with the great philosophers and scientists of the day, and, despite a stutter, he mastered most of the European languages during his travels.

Swedenborg excelled at whatever he turned his mind to. As well as being an accomplished musician, he was also highly skilled in mathematics, chemistry, astronomy, anatomy, physics, and psychology, and he even anticipated Freudian psychiatry by experimenting with dream analysis. The Swedish savant was also something of an inventor. Although many of his projects were never put into practice, Swedenborg usually sketched the schematics of his creations and worked out the details. Among his inventions were designs for a ship that could become waterproof and transform itself into a deadly, armed submarine, a mechanical device which enabled the musical novice to play complicated melodies on almost any instrument, and a hydraulic contraption for the effortless transference of heavy cargo into the hold of a ship. In 1716, Swedenborg was appointed as the assessor to the Royal College of Mines, a post he held for 30 years, during which time he vastly improved upon the orthodox methods for extracting metals from rock. In 1718, he published the first book on algebra in Swedish, and it was but the first of a torrent of 40 academic volumes to flow from his quill. He was ennobled in 1719 and became a member of the Swedish parliament.

But at the height of his accomplishments, many years later when he was in his fifties, Swedenborg discovered that he had other gifts beyond the merely academic. In a letter to a friend, Swedenborg wrote of a life-changing paranormal incident which he had recently experienced:

I have been called to a holy office by the Lord Himself, who most mercifully appeared before me in the year 1743; when he opened my sight into the spiritual world, and enabled me to converse with spirits and angels, in which state I have continued up to the present day. From that time I began to print and publish the various secrets that were seen by me or revealed to me about heaven and hell, the state of man after death, and the true worship of God.

Swedenborg later gave more details about the incident which proved to be a spiritual milestone in his life. He said he had been in bed when he heard a frightening noise which sounded like "many winds" rushing through the room. He trembled from head to foot, then something invisible seized him and flung him out of the bed onto the floor. As he clasped his hands to pray for God to deliver him from this unearthly attacker, he felt a hand press against his own, then he beheld the materialization of a person who resembled Jesus as he is depicted in religious paintings. According to Swedenborg, Jesus told him he had been enlisted into the service of God and would be allowed to talk with angels and the other entities of the spiritual world. However, the exact words spoken by Christ was never fully divulged by Swedenborg.

Swedenborg's personality and lifestyle subsequently underwent a dramatic change. He resigned his assessorship, gave up his mundane studies and devoted the entirety of his time to spiritual development. About a year after the psychic revelation, Swedenborg was enjoying his usual over-indulgent midday meal when the room suddenly darkened. Swedenborg looked down at the floor and saw that it was crawling with snakes and toads. A figure then appeared in the corner and told the startled Swede: "Eat not so much!"

The darkness and the apparitions faded away and, understandably, Swedenborg decided he would eat in moderation from that day on.

Swedenborg gradually developed a variety of psychic talents which included automatic writing, prophecy and precognition. One day he suddenly "knew" that a friend named Olofsohn would die at precisely 4.45 p.m. At that exact time his friend - who was apparently in good health - literally dropped dead. On another occasion, Swedenborg urged a mill owner with whom he was having dinner to go at once to his mill because a fire was breaking out there. The mill owner knew of his friend's clairvoyant powers and went to the mill immediately, where he found a large piece of cloth that had fallen on the furnace ablaze. This peculiar extrasensory gift is known to students of parapsychology as "remote viewing", and has been demonstrated in modern times by such psychics as the New York artist Ingo Swann. For the remainder of his life, Swedenborg could perceive events far beyond his range of optical vision, but sometimes this uncanny ability was more of a niggling annoyance than a cherished skill. On the Saturday evening of July 19th, 1759, Swedenborg was one of 16 guests invited to the home of his friend William Castell in Gothenburg, which is 240 miles from Stockholm. Swedenborg was enjoying dinner with the other guests when he suddenly beheld a stark vision of a massive blaze raging in Stockholm. He told the bemused guests around the table about the fiery vision and became pallid and greatly agitated. He left the house for a breath of fresh air and returned with more details which disturbed a number of the guests. He told one person present that his house had been totally destroyed by the fire and that his own house was now threatened by the hungry flames. He described vividly the course and extent of the raging fire, then suddenly at 8 p.m., he slumped into a chair out of breath and sighed, "Thank God. The fire is extinguished, the third door from my house."

Many of the guests were still sceptical, but on Monday evening, a messenger arrived from Stockholm and confirmed every detail of Swedenborg's account of the blaze. He had even been right about the way the fire had petered out three doors from his home. When the provisional governor of Stockholm heard of the strange story, he asked Swedenborg if he knew how the fire had started, and Swedenborg obliged by giving him a blow-by-blow account of the fire's origin.

Swedenborg's alleged ability to converse with spirits is also well-documented. In 1760, the Dutch ambassador to Stockholm died, and his widow received a bill from a goldsmith who claimed that her deceased husband had not paid for a silver service he had supplied. The widow was distressed at the allegation, for she knew that her husband had been a man who always settled his debts, so she enlisted the services of Swedenborg. The widow asked him if he could get in touch with her dead husband to see if he had paid for the silver service. Swedenborg duly chatted to the ambassador's spirit and was told that he had paid for the silverware, and that the receipt was somewhere in the house. The spirit ended the conversation by promising to return to the house to look for the receipt. Eight days later, the widow had a vivid dream about her departed husband in which he showed her the location of the receipt behind a drawer. When the widow awoke, she anxiously inspected the desk of her late husband, and found the receipt exactly where the dream had indicated.

Another demonstration of Swedenborg's psychic prowess took place in October 1761, when he was summoned by the Queen of Sweden. The Queen inquired if the mystic could get in touch with her brother, Augustus William of Prussia, who had died four years previously. Swedenborg said he would try, and three weeks later returned to the royal court. The Queen was playing cards at the time, without standing to meet the seer, asked him what information he had. But Swedenborg said her dead brother had asked him to deliver the message — which was highly confidential — to his sister in private. The Queen rose from the card table and gestured to Swedenborg to whisper the message in her ear. Swedenborg reluctantly did so, and whatever it was that he murmured, it caused the Queen to turn pale and totter about as if she was about to faint.

When a guard and Swedenborg steadied the monarch, she took a deep breath and trembled as she exclaimed, "That is something which no one else could have told, except my brother!"

In 1772, the founder of Methodism, John Wesley, who had heard so much about the mystical Swede, felt the urge to contact him, but before he did so, imagine his surprise when he received a letter from Swedenborg. The letter stated:

> Sir, I have been informed in the world of spirits that you have a strong desire to converse with me. I shall be happy to see you if you will favour me with a visit. I am, Sir, your humble servant, Emanuel Swedenborg.

Wesley was naturally astonished. He wrote back saying that he was delighted at the invitation but could not go immediately, as he was due to embark on a preaching tour soon that would last for six weeks. Swedenborg replied with a letter that shook Wesley even more than the first. In the missive, Swedenborg stated that as he himself would be entering the world of spirits on March 29th, he and Wesley would never meet in this material world. On March 29th, 1772, Emanuel Swedenborg peacefully passed away while in London, and was buried in the Swedish church of St George's of the East. In 1908, his body was reinterred at

Stockholm at the request of the Swedish government.

Although Swedenborg made no attempts to preach or to establish a sect, and never considered himself to be a mystic or a medium, he quickly gained many followers after his death. A distinct denomination was formed in 1787 by several Wesleyan preachers, and the followers called themselves "the New Church signified by the New Jerusalem in the Revelation".

Swedenborg's own cosmological beliefs about the "hereafter" are still being discussed and reinterpreted, but he made it clear in his books and conversations that he believed Heaven and Hell are all around us, and that death is simply a process by which the soul is transformed to another state. He claimed that the newly arrived spirit in the next world is received by angels and benevolent spirits, and that the novice spirit usually gravitates towards the spirits that are like itself. He courted controversy and risked retribution from the church when he also declared that God punishes no one, but instead transfigures evil spirits by preventing them from indulging in the evil they crave for; he claimed that this was the only type of torture that went on in the next world. Swedenborg also asserted that relatives of the human race lived in countless other worlds in space, and that the spirits of these people from other planets were also in the next world. This far-sighted view predictably caused many in the eighteenth century to scoff at him, including the German philosopher Kant.

So much for Swedenborg's beliefs; but what have historians and theologians to say about Swedenborg the man? Like many other extraordinary luminaries, Swedenborg has been branded as a charlatan and a crackpot. He has also been nervously dismissed as a paranoid schizophrenic, even a sexually frustrated swindler. Much has been made of the fact that Swedenborg was jilted in his youth and chose to remain single, although he was attracted to women, but how can this irrelevant trifle detract one iota from Swedenborg's psychic feats and his philosophy? As for the allegations that he was a charlatan, he was always willing to be called on - free of charge - to communicate with spirits, and all his contemporaries described him as sensible, sane, kind, honest and unimpeachable. If we are all headed for an afterlife, perhaps we may get to know more one day about the man who lived in two worlds.

THE ATLANTEANS

During World War Two, scores of American pilots on submarine duty in the Caribbean reported sightings of artificial underwater structures. Many of these geometrical constructs were seen in the coastal vicinity of Mexico, Yucatan and British Honduras, and seemed to fly in the face of the textbook history of the Americas. Today, many more submerged building of uncertain origin have been discovered, and they are providing quite a headache for conventional archaeology, because evidence is gradually mounting that hints at a pre-Inca (and possibly pre-Egyptian) civilization, which might have actually had a transatlantic trade route with Europe. Furthermore, it is entirely possible that the shipping lanes of this route had a regular port of call on their journeys: the mid-Atlantic continent of Atlantis.

The primary source of a legendary ancient super-civilization that existed on a mid-Atlantic island ten thousand years before the birth of Christ originated in Plato's books *Critias* and *Timaeus,* written circa 355 BC, when Plato was in his seventies. Among these works, Plato gives a detailed description of the Atlantean metropolis. When describing the dimensions and measurements of the island and its architecture, Plato often refers to the 'stade' - which is an archaic measurement of length, equivalent to 606 feet 3 inches. According to Plato:

At the centre of the island, near the sea, was a plain, said to be the most beautiful and fertile of all plains, and near the middle of the plain about fifty stades inland a hill of no great size... There were two rings of land and three of sea, like cartwheels, with the island at their centre and equidistant from each other... In the centre was a shrine sacred to Poseidon and Cleito, surrounded by a golden wall through which entry was forbidden... There was a temple to Poseidon himself, a stade in length, three hundred feet wide and proportionate in height, though somewhat outlandish in appearance. The outside of it was covered all over with silver, except for the figures on the pediment which were covered in gold... Round the temple were statues of the original ten kings and their wives, and many others dedicated by kings and private persons belonging to the city and its dominions... The two springs, cold and hot, provided an unlimited supply of water for appropriate purposes, remarkable for its agreeable quality and excellence; and this they made available by surrounding it with suitable buildings and plantations, leading some of it into basins in the open air and some of it into covered hot baths for winter use. Here separate accommodation was provided for royalty and commoners, and again, for women, for horses and for other beasts of burden... The outflow they led into the grove of Poseidon, which (because of the goodness of the soil) was full of trees of marvellous beauty and height, and also channelled it to the outer ring-islands by aqueducts at the bridges. On each of these ring-islands they had built many temples for different gods, and many gardens and areas for exercise, some for men and some for horses... Finally, there were dockyards full of triremes and their equipment all in good shape... Beyond the three outer harbours there was a wall, beginning at the sea and running right round in a circle, at a uniform distance of 50 stades from the largest ring and harbour and returning in on itself at the mouth of the canal to the sea. The wall was densely built up all round with houses and the canal and the large harbour were crowded with vast numbers of merchant ships from all quarters, from which rose a constant din of shouting and noise day and night.

Where was this civilization sited? According to Plato, Atlantis was located 'Beyond the Pillars of Hercules', which means beyond the Straits of Gibraltar (on either side of which the Herculean pillars once stood) and out into the Atlantic Ocean.

Many think that Atlantis was merely a figment of Plato's imagination; a pure myth that the Greek philosopher used as a vehicle for his theories of a utopia. Aristotle flatly rejected Plato's tale, and right up to the Middle Ages, a majority of the academics agreed with him, although Aristotelian reasoning on many things, such as metaphysics and astronomy, was faulty, and held up the advancement of empirical science for centuries.

Where did Plato get his information about Atlantis from? He says he heard it from a young man named Critias, who says he heard it from his grandfather who in turn heard it from his father, a friend of Solon, a famous Greek elder statesman, who had learned of the story of Atlantis from the Egyptian priests of Sais. Solon was visiting Sais on the Nile delta around 600 BC. His work of framing a constitution for Athens and of instituting social and economic reforms was ended, so Solon had decided to devote the remaining years of his life to poetry and the study of history. He was particularly interested in the origins of the Hellenic civilization, so he asked the Egyptian scholars what they knew of his nation's genesis. The scholars of the college of the goddess Neith, the protectress of learning, confided to Solon that there were records in their archives that were thousands of years old which referred to a continent beyond the Pillars of Hercules which sank around 9560 BC. This continent, was named Atlantis. The people of this continent - the Atlanteans - prized fellowship and friendship above worldly possessions, and enjoyed an advanced system of socialism that meant no one ever lived in poverty. Like the Incas (who were said to descendants of the Atlanteans) the people of Atlantis also had a moneyless economy and all land was held in common. Virgil's *Georgics* and Tibullus's *Elegies* state that land in ancient times was shared by large communistic-like societies where no one had the right to own a single acre. There is also a mention of a lost social system in which "there were no liars, no sickness, nor old age" in the 5,000-year-old *Engidu* and the poem of Uttra of Sumer.

Alas, Plato says that the Atlanteans became decadent and bellicose. They waged a war against the neighbouring areas of Europe and Asia. Not long afterwards, Atlantis disappeared beneath the ocean after being devastated by either a catastrophic earthquake or a meteor. Some sceptical historians believe the dramatic end of Atlantis is a very convenient epilogue that gets around the problem of obtaining proof of the continent's existence. However, throughout history, there have been many instances of land masses sinking and emerging from the seas of the world. In 1780, Falcon Island in the Pacific was discovered by the Spanish. In 1892 the government of Tonga planted 2,000 coconut palms on the island. Two years afterwards, the island dramatically sank beneath the ocean waves. In November 1963, the volcanic island of Surtsey emerged from the coastal waters of Iceland and grew rapidly. After three weeks, the island - which was half a mile across - had risen to 390 feet above sea level. Its lava rapidly solidified and the island now has vegetation. In 1819, the delta of the Indus was shaken by a mighty earthquake which caused most of the local territory to sink. One of the worst cases of a drowned city occurred on 1 November 1755, when a tremendous earthquake struck Lisbon. Every dwelling in the lower part of the city was demolished by the quake, then a gigantic tidal wave swept in from the ocean. Over sixty thousand people perished in the catastrophe. The shock from the quake was felt over an area of one and a half million miles, and people all over Europe who were attending masses in their cathedrals that All Soul's day actually saw the chandeliers dance and sway.

If Atlantis did disappear under the waves, surely there must be some traces of the island on the bed of the Atlantic? Deep-sea soundings of the Atlantic seabed have been made over the years with sonar and submarine investigation, and there have been some very curious finds. In 1898, 500 miles north of the Azores an American telegraph company lowered grappling irons onto the seabed and tried to retrieve the broken ends of the snapped transatlantic cable. Instead, they brought up samples of basaltic lava. A French geologist named Pierre Termier who analysed the dredged up lava was flummoxed, as the sample was vitreous instead of crystalline. This meant that the lava had been submerged under water after cooling. As lava disintegrates after 15,000 years, this told Termier that there had been some volcanic activity above sea level near the Azores in the fairly recent past, perhaps around the time of the Atlantis cataclysm.

In other areas on the sea bottom in the vicinity of the Azores, beach sand has been found. It was first discovered by Professor M. Ewing of Columbia University in 1949, at a depth of 3-and-a-half miles. The find was just as perplexing as the lava discovery. Beach sand is a product of sea erosion, and non-existent on the bed of the ocean, so its presence indicates that coastal land must have sunk into the Atlantic at some period in the recent past.

Some think that these underwater findings suggest that the Azores are the vestiges of Atlantis, but there is another site in the Atlantic where the legendary continent may have been located: the West Indies. The West Indies is an archipelago that extends in a curved chain for over 1500 miles from the peninsula of Florida to the Venuzuelan coast. The islands are mostly volcanic origin, but the Bahamas and Antigua are composed largely of coral. In September 1968, a local Bahamian fishing guide known as 'Bonefish' Sam brought Dr J. Manson Valentine, an archaeologist and honorary curator of the Museum of Science in Miami, to see an intriguing geometrical structure lying in 23 feet of water off North Bimini. Dr Valentine, who had been searching for traces of lost civilizations in the Bahamas for 15 years, was naturally excited. After investigating the underwater structure, Dr Valentine described his findings in his museum magazine as:

An extensive pavement of regular and polygonal flat stones, obviously shaped and accurately aligned to form a convincingly artefactual pattern. These stones had evidently lain submerged over a long period of time, for the edges of the biggest ones had become rounded off, giving the blocks the domed appearance of giant loaves of bread or pillows of stone... Some were absolutely rectangular and some approaching perfect squares.

The J-shaped 'Bimini Road' as it is now called, quickly fired speculation that evidence of a submerged civilization had been uncovered; perhaps the very site of Atlantis had now been found. Strangely enough, the renowned American psychic and prophet Edgar Cayce (1877-1945) went into a trance in 1933 and said that parts of Atlantis would be discovered in the late 1960s. His actual words were "A portion of the temples may yet be discovered under the slime of ages and sea water near Bimini. Expect it in '68 or '69 - not so far away."

The stones of the Bimini Road cannot be dated, but analysis of the fossilized mangrove roots growing over the stones in the road has given a date of around 10,000 to 12,000 years.

In 1975, the explorer Dr David Zink discovered an

unusual fragment of worked stone lodged in the Bimini Road; a block of tongue-and-groove masonry. One edge of the man-made fragment is semi-cylindrical and the other is rectangular. The remnant is hard but was evidently never fired, so it cannot be dated by thermoluminescence, and no archaeologist or architect can identify its origin.

Three miles south of the Bimini Road, underwater explorers have found fluted marble columns, which is hard to explain, as marble is not native to the Bahamas. Beneath the waters of the Great Bahama Banks, a large pyramidal building measuring 180 by 140 feet has been located. In the same area, a pilot spotted a wall under 12 fathoms of unusually clear water. Curiously, the wall had an archway going through the middle of it. There was also a recent report of another architectural anomaly a few miles from this wall: a large marble citadel covering five undersea acres with roads leading from it. Unfortunately, diving on the citadel is too hazardous, as Cuban patrol boats regularly visit the waters around it.

Surely if Atlantis did exist in the vicinity of the West Indies, its culture would have rubbed off on the peoples of the eastern coast of Mexico and the North and South Americas? The Aztec capital of Tenochtitlan, which was inhabited by 300,000 people, was situated on an island in a vast lake in the middle of concentric canals. The Aztecs built the capital as a replica of 'Aztlan' a land which lay in the east, from which the Aztecs claimed their descent. Tenochtitlan's concentric layout was a copy of the description of Atlantis given by Plato.

The Mayan Civilization of Central America left curious accounts of the destruction of an early civilization. Brasseur de Bourbourg, an eminent French ethnographer, deciphered a Mayan document in 1869 which told of the annihilation, millennia before, of two countries on an island that was rocked by a massive earthquake and 'suddenly disappeared in the night' along with 64 million people.

The American Indians also have stories about a drowned civilization in their folklore. According to the anthropologists, the Indians came across the Bering Straits from Siberia, but the Indians themselves believe that they came from a homeland in the east which was destroyed in a flood. The Okanogan Indians of British Columbia tell a similar story. They maintain that a continent existed in the middle of the Atlantic long ago called 'Samah-tumi-whoo-lah' - which translates as 'White man's island'. This island - which was destroyed in a terrible war - was said to be ruled by a tall white-skinned ruler named Queen Scomalt.

In the year 1519, Hernan Cortes and his conquistadores landed in Mexico at Vera Cruz. Cortes and his men gazed in awe at Mexico City, the capital of the New World. The Emperor Montezuma II greeted the explorers and promptly surrendered himself and his empire of five million people to Cortes and his six hundred soldiers. Cortes was baffled. He was not aware that to the Aztecs and Mayas, his arrival signified their Second Coming. Like the Red Indians of North America, the races of Central America were awaiting the return of the White God, known as Quetzacoatl, who was expected to turn up soon. To the Incas he was called Viracocha. The Toltecs described the god as fair and ruddy with a beard and long hair who wore a long robe of black linen cut low at the neck with short sleeves - a dress worn by the natives to this very day. To the baffled Cortes, the Emperor explained (through the daughter of an Aztec chieftain, who acted as an interpreter) that the Aztecs had not lived in Mexico long, and that their ancestors had been led by a bearded white man from the east named Quetzacoatl who displayed great wisdom. Before sailing back towards the east, the White God had promised to return to Mexico to govern the land. Cortes could make no sense of the Emperor's story, and gave an account of his journey from Cuba and his mission to secure the pagan lands for King Charles V of Spain. The Emperor replied, "You tell us that you come from where the sun rises, the things you tell us of this great Lord or King who sent you hither to us, we believe and take it for certain that he is our natural Lord, especially as you tell us that he was known of us for many days. And therefore you may be certain that we shall obey you and accept you as Lord in place of this great Lord of whom you speak."

Unfortunately, the Emperor could not dissuade Cortes and his gold-crazed conquistadors from proceeding to Tenochtitlan. He was held hostage, but won the affection of his captors. However, the white visitors caused an uprising among the natives, and as Montezuma tried to address them, they showered him with stones, and he died several days later.

Fourteen years later, the same tragedy unfolded in Peru, when Atahualpa, the tyrannical Inca ruler, venerated the Spanish soldier of fortune Don Francisco Pizarro as a descendant of the White God

Viracocha. In shining armour, Pizarro and 168 soldiers had been sighted by the natives riding inland from the sea towards the Inca city of Cajamarca. The awe-struck Incas greeted the strange visitors, and at Cajamarca, Atahualpa hailed Pizarro as the divine son of Viracocha. When Pizarro gave a demonstration of his power by firing a cannon, the Incas shuddered, as they recalled the legends which told of Viracocha's control over thunder. In no time, Pizarro's men were plundering their way across the country. Atahualpa saw that the visitors were not gods, but gangsters, and he demanded that the thieves from the west return the goods they had stolen. Instead, Pizarro sent a Bible-carrying priest to the Inca ruler to convert him and his people from sun-worship to Christianity, but the catechism lesson ended abruptly when Atahualpa threw the holy book to the ground. The outraged Spaniards immediately went on the rampage and slaughtered the unarmed natives. Atahualpa was taken captive and held for ransom for nine months, and during this time, a huge room was filled with silver and gold and offered to Pizarro for the Inca ruler's release. Pizarro had already planned to kill Atahualpa in order to disrupt and conquer the Inca society. The Spaniard mercenary arranged a mock trial and found Atahualpa guilty of trumped-up charges. Pizarro gave him a choice; he could be burned alive as a heathen, or he could be strangled as a Christian. Atahualpa chose to be strangled. He was baptised Juan de Atahualpa "in honour of St John the Baptist" then tied to a stake and garrotted. Pizarro and his soldiers then laid on a full-scale Catholic funeral for the 'converted' ruler. It was then only a matter of time before the 'men from the rising sun' sacked the rest of the country.

The strange aspect of these dark episodes in the exploration of the Americas is the way the explorers were assumed to be long-awaited white gods from an eastern land.

If Atlantis really was situated near the West Indies, there is evidence that an earthquake may not have been the demise of the legendary landmass. On the ocean floor of the south-west Atlantic, there are twin depressions 23,000 feet deep, near Puerto Rico, which look remarkably like craters (and the reader should check out the maps of the seabed in this region on Google Earth). There are similar craters of meteoric origin on the North American mainland at Arizona and Charleston, South Carolina, where an elliptical area extends out into the Atlantic. It has been estimated that the craters near the hypothetical site of Atlantis in the West Indies were created with an explosive force equivalent to the detonation of 30,000 million tonnes of nitroglycerine around 10 to 15,000 BC. An explosion of this magnitude could also be produced by 3000 medium-sized hydrogen bombs. Such an apocalyptic explosion would punch a hole in the planet's crust and some theorists think this was how the Gulf of Mexico was formed millions of years before. The celestial object that inflicted such a devastating hammer blow to the Earth is estimated to have been around 6 miles in diameter, which rates it as an asteroid. An earlier asteroid fall is thought to have wiped out the dinosaurs 65 million years ago, and in modern times, our world has had a number of close shaves with so-called 'Earth-grazers' - asteroids that come dangerously close to the planet as they orbit the sun. The asteroid Eros, which has a diameter of 10 miles, came within 14 million miles of the Earth in 1931. In February 1936, another asteroid named Adonis came within 1,500,000 miles of the Earth, which is too close for comfort. Incredibly, in 1993, an asteroid designated 1993 KA2, made the closest approach ever made by an asteroid. It passed within 90,000 miles of the Earth, travelling at a speed of 48,000 miles per hour. Although it was only 30 feet in diameter, the asteroid had an estimated mass of 6,000 tons, and had it survived a fiery plunge through Earth's atmosphere, it would have caused the equivalent of an atomic explosion. On 15 February 2013, a near-Earth asteroid plummeted through the atmosphere over Russia at 41,000 mph, and because of the shallow angle of descent, the object exploded with a force equal to 500 kilotons of TNT – thirty times the amount of energy released by the Hiroshima A Bomb. Around 1,600 people were injured by the exploding meteor and over seven thousand buildings in six of the cities affected by the blast sustained damage. The so-called Chelyabinsk meteor, which weighed in at around thirteen thousand metric tonnes, arrived on Earth without any warning whatsoever.

Despite all the speculation, the truth about Atlantis still eludes us, yet the legends of the submerged civilization continue to hold a growing fascination over each generation. There are many who think Atlantis is just a fable, but they should remember that prior to the excavations made by the explorer Heinrich Schliemann in the late 19th century, Troy was also regarded as fiction.

THE GREEN CHILDREN

The myth of a subterranean race living in the bowels of the Earth is an ancient one that is common to many of the world's cultures. For instance, in the Epic of Gilgamesh, an ancient Babylonian poem dating back to around 2000 BC, there is a reference to Gilgamesh visiting an ancestor inside the Earth. In Greek mythology, too, the fabulous musician Orpheus attempted to rescue his deceased wife Eurydice from Hades, the underground hell. The underworld also figures prominently in Egyptian mythology - the Pharaohs were reputed to be in contact with the gods under the Earth, and to visit them regularly via a system of secret tunnels in the pyramids. Furthermore, the Buddhists have always maintained that millions of people are living in an underground paradisiacal megalopolis called Agharta, which is ruled by "the King of the World".

The myth of a subterranean world has fired the imagination of many science-fiction and fantasy writers such as Edgar Allan Poe, who describes a terrifying confrontation with messengers from the interior of the world in his *Narrative of Arthur Gordon Pym*, written in 1833. But the most popular story about subterranean adventure is Jules Verne's 1864 masterpiece, *Journey to the Centre of the Earth*, which charts the descent of a professor, his nephew and a guide into the depths of our planet's interior through the crater of Mount Sneffels, an extinct volcano in Iceland. Is such a journey possible? It doesn't seem likely, according to present theories of the Earth's geological composition. Geologists and seismologists have built up quite a detailed picture of the Earth's interior by examining the effects of seismic Shockwaves from earthquakes and nuclear tests. From the way the shockwaves are distorted and reflected, it has been established that the Earth is composed of three principal layers: the crust, the mantle and the core. The outermost layer, the crust, is composed of granite and basalt rock up to 25 miles thick. Beneath this layer is the mantle, which extends downwards for 1,800 miles, and is made up of magnesium silicates, calcium, aluminium and iron. Then comes the mysterious part, the molten outer core, which is thought to be composed of molten iron. Deeper down at a depth of 3,160 miles is the boundary of the solid inner core, which is also probably made up from iron. At this depth, the pressure is estimated to be over 3 million tons per square foot.

These geological facts surely rule out any notions of undiscovered races living in the Earth's interior, so what are we to make of the following story, which was recorded by a monk named William of Newburgh, a reliable twelfth-century chronicler?

In the year 1200, William of Newburgh took up his quill and began to record the events which had occurred during the reign of King Stephen (1135—54). William was not given to flights of fancy, nor to embroidering events, so many historians today are intrigued by the monk's account of a strange event which allegedly took place in the English village of Woolpit, which lies near Bury St Edmunds in Suffolk:

I must not there omit a marvel, a prodigy unheard of since the beginning of all time, which is known to have come to pass under King Stephen. I myself long hesitated to credit it, although it was noised abroad by many folk, and I thought it ridiculous to accept a thing which had no reason to commend it, or at most some reason of great obscurity, until I was so overwhelmed with the weight of so many and such credible witnesses that I was compelled to believe and admire that which my wit striveth vainly to reach or follow.

There is a village in England some four or five miles from the noble monastery of the Blessed King and Martyr Edmund, near which may be seen certain trenches of immemorial antiquity which are named in the English tongue, Wolf-pittes, and which gave their name to the adjacent village. One harvest-tide, when harvesters were gathering in the corn, there crept out from these two pits a boy and a girl, green at every point of their body, and clad in garments of strange hue and unknown texture. These wandered distraught about the field, until the harvesters took them and brought them to the village, where many flocked together to see this marvel.

Had William of Newburgh's account been the only report of the bizarre incident, it would have been interpreted as an out-of-character fairytale penned by a monk who had perhaps imbibed too much mead, but Abbot Ralph of Coggeshall — another monastic scribe and a contemporary of William living just 30 miles south of Woolpit in Essex — also recorded the appearance of the green children. He wrote of them:

No one could understand their speech. When they were brought as curiosities to the house of a certain knight, Sir Richard de Calne, at Wikes, they wept bitterly. Bread and other victuals were set before them, but they would touch none of them, though they were tormented by great hunger, as the girl afterwards acknowledged. At length, when some [broad] beans just cut, with their stalks, were brought into the house, they made signs, with great avidity, that they should be given to them. When they were brought, they opened the stalks instead of the pods, thinking the beans were in the hollow of them; but not finding them there, they began to weep anew. When those who were present saw this, they opened the pods and showed them the naked beans. They fed on these with great delight, and for a long time tasted no other food. The boy, however, was always languid and depressed, and he died within a short time. The girl enjoyed continual good health; and becoming accustomed to various kinds of food, lost completely her green colour, and gradually recovered the sanguine habit of her entire body.

Abbot Ralph goes on to say that the green girl was later baptized into the Christian faith and lived for many years in the service of Sir Richard, the knight who took her into his care. Despite her baptism, the Abbot also mentions that the green girl was "rather loose and wanton in her conduct". All the same, according to William of Newburgh the girl married a man from King Lynn in Norfolk and settled down there with him. The curious continually quizzed the mysterious young woman about her origins. She always told them that she and her brother had come from a country that was entirely green and inhabited by green-skinned people. Even their sun, which was very feeble, glowed green. One day the girl and her brother entered a cavern where they were startled to hear a strange sound. Abbot Ralph described what happened:

On entering the cave they heard a delightful sound of bells; ravished by whose sweetness, they went for a long time wandering on through the cavern, until they came from its mouth. When they came out of it, they were struck senseless by the excessive light of the sun, and the unusual temperature of the air; and they thus lay for a long time. Being terrified by the noise of those who came on them, they wished to flee, but they could not find the entrance of the cavern before they were caught.

People naturally assumed that the children had come from some unknown land beneath the ground, for how else could they have emerged from a cave? Some thinkers of the time also surmised that the children's skin had a greenish hue because of lack of sunlight, while the superstitious believed that the green kids were sinister cousins of the elves and fairies who were also said to be green-skinned. The colour green has always been linked with the supernatural: the enigmatic Green Man of English folklore and the ominous Green Knight of Arthurian legend are just two examples. The green children's predilection for broad beans was interpreted by the irrational folk of the period as another indication of the youngsters' eerie nature - beans were said to be the food of the dead, and it was thought that ghosts and other spirits dwelt in bean fields. If we dispense with the mythological and superstitious explanations, can we rationalize the green children's appearance? Was there a mundane explanation? Most people have heard of "blue babies" - infants that have a bluish caste because of congenital cyanosis, a condition caused by lack of oxygen in the baby's blood, and yellowing of the skin, commonly known as jaundice, can be caused by blockage of the bile duct by gallstones or hepatitis. Greenness of the skin in children and adults has been recorded, but is very rare; the cause is usually an endocrine gland disorder or a type of secondary anaemia. However, the likelihood of such a disease or disorder occurring in two youngsters simultaneously is extremely small. The only credible explanations seem to point to extraterrestrial life or a parallel world. The green children may have been inadvertently teleported to Earth from another planet, or they may have been transported accidentally from their dimension to ours by some freak of nature. We will probably never know where they came from because of the scarcity of data we have on them, but the monastic records of the children from elsewhere will continue to tantalize us for a long time yet.

THE SUPER GAMBLER

In 1654, the Chevalier de Mere, a French gambler, wrote to Pierre Fermat and Blaise Pascal, two of France's mathematical giants, with a number of problems concerning the nature of his disreputable pastime. Thanks to de Mere, mathematics now has the Theory of Probability, which allows us to discover how likely an event is through the following formula: the number of events that are favourable to our outcome, divided by the total number of all possible events. For example, let's say the French gambler wanted to throw a dice once and come up with a six; his chances, according to the formula, are one in six, because the number of events favourable to his outcome equals one (he has one throw), and the total number of all possible events are six (the six sides of the dice). Similarly, if the gambler tosses a coin in the air, the probability of it landing on heads is one in two. But this theory only tells the gambler what odds to expect; it doesn't tell him when the die will come up with a six. Ideally, what the gambler would like is a mathematical method that can reliably predict what the outcome of particular event will be, but as yet, the world's mathematicians have failed to produce such a theory. The nearest they have come to the gambler's dream is in the extrapolation technique, which is a way of predicting, alas, with a margin of error, the future of a quantity from the past values of that quantity. For example, by extrapolating, we can predict what a country's population figure will be in a hundred years' time by studying that country's past rate of population increase. Sadly, extrapolation is useless when no past data is known, so it seems that the gambler's search for the perfect "system" is but a dream. Or is it? Perhaps not, for it is a mathematical fact that even with random events there are definite clusterings of coincidences. Therefore, if we toss a coin 1,024 times, it is highly likely that there will be one run of eight tails in a row, two of seven in a row, four of six in a row, and eight runs of five in a row. No one is sure why these clusters occur, but several mathematicians believe that there are undiscovered laws which govern such coincidences, and once they are worked out, it will be possible to predict the outcome of the toss of a coin, the throw of a dice, the supposedly random selection of six lottery numbers, and the result of a spin of the roulette wheel.

In 1891, a mysterious corpulent Englishman calling himself Charles Deville Wells strolled into Monte Carlo's world-famous casino and placed even money bets on red and black, and proceeded to win almost every time, despite the astronomical odds that were stacked against him. When his winnings surpassed the 100,000 francs limit allocated to the table, the attendants closed the "bank", covered the table with a black "mourning" cloth and closed it for the remainder of the day. On his third and final visit to the casino, Wells pulled off an extraordinary feat. He placed his first bet on number five (35 to 1 odds), and his gamble was a success. The attendants were stunned and suspicious. Wells then added his winnings to the original bet and placed the entire amount on number five again. The roulette wheel was spun and after a tense wait it did indeed come up again. This incredible outcome happened five times in succession. Wells collected his mammoth winnings and left the casino as the enraged, but baffled attendants looked on. Wells bought a yacht and settled in the south of France, but people wanting to know his gambling system persecuted him wherever he went. He was finally arrested by French police, charged with fraud, and extradited back to England. He stood trial at the Old Bailey, where he admitted to having 20 aliases, but he never revealed his real name. He was sentenced to an eight-year prison sentence, and after his release went to Paris, where he died in poverty in 1926.

How did Wells foresee what numbers would come up at the roulette table? Was he using some abstruse mathematical system to predict the outcomes of the wheel? The systems used by gamblers are legion and legendary, but none of them are infallible. They range from complicated mathematical tables, the result of many years of study, to even more complex, computer-aided hypotheses concerning chaos and catastrophe theory. The simplest system is said to be the Martingale, which closely resembles the betting practice commonly known as "double or quits on the toss of the coin". Imagine you have won ten dollars from a gambling opponent. You say to him "Double or quits on the toss off the coin." If he wins, the ten dollar debt is cancelled, but if you win, his situation is twice as bad as before, and you can continue in this way until the account is squared. The rule for playing a Martingale against the bank at a casino is as follows: You back a colour say, red, consistently and double your stake each time you lose, reverting after a win to your original stake.

Therefore, every red shows you a profit of one plaque over and above whatever you may have lost on that series. Compared with other ways of betting, the Martingale system makes you more likely to win than lose, but you will lose greater amounts, and should your run of bad luck come early in the proceedings, you may well find your capital so diminished that you simply cannot wait for luck to take a more favourable turn.

Charles Wells was closely watched by gamblers at the roulette table. One of them wrote of the lucky Englishman's system:

Wells began with ten units, decreasing his stake by one if he won, increasing by one if he lost, so that his last stake, if he lost consecutively, was twenty. He stopped playing after winning all ten coups with a gain of 55 units, made up of thus: 10 plus 9 plus 8 plus 7 plus 6 plus 5 plus 4 plus 3 plus 2 plus 1 = 55. The weak point in this system was that, though he won 55 units if a run of ten occurred at once in his favour, he lost 165 units if a run of ten occurred at once against him.

Amazingly, the miracle happened frequently enough

for Wells to break the bank. But Mr Wells hinted that he had actually used a far more advanced system than the luck-dependent Martingale. He insinuated that his successful method of winning was in fact an algorithm based on the layout of the roulette board used in Monte Carlo and in most casinos of southern France where he played. The board is numbered from 1 to 36, 18 of the numbers being black and 18 red. But there is a zero, which offsets the odds in favour of the house by 37 to 36 on any single number bet. Wells implied that numbers could be predicted from past numbers that had come up on the wheel. This seems to be nonsensical, but Wells stared intently at the wheel whenever the ball landed on a number, and appeared to be muttering, perhaps performing mental calculations. According to traditional mathematics, gamblers basing their bets on past outcomes are committing a gross error, because in the world of probability, the past has no influence on the future. If there have been 20 successive reds at the roulette table, it does seem likely that black will turn up, but the laws of probability state that this simply isn't so - red is just as likely to turn up again. However, those who eavesdropped on Wells at the table claimed that the gambler believed he had discovered some sort of natural recurring series of numbers that turn up everywhere. The thirteenth century mathematician Leonardo Fibonacci discovered that such sequences occur naturally in nature. His so-called Fibonacci sequence is: 0,1,1,2,3,5,8,13,21,34, . . . etc, each number being the sum of the previous two. The Fibonacci sequence has turned out to be relevant to the natural world in many ways. For instance, botanists have noted that the leaves on a branch are often situated helically around the stalk at measurements that correspond to Fibonacci's sequence. The same sequence is to be found in the proportions and ratios of many other natural patterns, such as the pads of a cat's paw and the spirals of a snail's shell.

Fibonacci's sequence had been partly discovered in ancient Greece, where architects employed a "mystical ratio" known as the "golden section". This ratio, which is approximately equal to 1.618, occurs over and over again in the proportions of the human body, the spiral galaxies of the universe, the layout of seeds in a sunflower, and in many other diverse locations, but no one knows why 1.618 is so omnipresent.

There are other naturally recurring decimals (for example 0.142857), but sometimes the significance of these numbers is baffling. Take the Greek letter pi which as every schoolboy knows, is the ratio of the circumference of any circle to its diameter, and is approximately equal to 3.1415. Thanks to the computer, pi has now been calculated to over 200 million decimal places, and deep within the millions of figures which make up pi, computers have discovered that there is a bizarre "cyclically increasing sequence" of digits that start with 89012345 and are gradually turned around to become 2109876543. It's as if there is some design among the never-ending string of numbers, but why the recurrent numbers are there continues to puzzle mathematicians.

So, as we have seen, mathematics is much more than the study of measurements, numbers and quantities. It is a science that is far from complete, and seems to be heading towards the metaphysical. It is a well-known fact that many discoveries in any systemized branch of knowledge come about long before their time; consider Tiphaigne de le Roche's production of crude photographs a century before Louis Daguerre invented the photographic plate; Ernest Duchesne's use of moulds to combat infection in 1897 - 44 years before Alexander Fleming "discovered" penicillin, and so on. Is it possible that Charles Wells stumbled upon a mathematical discovery relating to the strange phenomenon of recurring numbers that has so far eluded the mathematicians? Or is the truth more sinister? Until we know more, Wells will be best remembered as the subject of an old Charles Coburn music hall song: *The Man Who Broke the Bank at Monte Carlo*.

THE MAN IN THE IRON TUBE

While clearing up rubble from the aftermath of a German air raid on Liverpool, England, in 1943, the group of American soldiers probably regarded the long black metal tube protruding from the bottom of the bomb crater near Great Homer Street as a piece of shattered pipe. The GIs tried to dislodge the piece of 'piping' with a mechanical digger, but it wouldn't budge. In the summer of that year a second attempt was made to remove the obstruction with a more powerful mechanical digger, and this time the tubular piece of scrap was successfully uprooted.

As the dust from the difficult excavation settled, it became apparent that the metallic tube was no ordinary pipe, but a riveted sheet-iron cylinder 6 feet 9 inches in length and 18 inches in diameter. However, the sealed cylinder aroused no more than a passing interest among the soldiers who had more pressing matters to attend to, and so the tube was left among the debris of the blitzed site. There it lay forgotten until Friday 13 July 1945, when a nine-year-old boy playing on the bombed wasteland came across the unidentified relic while playing hide-and-seek with his friends. Little Tommy Lawless was hiding behind the tube when he noticed a boot poking out from a hole in one end of the cylinder. Tommy, who had never owned a pair of boots in his life, was delighted at his find, thinking that his barefoot days were over at last. He gently pulled the boot free - and saw to his horror that it had come off the foot of a skeleton. Terrified, Tommy fled from his startled playmates, and did not stop running until he saw PC Robert Baillie walking his beat in Great Homer Street. Breathlessly the youngster told the policeman what he had found, and in so doing launched the inquiry into the baffling case of the Man in the Iron Tube.

Shortly after 1 p.m. that day the cylinder and its gruesome contents were taken to the city morgue. After a detailed description of the strange artefact had been recorded, an engineer was called in to open the cylinder with an oxy-acetylene blowtorch. When the smoking tube was finally cut open, Dr Charles Harrison and the engineer looked at its occupant in total astonishment. To Harrison, senior lecturer in pathology at Liverpool University, it seemed that he was about to have the unusual task of performing a post-mortem on a body that evidently dated back to the age of Queen Victoria.

The skeleton was resplendent in a morning coat, striped narrow trousers and the fine pair of elastic-sided boots that had caught the eye of little Tommy Lawless. The position of the cadaver was strange: it lay lengthwise along the tube on a bed of sacking with its skull (which still had hair attached to it) resting on a pillow that consisted of a brick wrapped in a sack. This suggested that the man in the tube had been sleeping when he died.

Doctor Harrison's examination revealed that the body was that of a six-foot-tall middle-aged male. But that was all the doctor was able to say about the mysterious corpse. He could not explain how the man in the tube had met his death.

The police called in Dr J.B. Firth, a highly respected forensic expert from Preston. Firth's examination of the Victorian produced some intriguing results. Among the remains he discovered two diaries: one book covered July 1884 and the other contained entries for June 1884. From a pocket in the dead man's morning coat, Firth extracted a bundle of papers that were encapsulated in a revolting wax-like substance, the residue of the body's decomposed tissue. Firth skilfully applied various organic solvents to the waxen lump and with great perseverance finally managed to extricate thirteen separate documents: Most of the documents referred to a certain T.C. Williams & Co. of Leeds Street, Liverpool. A postcard among the recovered papers was also addressed to T.C. Williams.

Now that the police had a name to work with, their investigation could begin in earnest. Detective Inspector John Morris delved into the city's archives and scoured the electoral registers of the 1880s. In a business register for 1883 he came across a firm trading under the name of T.C. Williams & Co. The address was 18 to 20 Leeds Street. The firm was described in the yellowed text of the old register as 'Oil Merchants, Paint & Varnish Manufacturers'. Morris established that the head of the firm was a Mr Thomas Cregeen Williams, who lived at 29 Clifton road, Anfield. Moreover, the inspector discovered that in the following year the financial affairs of the plant works were for some reason being investigated by a firm of accountants. What became of the company after that is a mystery, for there is no further reference to the business in any of the Liverpool trade directories after 1884.

Inspector Morris searched the local registers for some record of the death of Thomas Cregeen Williams, but he could find none. Morris hypothesized that Mr Williams had hidden himself from his creditors by crawling into the metal tube and had died from accidental asphyxiation. But it is an unsatisfactory theory. In the 1880s it was more usual for debtors simply to board a ship and work their passage abroad when their creditors got too close. Thomas Cregeen Williams is listed in a column detailing liquidations in the *Liverpool Mercury* for 8 September 1883, and his residential addresses are given as 29 Cambridge Road, Seaforth, and Woodville House, Abbotsford Road, Blundellsands - where he was staying that month. The meeting with his creditors took place, according to this column, at the offices of Mr W. H. Harris, 4 Harrington Street, Liverpool.

Tantalizingly, Firth's examination of the Man in the Iron Tube reached a dead end. The forensic expert analysed the clothes and bones of the corpse for traces of poison but could find none. So what are we to make of the unknown man? How did he come to die in his cylindrical coffin? Was he murdered? Or was he a murderer hiding from justice? The questions remain unanswered.

WHAT HAPPENED TO BUSTER?

In 1956, Lieutenant Commander Lionel "Buster" Crabb dived with Royal Navy frogmen in the Scottish Isle of Mull's Tobermory Bay, in search of a payship of the Spanish Armada named *Duque de Florencia*. The ship had reputedly been sunk with 30 million pounds of gold on board in 1588. However, it turned out that most of the treasure was missing, and all Crabb recovered was a number of worthless trophies. The 46-year-old underwater expert was amused with one particular prize from the sunken Spanish Galleon: a shrunken skull. Experts analyzed the grisly relic and determined that it had belonged to a North African woman who had used it in black magic rituals. Crabb's friends urged him to get rid of the skull, fearing it would bring bad luck but Crabb thought they were being ridiculous. Imagine how these friends reacted when, a little over a year later, in June 1957, they learned that Crabb's body had been found floating in Chichester harbour - minus its head. To shed some light on the sinister incidents that led to this bizarre death, we must look into Crabb's background.

Crabb was born in 1910. During his twenties he went through a succession of jobs, the last one before the outbreak of the Second World War as a merchant marine apprentice. While most lives were shaken by the advent of the war, Crabb saw it as an incredible opportunity to find a direction in life. He began his career in the Royal Naval Patrol Service, and after quickly acquiring a commission, he was appointed as a bomb and mine-disposal expert with the Royal Navy at Gibraltar in 1942. Crabb had the unenviable duty of removing sensitive limpet mines which had been fixed to the hulls of Royal Navy merchantmen by Italian saboteurs. Disposing of a bomb on terra firma requires great skill and courage, but underwater the hazards are even greater. Nevertheless, Crabb excelled at his work, and was subsequently awarded the highly-coveted George Cross and promoted to lieutenant commander. He was also awarded the Order of the British Empire. During this period, Crabb injured his left leg while on a dive, and the minor accident left him with a small, but distinctive scar. This scar would later be the subject of much debate at the inquest of a corpse that the coroner would claim was Crabb's.

While most of the world rejoiced at the end of war in 1945, Crabb found himself confronted with an uncertain future. He felt he was no longer needed, and over the next ten years, often talked of suicide to his closest friends. His depression reached an all-time low in 1955 when he officially retired. He sought solace in constant drinking, and became something of a bore, reiterating the same stories over and over of his undersea exploits. He was also an eccentric who prefered to wear his rubber wetsuits under his normal clothing, even his pyjamas.

He jumped at the opportunity to dive on the wreck of the *Duque de Florencia* in 1956, but further diving assignments were sporadic. He therefore reluctantly turned to working as a rep for a firm which sold catering equipment to coffee bars to make a living. Around this time, something quite unexpected happened, the details of which can never be fully known, but what is known is that Crabb was approached by someone working in the intelligence service. Who this agent was is still a matter of much conjecture, but what follows is a summary of the clandestine events that led to Crabb's disappearance under highly suspicious circumstances.

On April 17th, 1956, Crabb booked into the Sallyport Hotel in Portsmouth, accompanied by Bernard Sydney Smith, an agent of Britain's Special Intelligence Service (SIS). Crabb pretended to be on business when he and Smith signed the hotel register, but Smith rather blatantly described his occupation as "attached Foreign Office" - a somewhat clichéd cover for MI6 operatives. According to Chapman Pincher, a respected authority on defence intelligence, another MI6 officer named Ted Davies was also involved, and shortly after dawn on the morning of April 19th, he escorted Crabb to a jetty a mere 200 yards or so away from the 12,000-ton Russian warship *Ordzhonikidze* and its two attendant destroyers. They had been anchored in Portsmouth Harbour for just a day, and had brought over the Soviet Premier Nikolai Bulganin and Nikita Khrushchev, First Secretary of the Communist Party in the USSR, on a mission of goodwill in Britain. The British Prime Minister, Sir Anthony Eden, seeing the visit as a way of reducing the East-West tensions that existed during the Cold War, had issued a directive from Downing Street to all the intelligence services in Britain, banning any spying missions relating to the Russian ships, because discovery would obviously have a devastating effect on Britain's tentative relations with the Soviet Union. The seasoned officers in the SIS thought this directive was unfair and unrealistic; whenever visiting British warships docked at Leningrad, shoals of Russian "spy divers" would unashamedly inspect the hulls of the ships for "routine inspection purposes".

Despite Eden's directive, MI5 had already installed highly sensitive microphones in the rooms of Claridge's Hotel, where Bulganin and Khrushchev were to stay, and extra surveillance devices had been set up in a neighbouring building.

At the jetty in Portsmouth Harbour, Crabb emerged from the freezing waters after his initial dive, which had lasted just a couple of minutes, for an extra pound of ballast weight. He complained of having trouble with his breathing apparatus, which was Royal Navy issue, but quite unsuited for diving below depths of 33 feet. Crabb said he'd had to surface during the operation to purge the system of excess poisonous carbon monoxide. He then made another dive, but Davies never saw him alive again.

Later that day, Rear-Admiral V.F. Kotov, the commander of the Soviet flotilla, told Philip Burnett, the Chief of Staff of the Portsmouth base, that Soviet sailors had spotted an unidentified frogman surfacing near the ships. Burnett, who maintained that he knew nothing of any surveillance operation, dismissed the Soviet's complaint, but shortly afterwards, James Thomas, the First Lord of the Admiralty, also saw the mystery frogman off the bows of the chief Russian ship. He made enquiries to Downing Street, but the ministers there could offer no explanation.

On April 29th, the *Ordzhonikidze* and the destroyers left Portsmouth Harbour and headed for home, and the following day, the Admiralty issued a controversial statement which caused a Parliamentary storm. The statement said that Crabb was presumed dead after failing to return from "a test-dive in connection with trials of certain underwater apparatus in Stokes Bay - three miles from Portsmouth".

Journalists refused to believe that an expert diver of Crabb's calibre had strayed three miles off course, and they descended on Portsmouth to investigate the real events behind the statement. The newshounds discovered that the head of Portsmouth CID had visited the Sallyport Hotel where Crabb had been staying and ripped out the incriminating pages of the hotel register. This fuelled speculation that Crabb had been spying on the Soviet ships, and when the Kremlin officials heard the rumour, they demanded an explanation from Britain's Foreign Office. The Government had no choice but to admit that the frogman seen near their ships during the stay at Portsmouth Harbour had been Lionel Crabb. However, Eden stressed that Crabb had been operating without government permission, and assured the Soviets that disciplinary action was being taken against those who had staged the operation.

During a debate on the affair in the House of Commons, John Dugdale, the MP for West Bromwich, asked the Prime Minister for more information on Crabb's covert activity, but tantalizingly, Eden replied that such information "would not be in the public interest".

Where had Crabb disappeared to? This was another mystery. Some believed that the diver had been intercepted by Soviet frogmen who had taken him to a chamber in the *Ordzhonikidze* below the waterline, known as the "wet compartment". Crabb had probably then been confined and taken back to the Soviet Union to be interrogated and tortured. Some even believed that Crabb had been some sort of double agent who had gone over to the "Red Navy".

Fourteen months later, on June 9th, 1957, the corpse of a man in a wetsuit was found by fishermen in the mouth of Chichester Harbour, just a few miles east of Portsmouth. The body had been decapitated, and the hands were also missing, but curiously, upon the left leg of the corpse there was a scar which looked identical to Crabb's wartime scar. The wetsuit was also of the same Italian make that Crabb favoured, but what proof was there that the corpse was the body of the missing frogman? Despite the absence of any substantial identification factors, the Chichester coroner confidently recorded a verdict that the body was that of Crabb. The British authorities seemed pleased with the verdict, and held the "belief" that Crabb had died because of a combination of ill health and the inhalation of carbon monoxide from his closed-circuit oxygen.

Not long after the controversial inquest verdict came a plethora of reports that Commander Crabb had been sighted in the Soviet Union living under a Russian alias. Patricia Rose, Crabb's fiancée, stated that she was convinced that the headless body was not Crabb's. She claimed that she'd had a message from a man who had met "Grabble" in Sebastopol, where he was allegedly training frogmen for the Russians. Rose said the mysterious messenger accurately described the idiosyncratic way Crabb smoked and coughed.

The Labour MP Bernard Floud also fanned the controversy when he claimed that he had learned through a contact in MI6 that British Naval officers had actually witnessed the capture of Crabb. Then, in 1968, Bernard Hutton published a fascinating book called *Commander Crabb is Alive*. Hutton states in the book that a Captain Roman Melkov of Leningrad told him he had spoken to Crabb, and had a personal message from him for Patricia Rose. Melkov mentioned Crabb's pet name ("Crabbie") as proof. Melkov then went on to describe a conversation Crabb had had with an old diving companion named Sydney Knowles, just prior to his disappearance. Knowles later verified Melkov's story of his conversation with Crabb. At last, it looked as if there was a lead in the Crabb case.

However, on May 8th, 1968, the body of Captain Melkov was found in the cabin of his ship *Kolpino*, which was anchored at London docks. He had shot himself. Not long afterwards, more curious reports were made. It was claimed that several sailors onboard the *Ordzhonikidze* had seen Crabb being escorted into the ship's hospital - which was later inexplicably sealed off during the vessel's return journey to the Soviet Union. While this rumour was circulating, a Russian forces magazine came to light in the West which carried a blurred photograph of a group of Soviet naval officers, and among them was a man who looked suspiciously like Commander Crabb - an underwater operations instructor named Lieutenant Lvev Lvovich Korablov. Crabb's ex-wife Margaret, and one of his old wartime friends inspected the photograph of "Korablov" and both were convinced it was Lionel Crabb.

If Crabb did end up in the Soviet Union, why didn't the Russians make the fact public as a propaganda exercise? That remains an unanswered question today. Stranger still, the official government dossier on the Crabb case was not open to inspection within the normal period of the 30-year-rule, so the contents of the file are presumably still deemed to be too confidential. Perhaps one day we will be told more about the case of the vanishing spy diver.

THE MYSTERY AIRSHIPS

In 1909, an armada of unidentified airships were seen in the skies above England. The first of these strange sightings occurred on March 25th in the town of Peterborough. PC Kettle, a Cambridgeshire policeman, was patroling Cromwell Road in the early hours when he heard what he assumed to be the engine of an approaching motor car. As he continued on his beat, he noticed that the sound of the car had changed in pitch to a low buzzing noise that seemed to be coming from overhead. Looking skyward, Kettle saw a bright light shining down at him, attached to a massive craft which blocked out the stars. The policeman watched in total fascination as the oblong-shaped craft suddenly accelerated across the starry sky in a southerly direction. Within a minute the mystery airship was lost to sight. When PC Kettle returned to his station and gave an account of the strange sighting to his superiors they ordered him to take leave for a couple of weeks.

More nocturnal flights of strange aerofoils were reported across the land from Liverpool to Kent as the months went by, and the newspapers were quick to nickname the epidemic of reports "airshipitis". The aviation experts of the day initially dismissed the "scareships" as collective hallucinations, despite the fact that these "imaginary" invaders of English airspace were seen over towns hundreds of miles apart. In the summer of 1909, the debunkers had a difficult job explaining away an unidentified airship which landed in London. On the night of May 13th, a Mr Grahame and Mr Bond were walking across Ham Common on the outskirts of south-west London, when they noticed a strange cigar-shaped craft approximately 250 feet in length hovering about 12 feet from the ground. Grahame and Bond cautiously approached the awesome craft and at close quarters could see a couple of silhouetted people moving about in what looked like a gondola hanging beneath the underbelly of the craft. When the two men were 30 feet from the airship, the beam of a blinding searchlight shone from the gondola and swept the common, then singled out the two Londoners. Grahame and Bond stood rooted to the spot as two shadowy figures then alighted from the flying machine and came over to meet them. One was a clean-shaven young man who greeted Grahame and Bond with an American accent, The other a German, who asked for some tobacco. Mr Grahame produced a pouch of tobacco and handed it to the German, who had a calabash pipe in his hand. The German took some tobacco from the pouch, handed it back to Mr Grahame, then turned and headed back to the huge airship, followed closely by the American.

The American climbed into a cage-like enclosure in the gondola and operated a series of levers that resembled draught beer pump handles. As the German sat down behind his associate and began to study a large map dotted with coloured pins, the American pulled one of the levers down and the brilliant searchlight went out. The airship started to buzz, then rose gently into the night sky without either of the sinister aeronauts saying goodbye. The unidentified airship raced through the air in a north-easterly direction across Richmond Park and towards Central London at an unheard of aerial speed of around 80 miles per hour.

Grahame and Bond informed the authorities, but their story was dismissed as nonsense, and the staid editor of *The Times* refused to print an account of their encounter, saying he thought the story preposterous. Ironically, on the day of the alleged urban airship incident, the following article appeared in the "Military Intelligence" column of *The Times*:

AERIAL NAVIGATION
The Army Dirigible Balloon

Further experiments were begun at 4 o'clock yesterday morning on Farnborough Common with the new Army dirigible balloon. The balloon was towed from its shed by a small party of Royal Engineers, and at 4.15 a.m., with Colonel J.E. Capper and Mr McQuade in the car, the propellers were started, and the balloon rose to a height of about 400 ft. The gas bag was not distended, as at the last trial, and the sides of the envelope hung wrinkled and flaccid. The lateral planes attached to the car and the upper surface of the balloon appeared to be saturated with moisture from a dense mist which overspread the common. Since the last trial, a triangular sail has been attached which hangs vertically between the balloon and the car. At 400 ft the ascent ceased, and the balloon was headed into a very slight breeze. A speed of 6 or 7 mph was maintained. The motor experiments were continued for a quarter of an hour, and during this time the balloon traveled over a course of about a mile out and home.

The Army dirigible was 100 feet in length, not even half as long as the Ham Common airship, which was estimated by Grahame and Bond to be around 250 feet in length. Nor was the 7 mph Army dirigible - with its 24 horsepower engine - as fast as its sinister counterpart, which was seen to race across the sky at 80 mph. The French airships of the day had difficulty achieving 30 mph, and the prototype German Zeppelins, hindered by bad aerodynamic design, could not exceed a 35 mph limit. So who was the genius behind the unidentified airship that touched down in London?

On the day after the Ham Common airship encounter, an announcement was made to the Reuters news agency from Germany that rocked the military world. A spokesman for the electrical manufacturer Allgemeine Elektrizitats Gesellschaft said that his corporation would supervise the newly-formed Wright Aeroplane Company in Berlin. Several other industrial companies, and the Berlin banking house of Delbruck, Leo and Co., would also back the new venture to mass-produce flying machines for Germany and its colonies in Sweden, Norway, Denmark, Luxembourg and Turkey.

The British War Office must have felt impotent at the Berlin announcement. All the money and research devoted to a dirigible that was struggling to make it off the drawing board had been a complete waste of time. It now looked as if Germany would rule the skies of Europe - with a little help from the American Wright brothers. Four days after the formation of the Wright Aeroplane Company, Herr Colsmann, the director of the Zeppelin Airship Construction Company, announced that Germany would soon have a regular airship service with Zeppelin terminals in Friedrichshafen, Lucerne, Dusseldorf and Berlin. Colsmann even hinted at a Zeppelin service to terminals abroad — perhaps even in London. The new airships would travel at speeds of 70 or 80 mph, and be able to carry around 30 passengers and crews of six. Plans of the proposed airship fitted the description of the Ham Common airship. The new Zeppelin was cigar-shaped, 250 feet long, and with an airspeed of 70 to 80 mph. The craft would also be equipped with a powerful searchlight that would sweep the ground to illuminate potential hazards during take-off and landing.

According to Herr Colsmann, such ships were still at the design stage, but on May 18th, 1909, Mr Fell, the Member of Parliament for Great Yarmouth, quizzed Richard Burdon Haldane, the British Secretary of State for War about the number of dirigibles in Germany. Haldane shocked the House when he gave his reply. He stated, "Seven dirigibles have been constructed, and five are being built. A sum of £25,000 was allotted for airships in 1907, and £107,000 in 1908."

Mr Fell then asked Haldane if he would be asking Parliament for a sum similar to that voted by the German Government for the construction of dirigibles.

"We shall give full information when the time comes," was Haldane's enigmatic reply.

The wave of mystery airship sightings gradually died down until a second wave of sightings swept Britain three years later in the autumn of 1912. At 7 p.m. on the evening of October 14th that year, the townspeople of Eastchurch on the Isle of Sheppey heard a buzzing noise in the sky. Flares were shot into the heavens to illuminate the aerial craft, but they revealed nothing. The drone passed over Sheerness and was later heard in the vicinity of Basildon. The eerie sound spawned widespread rumours of a secret Zeppelin flight over the capital. Some scaremongers maintained that the clandestine airship was of German origin, and that it had been carrying out a reconnaissance mission in preparation for war.

The rumours reached fever pitch, and on November 27th, 1912, opposition MP William Joynson-Hicks asked the First Lord of the Admiralty, Winston Churchill, if he knew anything about the Sheerness airship. Churchill confirmed that an airship had flown over the Isle of Sheppey, areas of Essex and East London, but that the nationality of the craft was unknown to him. Churchill thought that the anonymous flying machine had violated British airspace, and many in the house agreed. As a result, a bill passed to strengthen the Aerial Navigation Act of 1911 was given the royal assent on February 14th, 1913. This bill gave the Home Secretary the power to prohibit aerial traffic over the United Kingdom and its territorial waters. Any unidentified dirigible entering British airspace in future would be shot at if it failed to respond to ground signals.

During World War One, on January 19th, 1915, a fleet of Zeppelins made a mockery of the Aerial Navigation Act by invading British airspace to drop bombs on Norfolk. Then, on the last day of May that year, 11 Zeppelins converged on London and dropped their bombs — the first of 12 such raids on the capital. By the end of the war, England had sustained 53 raids from the German airships, killing a total of 556 civilians. However, the Zeppelins of World War One were, without a doubt, too slow and vulnerable to the elements to be of any real use to the military powers of Germany. Just like the Spanish Armada, the airship menace was no match for the changeable British weather. So were the Zeppelins responsible for the mass-sightings of airships in 1909 and 1912? It seems very unlikely when we consider the high-speed manoeuvres of the "scareships" reported by witnesses, which were often seen during adverse weather conditions. There are two logical possibilities to consider: that the "scareships" were the product of a genius — someone of the calibre of Orville and Wilbur Wright, or that the mystery airships were an early manifestation of what is now known as the UFO phenomenon. The latter is an incredible but intriguing possibility with a lot to be said for it. The scareships were not only seen over Britain in 1909 - in July of that year, a fleet of the same phantom dirigibles buzzed over the skies of New Zealand - where no Zeppelin or any other type of recognized dirigible ever flew. The sightings persisted night and day over an area that stretched 850 miles from Invercargill to Dargaville. These enigmatic airships also carried searchlights with high-intensity beams which lit up the landscape for miles, and exhibited acrobatic skills that could not have been equalled by any dirigible known to man. At Gore, on the South Island, one airship dived from 2,000 feet to 1,000 feet within half a minute, then circled the town at an incredible velocity. This airship was cigar-shaped, around 250 feet in length, and manned by a crew of two, just like the Ham Common craft.

The airship waves of the early twentieth century are still a complete mystery. Ufologists have scoured declassified military records of the 1900s to determine if the mysterious craft were simply experimental prototype dirigibles designed for aerial warfare, but up to now, no evidence has been uncovered to prove this hypothesis. The history of the unidentified airship can be traced to March 26th, 1880 in the United States, when three men in Santa Fe saw a strange propellor-driven craft in the sky. It was cigar-shaped, and carried ten people who laughed and shouted down at the startled witnesses. One of the people in the airship threw several items down to the men on the ground: a beautiful, unfamiliar-looking flower, a cup (of very peculiar workmanship), and a slip of silken paper which had letters of an oriental type written on it.

The three men watched the airship scud through the clouds until it was a faint spot on the horizon. The strange items that the aeronaut had hurled to earth were put on display at a nearby railroad depot. A few hours later, a man of Asiatic origin turned up at the depot. He produced a bundle of banknotes and asked the depot agent if the items on show were for sale. The depot agent nodded enthusiastically and took the stranger's money.

Between November 1896 and May 1897, unidentified airships were sighted in over 19 states in North America. The machines were often seen during daylight, sometimes flying against the wind at tremendous speed. When the ships were seen at night, they always gave off incredible laser-like beams of light brighter than any contemporary searchlight.

At Grand Rapids, Michigan, on April 16th, 1897, the local newspaper, the *Evening Press*, carried a curious article which seemed to throw light on the origin of the airships buzzing through America's skies:

Appleton, Wisconsin, April 15 — Many persons in this city declare that they saw an airship pass over this city last Sunday night. Last night on the farm of N.B. Clark, north of the city, a letter was picked up attached to an iron rod eighteen inches long, sticking in the ground. The letter, which was not signed, is as follows: "Abroad the airship *Pegasus*, April 9th, 1897. The problem of aerial navigation has been solved. The writers have spent the past month cruising about in the airship *Pegasus* and have demonstrated to their entire satisfaction that the ship is a thorough success. We have been able to attain a speed of 150 miles an hour and have risen to a height of 2,500 feet above sea level.

The *Pegasus* was erected at a secluded point ten miles from Lafayette, Tennessee, and the various parts of the machine were carried overland from Glasgow, Kentucky to that point, being shipped from Chicago, Pittsburgh, and St. Louis. We have made regular trips of three days each from Lafayette to Yaukon, and no harm has come to the Pegasus thus far.

Within a month our application for the patents for a parallel plane airship will be filed simultaneously at Washington and the European capitals. The ship is propelled by steam and is lighted by electricity, and has a carrying power of 1,000 pounds."

The letter seemed to make some sense. Water would

be needed in considerable quantities to feed the alleged steam-propelled ship, and on numerous occasion, wells had been inexplicably drained overnight in the states where the airships had been sighted. But if the ship could only lift 1,000 pounds as detailed in the letter, it didn't leave much room for the airship pilots. Steam engines also require coal or wood to fuel them to heat the water, and such fuels would have to be carried in large quantities to allow three-day journeys between Lafayette and Yaukon at a speed of 150 miles per hour. What then, are we to make of the letter? Is it a hoax, perpetrated perhaps by some news-starved journalist eager to cash in on the airship phenomenon? Needless to say, there were no patents concerning a "parallel plane airship" filed in America or Europe, as promised in the letter, but there were more revelations from above.

On April 17th, 1897, two boys were climbing trees in Chicago's Lincoln Park when one of them - 12-year-old Danny Schroeder - found a brown paper parcel nestling in the uppermost branches of a tree. Danny grabbed the parcel and quickly descended from the tree, anxious to discover the package's contents. The parcel contained a cardboard box which held the remains of a meal, and an elaborately engraved card folded and in a gilded design, depicting a boy standing on a pair of outstretched wings. In the upper corner of the card the word "airship" was printed, and below it a printed sentence: "Dropped from the airship *Saratoga*, Friday, April 16th, 1897". A message written in blue pencil on the card stated: "9:41 p.m. - Due northwest, 2,000 ft.; 61 N. Lat., 33 Long. Descending. Dense fog. Drizzling 'spods' ".

Some surmised that the parcel was a hoax, but others wondered why a prankster — who must have gone to elaborate and expensive lengths to print the card — would put the parcel up a tree when he could have easily left it on an open common or in some busy thoroughfare.

Yet another missive from the skies was received a couple of days later, and this time it looked as if the airship mystery would be cleared up once and for all. An employee of a furniture company in Grand Rapids named Charles Smith — a man who was renowned for his honesty and integrity — was on his way to work at 6.15 a.m., when he saw an envelope attached to a bottle opener on the ground. The words "From the Airship Travellers" were scrawled on the envelope, which contained a sheet of notepaper. Upon this sheet there was a message written in purple indelible pencil:

To whoever finds this:

We are 2,500 feet above the level of the sea, headed north at this writing, testing the airship. Afraid we are lost. We are unable to control our engine. Please notify our people. Think we are somewhere over Michigan.

> Arthur B. Coats, Laurel, Mississippi
> C.C. Harris, Gulfport, Mississippi
> C.W. Rich, Richburg, Mississippi

Smith's local newspaper seized the letter and printed it in its editorial, citing it as evidence that the airships were the work of some American aeronautical genius who would probably reveal himself and his flying machines to the world, once he had ironed out some technical difficulties. Around this time, a person professing to be the unknown genius wrote a sensational letter to the director of the Transmississippi Exposition that was soon to be held at Omaha, Nebraska. The letter said:

To the Exposition Director:
My identity up to date has been unknown, but I will come to the front now; i.e., if you will guarantee me 870,000 square feet of space. I am the famous airship constructor and will guarantee you positively of this fact in a week. The airship is my own invention and I am an Omaha man. I wish it to be held as an Omaha invention. It will safely carry twenty people to a height of from 10,000 to 20,000 feet. I truly believe I have the greatest invention and discovery ever made. Will see you April 17th, 1897, at the headquarters.

[signed] A.C. Clinton

Mr Clinton failed to show up at the Exposition on that date, but strangely enough, several airships were seen in five neighbouring states on that night. By May of that year, the airship sightings in North America were dwindling, and the clandestine aerial activity soon shifted to Europe. Many ufologists have surmised, somewhat controversially, that an alien intelligence was behind the various waves of airship sightings. They reason that in 1897, most educated people had heard of the lighter-than-air dirigible, and had seen pictures of these machines in newspapers and books. If an alien intelligence was visiting the Earth in 1897, perhaps on some reconnaissance program, they would disguise their ships as dirigibles so as not to alarm the local terrestrials or interfere with their cultural beliefs. The extraterrestrial hypothesis seems far-fetched, but would make some sense of the baffling airship phenomenon, although time seems to deepen this strange mystery.

TALES OF THE UNDEAD

The myth of the vampire is a very old one, dating back to ancient Egypt and Greece. Today, in our well-lit sprawling cities, there is no place for such a legend, except in films such as the *Twilight* series and in the books of the American fantasy novelists Stephanie Mayer and Anne Rice. Vampires are just figments of the imagination, the bogey-men of gullible rural peasants who lived in a bygone superstitious age. That's what common sense leads us to believe; but even in modern times Dracula-like beings prowling the world continue to be reported. Shortly before midnight on 8 June 1993, over a thousand people turned up at a cemetery in Pisco, Peru, in the hope of witnessing the resurrection of an alleged vampire named Sarah Ellen Roberts. Local historians and officials from the British Embassy had recently been shocked to learn that the corpse of Mrs Roberts had been brought to Pisco from Blackburn, England, by her husband John Roberts in 1913, because British authorities refused to let him bury his wife in England, as they believed her to be a vampire. Mr Roberts dismissed the refusal as an absurdity, but subsequently bought a lead-lined coffin for his deceased wife, and allegedly roamed the world for four years, seeking out a country that would allow him to bury her. Finally, Mrs Roberts came to Peru, where he was allowed to inter his wife at Pisco for the sum of five pounds. Shortly after the ad hoc burial service, Mr Roberts boarded a ship for England and was never heard of again. Then the news from England reached Pisco; Sarah Ellen Roberts had been bound in chains and shut up in the lead-lined coffin after being found guilty of witchcraft, murder and vampirism. Just before the lid of the coffin was screwed down, the Lancashire witch had screamed she would return from the grave to seek vengeance.

The Peruvian peasants in the town trembled at the news. Eighty years later in June 1993, people visiting a grave in the Pisco cemetery were terrified when they witnessed a large crack appearing in the headstone of the Blackburn woman's grave. That night, over a thousand excitement seekers and occultists descended on the graveyard when the word went round that the vampire would rise from her grave at midnight. Hundreds of local women left the town 'to prevent the vampire being reincarnated in their new-born children', and cloves of garlic and crucifixes festooned the front doors of almost every house in the region. When midnight arrived, the vampire mania reached a peak, and police had to be called in to control the hysterical crowds. Shots were fired in the air, and slowly the crowds dispersed. A small group of local witch doctors were apparently allowed to stay at the controversial grave, where they splashed the cracked headstone with holy water and sprinkled white rose petals around. The English vampire did not rise, and the witch doctors later celebrated their 'success' at laying the undead woman to rest.

Such superstitious mumbo jumbo is excusable in a remote Peruvian town, but there have also been a number of vampire alerts in the bustling metropolis of London. The first scare occurred in the spring of 1922, when an enormous black bat-like creature with a wing span of six feet was seen flying around West Drayton Church during the night of a full moon. Several terrified witnesses watched the creature dive into the churchyard, where it roamed the tombs. When it was chased by two policemen, the creature let out a loud blood-curdling screech, flapped its wings, and soared skywards. An old man who claimed he had seen the giant bat twenty-five years previously, maintained that it was the spirit of a vampire who had murdered a woman to drink her blood in Harmondsworth in the 1890s. No one took the oldster's tale seriously. Later that month, on the morning of 16 April at around 6 am, an office clerk on his way to work was walking down Coventry Street in London's West End. As he strolled into a turning off the street, something invisible to his eyes seized him and pierced his neck. The man felt blood being drawn, then fell to the pavement unconscious. He woke up in Charing Cross Hospital and told his unusual tale. The surgeons who quizzed him said someone must have stabbed him with a thin tube, but the victim disagreed; he was absolutely certain that no one had been close enough to deliver such a thrust. Two and a half hours later something incredible happened which still defies explanation; a second man was brought to the same hospital. he too was bleeding profusely from the lower neck, and when he regained consciousness, he also told how he had been walking down Coventry Street when something intangible attacked him - on the very same corner where the office worker had been struck down by an unseen attacker. Later that evening a *third* victim of the invisible assailant was admitted to the hospital. The doctors at Charing Cross were absolutely dumbfounded when the police told them that the latest victim had been stabbed at precisely the same spot as the two other casualties - at a turning off Coventry Street.

An investigation into the bizarre crimes was launched as rumours of a vampire at large in London swept the capital. The newshounds of Fleet Street pricked their ears up at the rumours. The *Daily Express* reported the sinister Coventry Street assaults and asked the police if they had any theories on the strange crimes. A police spokesman reluctantly admitted that the injuries sustained by the three men at Coventry Street defied rational explanation, and there had been no headway in finding the bloodthirsty attacker. With his tongue placed firmly in his cheek, a reporter asked the spokesman if the police had considered the theory of the Coventry Street attacker being a vampire. The spokesman just chortled nervously and said 'That's all'.

Another rumour swept the City; the Coventry Street vampire had been cornered by the police and killed by a professional vampire hunter who had been drafted in for the job! Furthermore, the bloodsucker had been secretly interred with a wooden stake through its heart in a deep vault up in Highgate Cemetery. The rumour was traced to a pub in Covent Garden where an off-duty policeman told a landlord of his part in the vampire hunt that had stretched across London. It is of course, easy to dismiss the policeman's yarn as bunkum, but by a strange coincidence, London's second vampire scare took place at Highgate Cemetery forty-eight years after the Coventry Street vampire episode.

Highgate Cemetery was founded in 1836 when the London Cemetery Company purchased 17 acres of land in the north of the city. The company's gardener was something of a horticultural genius who transfigured the purchased acreage into a breathtaking peaceful oasis of greenery with tree-lined avenues, shrubs and meandering pathways. But there were problems ahead. The outbreak of the First World War deprived the cemetery of labour, and the number of plots for sale were dropping to double figures. Furthermore, cremation was also emerging as a popular alternative to burial. With insufficient funds for its upkeep, the cemetery was neglected, and the shrubbery and wildflowers were overtaken with weeds which enshrouded tombs and gravestones by the score. Then the vandals invaded the wilderness of the abandoned cemetery, daubing their names and profanities on the tombs. In December 1969, a group of occultists prowled the forsaken dormitory of the dead painting Voodoo symbols on a number of gravestones and chanting incantations in the hope of resurrecting a corpse. Urban legend has it that the occultists broke into a tomb and disturbed something that sent them running for their lives; an eight-foot wiry figure clad entirely in black which emerged from a hole in the tomb that led to catacombs. The fleeing necromancers scaled the railings of the cemetery and leaped to safety; one of them looked back as he raced down Swains Lane and saw the man in black reaching through the railings at him with a long bony arm.

The next alleged sighting of the Highgate Vampire occurred in January 1970, when a motorist from Milton Park was driving down Swains Lane near the entrance of the cemetery, when the engine of his car started to sputter. The man pulled into a parking space and got out the vehicle to lift the bonnet open, when he noticed an abnormally tall shadowy figure peering at him through the entrance gates of the cemetery. The motorist was so terrified at the apparition, he ran off without closing the bonnet of his car.

The English city of Liverpool has had a surprising number of vampire reports over the years, and the most well-known one in the city is the legendary 'Manilu', who prowls the Lodge Lane area of Liverpool. There have also been other vampiric beings reported to me over the years in the northern suburbs of the city, and the following is just one of many cases I have researched in my Haunted Liverpool series of books. Around 3.40am on the Tuesday morning of 3 September, 1963, a petty thief from Bootle named Ron was trying to break into a lock-up in a certain alleyway behind Aintree's Greenwich Road. He tried picking the padlock on the big green wooden door but the picklock rods just wouldn't work their magic, possibly because the lock seemed rather rusty, and so Ron took out his trusty old jemmy and he looked up and down the alley, just in case there was someone about. Not a soul stirred at this unearthly hour, and above the rooftops of Greenwich Road, a full moon shone down, but Ron was luckily in the shadows, shielded from its revealing silvery light. He was just about to try and prise the padlock off the door with the short crowbar when Ron thought he heard a noise behind him and to his right. He turned slowly to the direction of the real or imagined sound and saw something he cannot explain to this day. A tall (about 6 feet and 4 inches at least) slim figure of an elderly but distinguished-looking man in a long cape stood there at the mouth of an entry, and he had a faint blue phosphorescence about him. His white hair rose into pointed tufts on either side of his head like little devil horns, and the face of this weird-looking stranger wore a straight white well-trimmed moustache and a snowy Vandyke beard. Beneath the dark swept-back eyebrows, the eyes of the faintly glowing figure bulged, and the irises, which were bright compared to the dark eyeballs, gave a piercing, mischievous stare.

Ron instinctively lifted the leather-gloved hand which held the jemmy, intending to strike out at the entity if it approached, when the mouth of the apparition opened slightly – to reveal two rows of long pointed teeth. Ron turned on his heels and ran off down the alleyway to the sound of cackling laughter. A heavy smoker on the wrong side of thirty, Ron found himself out of breath as he bolted down Inglis Road. He slowed down and looked over his shoulder, and saw to his great relief that he was not being pursued by what had surely been a ghost of some sort. In the ten years Ron had indulged in a life of crime, he had never once seen anything remotely supernatural during his nocturnal career. Upon reaching Longmoor Lane, Ron got the shock of his life, for there was the old man in the long flowing cape, coming towards him from the top of Poulter Road. He still had the blue radiance emanating from him, but it wasn't as prominent in the gleaming moonlight. Ron felt the handle of the crowbar in his inside jacket pocket, and knew it was useless. How on earth could he injure something that looked as if it was already dead? He ran off, confused, and upon reaching the Prince George pub, he looked back again – and saw that the figure seemed to be gliding along towards him as its cloak flew up with the forward movement. Ron swore to himself and listened to his heart pounding in his chest as he took flight down Greenwich Road – a road which ran alongside Kirkdale Cemetery. Ron heard distant laughter, and he turned to see the caped vampiric creature turn the corner where the Prince George stood and accelerate towards him. Ron let out a string of swear-words as nerves got the better of him, and ran up the road – when he saw a welcoming sight in the distance: two policemen were coming his way on their beat up Greenwich Road. Ron dropped his jemmy and leather gloves behind the wall of the cemetery, then hurried towards the policemen – something he thought he would never do in a million years. The constables eyed him suspiciously, but a panting Ron turned and pointed to the cloaked pursuer – who had now stopped dead about three hundred yards away. The policemen wanted to know what Ron's full name was and if he had ever been in trouble with the law before. Ron shook his head and said he had been returning from his cousin's party in Walton Vale and urged the constables to tackle the maniac. 'Look at him go!' one of the policemen remarked as the eerie figure in the distance ran off at an incredible speed. Within a few seconds he was lost to sight.

Ron became a reformed man not long after that weird encounter, and gave up his life of crime. He died a few years ago, and when I interviewed him in 2004, he was intrigued to discover that I had received many reports of the so-called "Aintree Vampire" over the years. In 1971, a very nimble cloaked figure was seen running at a phenomenal speed through Kirkdale Cemetery by scores of children one autumn evening, and in the 1980s I received two reports of what was undoubtedly the same sprightly silver-haired bogeyman from off-duty nurses from a certain hospital who had been chased along Lower House Lane by the uncanny cloaked figure. I mentioned the entity on a BBC radio programme one afternoon and was afterwards deluged with calls and emails about the "vampire". Many of the callers said the figure always went to ground at Kirkdale Cemetery whenever it was chased, and one woman even saw the fanged phantasm as recently as 2010 in West Derby Cemetery. A West Derby woman named Elaine, who was 53 when I interviewed her in 2006, was a beautiful young 20-year-old blonde in 1973 and lived just a stone's throw from Aintree's famous racecourse. One freezing February night in 1973, Elaine's sleep was disturbed by the sensation of someone getting into bed with her. When the young lady opened her eyes, she saw a stranger's head resting on the pillow next to hers. It was too dark in the bedroom to make out the man's features, but Elaine told me a curious thing. She said that the man had a pointy light-coloured beard and moustache and white hair. His breath had a sweet smell reminiscent of lavender. Just before Elaine began to scream for help, she heard the creepy bed-hopper whisper something which she couldn't make out. Elaine threw herself out the bed and ran out the room in hysterics, and when her parents and older brother went into the girl's bedroom, there was no one there – but the bedroom window was wide open and the February gales were fiercely blowing the nets and curtains about. Elaine's father maintained that the 'ghost' had been nothing more than a product of a particularly realistic nightmare, but Elaine asked him how a figment of a dream could open her bedroom windows wide. There was no history of hauntings at Elaine's house, and I feel that the thing which got into the girl's bed, possibly to seduce her, was the fanged white-haired entity known as the Aintree Vampire. I have tried to unravel the obscure history of the Aintree Vampire (or whatever he is) for some time now, but to date he has resisted every attempt to be researched, and so this case remains among a bundle of other Knowsley mysteries that are bound together in a thick folder that is marked: Unknown.

Another vampire was said to be at large in England's picturesque Lake District in 1900. In January of that year, a Captain Edward Fisher left Croglin Grange - a bleak glorified granite-brick farmhouse in Cumbria - and headed south to Guildford, where he had purchased a new residence for business purposes. The new residents of Croglin Grange were Fisher's godsons, Edward and William Cranswell, and their young sister, Amelia, who had jumped at the opportunity of taking up the seven-year lease on the secluded but beautifully located property. The trio were popular with the neighbours, and seemed to be settling in well at their new home. Amelia enjoyed cooking and was a student of oriental languages. In the first summer at Croglin Grange, which was infernal, Amelia found it difficult to sleep at night. She would lie in her stifling bedroom, gazing out at the moonlit nightscape beyond the windows. One night she opened her bedroom window and stared out into the darkness when she suddenly noticed the silhouette of a lanky, bony figure darting across the moonlit lawn. Within seconds the agile, sinister-looking stranger was scaling the wall below her, so she slammed the window shut and fastened its catch. Almost paralysed with fear, Amelia retreated from the window as she listened to the figure scrambling up the wall. She sat on the end of the bed, trying to shout out to her brothers, but found she could hardly raise her voice. Then the figure was at the window. At this closer range she could see he was grotesque. The face was yellowed and shrivelled, and the eyes were almost black circular sockets. The nose was long and pointed, and the mouth, which was unusually large, showed a set of pointed, gruesome-looking teeth. The creature's bony finger scratched at the window as it picked away the lead lining of a pane. The pane rattled, then fell out, and the ghoul reached in through the hole and undid the window catch. It opened the window and bolted across the room towards its terrified prey. Amelia collapsed onto the bed in a state of sheer terror. The skeletal freak seized the trembling teenager by her hair and held her still as he bit into her neck. In the life-threatening situation, Amelia somehow summoned up enough courage to let out a scream which sent her brothers running into her room. They caught a glimpse of the nimble intruder leaping out of the bedroom through the window. They ran downstairs, unbolted the door and pursued the wiry assailant across the lawn and over the neighbouring churchyard wall, where they lost sight of him. William and Edward stood staring into the darkness for a while, then returned to their traumatized sister. When they saw the crimson fang-marks on her neck they knew that no ordinary intruder had been in her bedroom, but they could not believe the assailant had been a vampire.

One night in the following March, the creature returned to Croglin Grange during a severe gale. As the winds howled across the barren landscape outside, the bony finger was once again at work removing a pane from the Amelia's bedroom window, but this time the moan of the gales swamped the sound of scratching finger. The teenager awoke and found the vampire leaning over her. His cold and clammy hands grabbed her neck, and the woman screamed. The two brothers burst into the room armed with pistols. The vampire left his prey and attacked the brothers, but Edward opened fire, blasting a hole in the bloodthirsty stalker's thigh. Apparently unaffected by the gunshot, the Cumbrian vampire turned and literally dived through the open window. The chase was on again, but this time the brothers saw where the creature went to ground; in an old family vault in the churchyard.

The brothers alerted the local villagers, and on the following morning over seventy people gathered around the family vault that was said to be the vampire's lair. William, Edward and three brave villagers lifted the large sandstone slab of the vault and peered into the darkness. A torch was lit, and the crowd beheld the disturbing scene within the vault: four broken coffins and their mutilated corpses. A fifth coffin in the corner was intact. The crowd drew back in fear as the brothers lifted the lid on this coffin - to reveal the same hideous creature that had attacked their sister twice at Croglin Grange. The corpse even bore the recent mark of the pistol shot in its thigh. One of the villagers stepped forward and told the brothers he too had seen this same creature of the night attacking and killing livestock, and he said the only way to destroy a vampire was with fire, so he and the brothers took the creature out into the churchyard, and after the villagers had gathered enough wood, the vampire was burned on a bonfire.

DOPPELGÄNGERS

We often say, when impossible demands are made of us, that we "cannot be in two places at once", but there have been many recorded instances of the doppelganger — an exact double of a living person that is supposed to stalk us all. These phantasms of the living are said to stay out of sight of their worldly counterpart until he or she is approaching death or experiencing a serious illness, at which time they usually visit their double or even their double's friends. One intriguing report of a doppelganger is alleged to have taken place in the reading rooms of the British Museum in London in 1888. That year on April 12th, Dr W. Wynn Wescott, a coroner, met the Reverend W.T. Lemon in the museum's reading rooms at the appointed time of 2.30 p.m. Reverend Lemon was three minutes late, but Dr Wescott, being his usual punctual self, was already there, and had been chatting with a friend, Mrs Elizabeth Salmon. Mrs Salmon walked over to the reverend, informed him that Dr Wescott was waiting for him, and turned to point at the table where the doctor had been seated. He was not there. Mrs Salmon was completely baffled; there was only one exit to the room, and Dr Wescott had not passed her to walk to the door. Mrs Salmon asked two people at the reception desk if they had seen the doctor leave the museum. They both said they had seen Dr Wescott enter the building, but were certain that he had not passed them on his way out. Five other people who knew Dr Wescott also stated that they had seen him enter the reading rooms, but none could recall seeing him leave the museum. An hour later Mrs Salmon and the Reverend Salmon visited Dr Wescott's home in Knightsbridge, and were perplexed to learn that the doctor had not been to the British Museum at all, as he had been confined to his bed with a cold and fever since 8 a.m.

"But that's impossible," said a flummoxed Mrs Salmon, and she told the sick doctor that she had talked to him earlier and, furthermore, five other people had actually seen him in the British Museum. Dr Wescott sniffled and shook his head. His entire family and a servant backed him up. They all testified that the doctor had never left his bed, but how he came to be in two places at once has never been solved. Perhaps the person who held a conversation with Mrs Salmon at the museum was the doctor's doppleganger.

One of the best-documented accounts of a doppelganger concerns an attractive 32-year-old French schoolmistress named Emilie Sagee, who had lost 18 jobs in 16 years because of her double. It all began in 1845, when Emilie took up her post at the Pensionat von Neuwelcke, an exclusive school for the daughters of the nobility, situated in Livonia (now part of Russia) about 36 miles from the port of Riga. The pupils at the elitist school immediately took to

Mademoiselle Sagee, and described her to their parents as a lovable and sweet-natured person who made French lessons a delight. But within a couple of weeks of Sagee's arrival, a disturbing rumour was circulating at the school: it was said that the French teacher could literally be in two places at once. The bizarre rumour apparently stemmed from a heated argument between two pupils. One said Emilie was in the school garden, while the other claimed that Emilie was in her classroom. The teachers reprimanded the squabbling girls, but days afterwards, something astonishing happened that indicated that both of the pupils had in fact been right about the French teacher's whereabouts. Emilie was giving a lesson to 13 pupils, chalking a series of sentences in French on the blackboard with her back to the class, when a second Emilie suddenly materialized next to her. The double was precisely like its flesh and blood counterpart, and mimicked the exact same movements in perfect synchronization, but it held no chalk like the original Emilie. The class gasped in disbelief at the strange sight, but shortly afterwards the double vanished.

On other occasions, Emilie's mirror-image deviated from its usual mimicry and acted independently by going on walkabouts around the school. The "fetch" as it was called, was once seen striding down a corridor in excellent health while the real Emilie was tucked up in bed with a fever.

All 42 pupils witnessed the etheric dead-ringer when they were assembled in the school hall one day to do their sewing and embroidery. Most of the girls faced the four french windows through which Emilie could be seen, picking flowers in the garden. The teacher supervising the pupils got up and left her chair vacant and about a minute later, Emilie came in and sat in this chair. The girls smiled at her, then one of them pointed to the other Emilie out in the garden. Two of the braver girls present stood up and approached the fetch. They reached out to touch it, but it didn't feel real. It seemed to be made of a delicate substance not unlike the stuff of cobwebs. One of the girls accidently walked through the fetch's leg, and seconds later, the doppelganger faded away. It transpired that the real Emilie had not seen her double - in fact she never once saw it - and she wished she had been supervising the sewing class around the time that the doppelganger had materialized in the hall.

Emilie Sagee's double continued to haunt the school, and each time it appeared, it was noted that the original Emilie became lethargic and listless, as if the fetch were draining power from its living replica.

When the parents of the pupils heard about the doppelganger, they complained to the directors of the school and Emilie Sagee was subsequently dismissed from her post. She was never heard of again.

Another well-documented doppelganger case is said to have taken place on June 22nd, 1893. On that day, in the eastern Mediterranean, Vice-Admiral Sir George Tryon was in command of *HMS Victoria*, the proud and formidable flagship of the British Mediterranean Fleet. Steaming along on a parallel course with *HMS Victoria* was *HMS Camperdown*, the sister ship of Tryon's vessel. Five ships steamed behind Victoria and four ships cut through the waters behind *Camperdown*. At precisely 3.34 p.m., Tryon gave the order for the ships of each column to turn inward to each other simultaneously and reverse direction before anchoring. This incredibly inept order, if carried out, would set *Victoria* and *Camperdown* on a disastrous collision course. Rear-Admiral Markham, who commanded the *Camperdown*, queried the signalled orders, but they were repeated. He dared not argue with Vice-Admiral Tyron, who had a legendary temper, so Markham desperately hoped that his superior was executing some elaborate master plan, and acquiesced.

It was noted that Tryon had been in a trance-like state when he gave the fatal orders. His crew had been concerned at the glazed vacant look in his eyes and the slow reflexes which had been evident over the past few weeks. Unknown to the crew, his lethargic condition was the side-effect of an opium-based medication Tryon had been taking every day for a painful leg ulcer.

The *Victoria* and *Camperdown* began to turn at the same time, towards each other. Captain Bourke of the *Victoria* screamed out that the ship was in immediate danger, but the narcotized Vice-Admiral did not react. He gazed tranquilly at the 10,000-ton *Camperdown* charging towards his ship.

"Permission to go astern at full speed sir!" pleaded Bourke, but Tryon remained placidly transfixed on the steel-plated leviathan rushing headlong towards them at breakneck speed. Less than a minute before impact, Tryon finally answered Captain Bourke's question. He shouted "Yes!" but it was too late. Even though the *Camperdown* was reversing her screw propellers, this did not prevent her from ramming the *Victoria's* bows, which caved in and split asunder. The impact crushed some men to pulp and trapped others at their posts in the engine room. The *Victoria* slid bow first beneath the waves taking Vice-Admiral Tryon and 358 crewmen with her. Most of those who managed to escape from the sinking ship were chopped to pieces by her fiercely revolving propeller blades. Several survivors of the tragedy who were picked up by *HMS Nile* claimed that the doomed Vice-Admiral had said "It's all my fault" as he went down with his ship.

Meanwhile, two time zones and 2,000 miles away at his home in Eaton Square, London, Vice-Admiral Tryon appeared in his library in full view of four witnesses, who did not know that the Vice-Admiral was in fact at sea at that time. Tryon glanced at them then looked at his globe of the world before vanishing. The time was precisely 1.44 p.m. The four people present were dumbfounded at this apparition and told Lady Tryon about it when entered the library, but she dismissed it as some sort of hallucination and explained that her husband was commanding a ship in the Mediterranean. Then the tragic news came through in the evening, and Lady Tryon almost fainted. She realized that the people in the library had seen her husband's ghost at the exact time of his death.

Not all doppelgangers are spiritual, etheric beings, according to some sinister accounts. In 1907, Albert Steer, a labourer from Bickley, London, left his home to search for work in Surrey. His son and daughter - both in their early twenties - waved goodbye to their father after wishing him luck. The next day, a policeman turned up at Steer's home and broke the tragic news: the body of Mr Steer had been found floating in the Thames near Chelsea Bridge. As Steer's son and daughter sobbed, the policeman told them they would have to identify the body to make sure it was their father. At the morgue, Steer's son and daughter quickly identified their father. The body was unmistakably his. Every physical attribute matched: the missing eye, the deep scar over the left eyebrow, and the deformed toe of the right foot which had been crushed in an accident.

Two months after the burial, Albert Stect turned up at his Bickley home to be greeted by his dumbstruck son and daughter. He told them he had been working as a gardener, but had found the work tiring, hence his return. Steer's reappearance is a real enigma; who or what was buried that not only resembled him, but also exhibited the very same injuries? We will probably never know. Nor will we know what happened one September morning in 1982, when an office worker named Anna Petherbridge was walking to work through Covent Garden in London. Ms Petherbridge was startled by a "wild-eyed" young man who came running towards her, all out of breath. The youth glanced back over his shoulder several times as if he was being chased, then dashed past Ms Petherbridge and she lost sight of him as he ran behind a parked van. Ms Petherbridge walked on, and a few seconds later the very same young man came running around a corner near Henrietta Street, which astonished Ms Petherbridge, because she was well-acquainted with the area and knew it would have been impossible for the youth to have doubled back within such a short period. Ms Petherbridge gave the encounter with the ubiquitous running youth a lot of thought but was at a loss to explain what had happened that autumn morning. The only rational explanation would be that the running youth had an identical twin brother, but

Ms Petherbridge feels the truth is probably stranger - that the youth was being chased by his doppelganger. All we can do is hazard a guess, and surmise that all the previous accounts outlined in this chapter are also examples of the same phenomenon. According to psychical researchers, ghosts of the living are the commonest type of apparition, a claim that was backed up by a report carried out in November 1994 by the *British Journal of Psychiatry*, which examined 56 doppelganger episodes that year, including the case of a pilot who saw himself several yards away for a full ten minutes. The report also investigated an intriguing incident concerning a real-looking doppelganger which stalked a retired doctor.

Until scientists can open their minds to the reality of the doppelganger, societies will continue to live in fear of this phenomenon. Perhaps one day we will discover some complex biological mechanism which causes the human body to create a seemingly physical carbon copy of itself. This isn't as far-fetched as it seems. Cell multiplication was not discovered until 1844, when the Swiss anatomist and embryologist Kolliker astounded the medical world by proving that a human being begins its life as two cells which split up and multiply. Perhaps when we die, we also split up and produce an intangible etheric body which leaves its earthly replica behind to decay. Perhaps in times of illness or great emotional stress, such as in a near-death situation, this "secondary body" is projected from its physical duplicate, or becomes prematurely detached in some way. This theory would make some sense of the fascinating doppelganger phenomenon.

THE TUNGUSKA ALIEN

Had the following unexplained incident occurred today, even in the slightly relaxed atmosphere of the post-Cold War, it would have probably triggered World War Three. Fortunately, the greatest hammer blow from space to hit our Earth since prehistoric times happened when the 20th century was barely eight years old. Even today, scientists are still at loggerheads as regards to the nature of the extraterrestrial object which shook the world after exploding in the skies of pre-Revolutionary Russia.

The momentous event happened at 7.15 a.m. local time on the last day of June 1908. At that precise moment, an object brighter than the morning sun ripped through the atmosphere over Siberia. A trainload of passengers on the trans-Siberian railway stared in horror at the towering pillar of flame roared through the clear blue skies at a phenomenal velocity of around one mile per second. The sonic boom given off by the sky invader shook the railway track, convincing the engine driver that one of his coaches had been derailed. The driver jammed on the brakes and as the train screeched to a grating halt, the mysterious fiery object thundered north. The trembling train passengers listened in relief as the overhead danger became fainter, and many of them looked out the windows of the carriages and eyed the vapour trail with bafflement.

Almost 350 miles to the north of the train, the nomadic hunting tribes of the Evenki people felt the ground shake violently as they witnessed what seemed to be a second sun racing across the heavens. Only this sun seemed to be cylindrical. By now, the immense apocalyptic object had been seen to change course as if it was being controlled or steered. After passing over the terrified travellers of the trans-Siberian train, the object made a forty-five degree right turn and travelled 150 miles before performing an identical manoeuvre in the other direction. The tubular shaped object then proceeded for another 150 miles before exploding over the Tunguska valley. The detonation occurred at a height of five miles, and the 12-megatonne explosion (it might have even been 30 megatons) destroyed everything within a radius of 20 miles. Herds of reindeer were incinerated as they stampeded away from the explosion, and all wildlife in the area was ignited by the searing heat blast. Thirty-seven miles from the blast, the tents that the frightened Evenki people had taken refuge in were lifted high into the air by the resulting atmospheric shock wave, and the Evenki's horses galloped off in terror, dragging their ploughs with them. At the centre of the explosion a monstrous mushroom cloud rose steadily over Siberia.

Such a strange and unsettling sight would not be witnessed for another thirty-seven years at Hiroshima and Nagasaki. But this explosion was even fiercer than the A bombs which were dropped on the Japanese cities. The blast from the Tunguska explosion felled trees as if they were matchsticks for 20 miles around and set whole forests alight. The shockwave generated by the mysterious cataclysm travelled around the world twice and shook the recording pens of the microbarographs at three meteorological stations in London, where they were interpreted as seismic jolts from some distant earthquake.

At a distance of 400 miles from the epicentre of the Tunguska blast, the relentless shockwave showed no signs of abating, and knocked fishermen from their boats on the River Kan. By the time the blast had deteriorated into a hurricane-like storm, a strange black rain started to fall over the Tunguska valley. Days later, strange scabs started to break out on animals that had been too far away to be directly burnt by the blast, and weeks later, curious investigators who ventured to the site of the explosion became sick and complained of strange burning sensations within their bodies. Were these signs of radiation sickness? But what meteoric object could be radioactive? Stranger still, why was there no crater at the site of the explosion? All meteorites leave a crater. And how would a meteorite travel horizontally for hundreds of miles and change course twice? Then there were other strange occurrences which seemed to suggest that the object which had exploded over Siberia was not a meteor at all, but perhaps some nuclear-powered spacecraft from another world which had had made an emergency crash-landing in a forbidding area of our planet.

The first reports of a strange glow in the sky came from across Europe. Shortly after midnight on 1 July 1908, Londoners were intrigued to see a pink phosphorescent night sky over the capital. People who had retired awoke confused as the strange pink glow shone into their bedrooms. The same ruddy luminescence was reported over Belgium. The skies over Germany were curiously said to be bright green, while the heavens over Scotland were of an incredible intense whiteness which tricked the wildlife into believing it was dawn. Birdsong started and cocks crowed - at two o'clock in the morning. The skies over Moscow were so bright, photographs were taken of the streets without using a magnesium flash. A captain on a ship on the River Volga said he could see vessels on the river two miles away by the uncanny astral light. One golf game in England almost went on until four in the morning under the nocturnal glow, and in the following week *The Times* of London was inundated with letters from readers from all over the United Kingdom to report the curious 'false dawn'. A woman in Huntingdon wrote that she had been able to read a book in her bedroom solely by the peculiar rosy light. There were hundreds of letters from people reporting identical lighting conditions that went on for weeks after the Tunguska explosion. Scientists and meteorologists also wrote to the newspaper giving their opinions about the cause of the strange skyglare which ranged from the Northern Lights to dust in the upper atmosphere reflecting the rays of the sun below the horizon. No one connected the phenomenon with the strange object which had come down in Siberia to explode with the fury of a H-bomb. Even the national press in Russia gave no mention to the catastrophic event in the Tunguska Valley, because the country was then entering a major period of political upheaval. A serious investigation of the Tunguska incident did not take place for another thirteen years, when a Soviet mineralologist named Leonid Kulik led an expedition to the site of the explosion. But within those thirteen years, strange whispers and rumours spread across Siberia. There were tales of a strange being wandering the remote forests of Tunguska near the scenes of devastation. The nomadic reindeer herdsmen of Siberia sighted the gigantic grey humanoid figure some 50 miles north of the Chunya river. They saw the man, who seemed to be over 8 feet in height, picking berries and drinking water from a stream. The superstitious Mongol herdsmen regarded the freakish-looking stranger as one of the fabled chuchunaa - a race of hairy giants similar to the abominable snowman which were said to inhabit the region. The nomads crept through the forest to get a better look at the figure, and they saw that the grey colour of the man was not hair, but tattered overalls of some sort. The herdsmen sensed that there was something unearthly about the being, and they retreated back into the forest and moved away from the area. There were several more sightings of the grey goliath over the years, and each report indicated that the entity from the cold heart of Siberia was moving westwards. Alas, all of the accounts of the strange giant were interpreted as mere folklore tales of the Russian peasants.

In February 1927, Leonid Kulik went in search of the strange object that had impacted into Tunguska.

He had read countless old newspaper clippings on the Siberian explosion and had conjectured that the object that had caused the widescale destruction had been a large meteorite made of stone and iron. Being a mineralologists, Kulik looked forward to obtaining samples of the meteorite for analysis. Kulik got off the Trans-Siberian railway at the Taishet station and on horse-drawn sledges they set off on an arduous three-day odyssey through 350 miles of ice and snow until he and his men reached the village of Kezhma, situated on the River Angara. At the village Kulik and his party of researchers replenished their supplies of food, then struggled on for a three-day journey across wild and unchartered areas of Siberia until they reached the log-cabin village of Vanavara on 25 March. Kulik then tried to make headway through the untamed Siberian forests, or taiga as the Russians call it, but was forced to turn back after heavy snowdrifts almost froze the horses to death. For three days Kulik was forced to remain in the snow-bound village of Vanavara, but during this period he interviewed many of the Evenki hunters who had witnessed the Siberian fireball's arrival on this planet. The tales of the sky being ripped open by a falling sun and of a great thunder shaking the ground made Kulik even more eager to penetrate the taiga to find his holy grail. When the weather gradually improved, Kulik set out for the Tunguska Valley. When he finally reached the site of the mysterious explosion, he was almost speechless. From a ridge overlooking the scene, Kulik took out his notebook and scribbled down his first impressions of the damage wreaked by the cosmic vandal. Kulik wrote:

From our observation point no sign of forest can be seen, for everything has been devastated and burned, and around the edge of the dead area, the young, twenty-year-old forest growth has moved forward furiously, seeking sunshine and life. One has an uncanny feeling when one sees twenty to thirty-inch giant trees snapped across like twigs, and their tops hurled many yards away.

Kulik then proceeded towards the felled forest, but two of the guides who had taken him and his assistants to the area refused to go any further. The guides told the bemused scientist that there was something or someone still lurking about in the area. Kulik thought the guides were superstitious fools, but they told him that strange things had been seen at twilight in the shadows of the dead taiga. The guides returned home and Kulik fortunately met a few bold members of the Evenki tribe, who took him and the researchers further into the taiga. By June, Kulik and his men had reached the middle of the explosion site, where uprooted trees were scattered from the centre of the blast like the tangled spokes of a wheel. There were no signs of a crater. Kulik realised that the explosion had occurred above ground. The Evenki tribesmen seemed to become very uneasy in the middle of the devastation zone, and started to talk about a supernatural presence in the area. But Kulik didn't have time to listen to such irrational ramblings of the nomads; he had limited time to collect data for his friends back home at the Russian Academy of Sciences. There were three further expeditions to the site of the Tunguska explosion, all of them headed by Kulik. In 1941, Hitler attacked Russia. The 58-year-old

Leonid Kulik volunteered to defend Moscow, but was wounded by the Nazis. He was captured by German troops and thrown in a prison camp where he died from his wounds.

The next three expeditions to the Tunguska Valley in 1958, 1961 and 1962 were led by the Soviet geochemist Kirill Florensky, who used a helicopter to survey and chart the blast area. Florensky's team sifted the soil in the area and discovered a narrow strip of dust which was of extraterrestrial origin. The dust consisted of magnetic iron oxide (magnetite) and minute glassy droplets of heat-fused rock. Florensky carefully checked the radiation levels at the site, but the only radioactivity present seemed to be from the fallout which had drifted into the area from distant Soviet H-bomb tests.

Scientists who examined the findings of Florensky and the data from further investigations of the Tunguska explosion site began to postulate that a fragment of Comet Encke had collided with our planet and smashed into Siberia in June 1908. Today, some scientists believe that the blast was caused by a wandering black hole or a chunk of anti-matter. However, there is one piece of curious evidence that seems to vindicate the spaceship theory. At the site of the Tunguska blast, there is a strange irregular shape at the centre of the circle of damaged terrain. Scientists and geologists who have analysed the shape say it looks as if it was caused by something exploding within a cylinder. Comets are not cylindrical, and they do not travel horizontally to the ground making forty-five degree turns.

And what of the fabled *chuchunaa* creature? What

became of him? The last known encounter of the grey giant took place in 1941 in Daghestan. A Colonel V. S. Karapetyan and his troops were called out to investigate sightings of an enormous 'beast-like' figure in the Buinaksk Mountains. The soldiers spotted what they regarded as a monstrosity and gave chase. They cornered the towering figure in a cave and opened fire on it with their rifles. The creature fell with a loud echoing thud, quite dead. Colonel Karapetyan later wrote an account of the confrontation with the unidentified human-like creature:

He stood before me like a giant, his mighty chest thrust forward. His eyes told me nothing. They were dull and empty - the eyes of an animal. And he seemed to me like an animal and nothing more...a wild man of some kind.

The corpse of the creature was left to to the scavengers, and the colonel and his men left the mountains and concerned themselves with the task of defending Russia from the Nazis. The humanoid they had killed may simply have been one of those mysterious 'men-beasts' such as the Yeti or Bigfoot, but according to some of the peasants of the Buinaksk Mountains, the oversized man wore ragged grey clothes. Is it therefore possible that the creature in the cave murdered by the military was the same being that had first been seen by the Evenki tribe near the scene of the Tunguska explosion? This leads us to a tantalising possibility; was the abnormally tall entity some marooned alien from another world who had managed to eject himself from a damaged spaceship after steering the craft away from the inhabited areas of Siberia? If this was the case, what a sad and barbaric end for a visitor who might have been able to teach us so much.

ZODIAC

He was one of the most chilling and enigmatic psychopaths in the history of crime, and despite the steady stream of books and television documentaries that claim to have unmasked him, the mysterious serial killer who called himself The Zodiac remains faceless. We are as near to putting a name to Zodiac as the police were back in the 1960s when he first embarked on his killings. No one is even sure when Zodiac began his sinister programme of stabbings and shootings; did the killings commence with the brutal cold-blooded murder of the pretty 18-year-old coed Cheri Jo Bates just before the Halloween of 1966, or was it the chilling double murder of a teenaged couple in December 1968 Zodiac's baptism in blood? Some researchers into the Zodiac murders believe he may have struck as early as 4 June, 1963 – the date when two high school seniors – Robert George Domingos (aged 18) and his fiancée Linda Faye Edwards (aged 17) – were killed around twenty miles out of Santa Barbara. Domingos and Edwards were full of high-jinks that Monday in the summer of 1964; they graduated from a Lompoc High School, and had driven to a rather remote beach to swim together. They would have felt that the nearby bushes and thick shrubbery would have shielded them from any prying eyes of motorists passing by on the nearby highway, but someone might have noticed Domingos' Pontiac partially hidden behind the bushes and deduced that the driver – and possibly a partner – had obviously gone for a swim on such a hot day. And that person was probably The Zodiac.

The couple had gone to an isolated spot to canoodle in their swimsuits, and when they laid down together on a blanket, neither of them would have dreamt they would soon find themselves the prey of a extreme psychopath. The couple were approached by a man brandishing a rifle (loaded with Winchester .22 ammunition). He carried rope, and he seems to have attempted to tie the couple up. It's believed he first asked Linda Faye Edwards to tie up her boyfriend, but in the middle of the enforced bondage the couple got to their feet in an attempt to escape and ran into the marshy creek. The killer fired upon them with his rifle. Robert George Domingos was hit in the back and fell face down, dead. The murderer then blasted Linda, and then, just to make sure the teens were dead, he stood over their bodies and fired at them at point blank range. Eleven bullets were left in Robert's body and eight in Linda's. The killer then took turns in dragging each of the bodies to a shack where wood was usually stored. The killer took a knife out at one point and began to carve Linda's flesh with it. He then tried to burn the wooden shack down with the bodies inside but it failed to burn. The few prints that had not been obliterated by the weather seemed to show that the killer had worn military-style shoes. The killer of Robert George Domingos and Linda Faye Edwards was never brought to justice, but it's possible that he was in fact Zodiac, because he would later attack a couple and he would ask the female victim to tie up the male victim, and this couple, like Domingos and Edwards, would also be lying together on a blanket in a remote location.

Next, we come to another possible murder of Zodiac's – the barbarous slaying of teenager Cheri Jo Bates. The full moon loomed high over the campus library annex of Riverside City College, Riverside, California, that Sunday evening on "Devil's Night" - 30 October 1966. Inside the library, 18-year-old former varsity cheerleader Cheri Josephine Bates – known as Cheri Jo to her friends and family – was studying hard. A graduate of Ramona High School, the attractive and petite brownish-blonde-haired green-eyed Cheri Jo held an ambition to become a flight attendant, and was working at the time of her studies as a clerk typist and also as a teller in the local bank. Around 9.00pm, just before the library closed, Cheri Jo checked out three books (which were about the structure of the US Government) then went to her light green Volkswagen Beetle, which was conveniently parked outside. It seems Cheri Jo put the key in the ignition and discovered that the engine would not start. Someone had tampered with the engine, presumably as the girl had been in the library. This person had removed the middle wire from the distributor and possibly removed the condenser and ignition coil. We can only surmise what happened next. Cheri Jo might have left the car and gone in search of a telephone call box to contact her father to tell him about the problem with her car. She may have gone back to the library but found no one to answer her knocks on the door because the place had closed by then. We can only speculate as to what happened after the teenager found her Volkswagen's engine was dead, but we do know that Cheri Jo Bates encountered a psychopath that moonlit evening. Two "awful screams" as a neighbour in the area of the library described them, were heard that Halloween eve at around 10.30pm. Just before 6.30am on the following morning, Cheri's body was found by the janitor of Riverside Community College, a 48-year-old WWII veteran named Cleophus F Martin. Martin found the body in an alleyway, lying face down in the dirt driveway adjacent to the library and some 100 yards from her sabotaged car. She had been stabbed forty-two times and her head was barely attached to the body – as if the killer had intended to decapitate her. As well as several stab wounds to the face, chest and shoulder, Cheri's head was bruised, as if it had been struck with a blunt weapon – or kicked. Inside the deceased's car, police found the three books checked out from the library, lying on the front passenger seat. A Timex wristwatch - which had stopped at twenty-three minutes past midnight – was found about ten feet away from Cheri's corpse. This watch, which had a broken 7-inch-wristband, was later traced to a military depot in the UK, but its origins threw no light on the murder case, and some investigators are not even sure if the watch has anything to do with the homicide; it may have simply have been discarded or mislaid by its wearer in the vicinity of the crime days or weeks before the murder. It's even possible that the killer of Cheri Jo Bates planted the wound-down

Timex watch as a red herring to distract investigators and perhaps lead them to believe that the attack had occurred three hours later than it actually did (which was around 9.30pm). Shoeprints made by what appeared to be a military-style heel were found near to the body, but all that could be determined was that the wearer of the shoes was size 8-10. The autopsy established that the victim had not been subjected to a sexual assault, and the police quickly ascertained that Cheri Jo had not been robbed, so it looked like an entirely motiveless murder had taken place. Just under a month after the murder, two copies of a typewritten letter containing a confession to the Bates killing, were posted to the Riverside Police Department and the Riverside *Press Enterprise* newspaper. Police forces across the world routinely receive bogus confession letters after murders, but detectives believed that the author of this confession letter seemed to know details about the Bates murder that hadn't been revealed to the Press. The letter-writer knew, for example, that the middle wire had been removed from the distributor in Cheri Jo's car. The letter ran thus:

THE CONFESSION
BY_____

SHE WAS YOUNG AND SHE WAS BEAUTIFUL. BUT NOW SHE IS BATTERED AND DEAD. SHE IS NOT THE FIRST AND SHE WILL NOT BE THE LAST. I LAY AWAKE NIGHTS THINKING ABOUT MY NEXT VICTIM. MAYBE SHE WILL BE THE BEAUTIFUL BLOND THAT BABYSITS NEAR THE LITTLE STORE AND WALXS [sic]

DOWN THE DARK ALLEY EACH EVENING ABOUT SEVEN. OR MAYBE SHE WILL BE THE SHAPELY BLUE EYED BROWNETT THAT SAID NO WHEN I ASKED HER FOR A DATE IN HIGH SCHOOL. BUT MAYBE IT WILL NOT BE EITHER. BUT I SHALL CUT OFF HER FEMALE PARTS AND DEPOSIT THEM FOR THE WHOLE CITY TO SEE. SO DON'T MAKI [sic] IT EASY FOR ME. KEEP YOUR SISTERS, DAUGHTERS, AND WIVES OFF THE STREETS AND ALLEYS. MISS BATES WAS STUPID. SHE WENT TO THE SLAUGHTER LIKE A LAMB. SHE DID NOT PUT UP A STRUGGLE. BUT I DID. IT WAS A BALL. I FIRST PULLED THE MIDDLI [sic] WIRE FROM THE DISTRIBUTOR. THEN I WAITED FOR HER IN THE LIBRARY AND FOLLOWED HER OUT AFTER ABOUT TWO MINUTS [sic]. THE BATTERY MUST HAVE BEEN ABOUT DEAD BY THEN. I THEN OFFERED TO HELP. SHE WAS THEN VERY WILLING TO TALK WITH ME. I TOLD HER THAT MY CAR WAS DOWN THE STREET AND THAT I WOULD GIVE HER A LIFT HOME. WHEN WE WERE AWAY FROM THE LIBRARY WALKING, I SAID IT WAS ABOUT TIME. SHE ASKED ME "ABOUT TIME FOR WHAT". I SAID IT WAS ABOUT TIME FOR HER TO DIE. I GRABBED HER AROUND THE NECK WITH MY HAND OVER HER MOUTH AND MY OTHER HAND WITH A SMALL KNIFE AT HER THROAT. SHE WENT VERY WILLINGLY. HER BREAST FELT VERY WARM AND FIRM UNDER MY HANDS. BUT ONLY ONE THING WAS ON

MY MIND. MAKING HER PAY FOR THE BRUSH OFFS THAT SHE HAD GIVEN ME DURING THE YEARS PRIOR. SHE DIED HARD. SHE SQUIRMED AND SHOOK AS I CHOAKED [sic] HER. AND HER LIPS TWICHED [sic]. SHE LET OUT A SCREAM ONCE AND I KICKED HER HEAD TO SHUT HER UP. I PLUNGED THE KNIFE INTO HER AND IT BROKE. I THEN FINISHED THE JOB BY CUTTING HER THROAT. I AM NOT SICK. I AM INSANE. BUT THAT WILL NOT STOP THE GAME. THIS LETTER SHOULD BE PUBLISHED FOR ALL TO READ IT. IT MIGHT JUST SAVE THAT GIRL IN THE ALLEY. BUT THAT'S UP TO YOU. IT WILL BE ON YOUR CONSCIENCE. NOT MINE. YES I DID MAXE [sic] THAT CALL TO YOU ALSO. IT WAS JUST A WARNING. BEWARE...I AM STALKING YOUR GIRLS NOW.

CC. CHIEF OF POLICE

ENTERPRISE

The second-to-last sentence in the disturbing letter which stated: 'Yes I did make that call to you also' was interpreted by the police and the FBI (who never directly investigated the Zodiac case) as a reference to a certain telephone call made to the Riverside Police Department from an anonymous individual who talked about the Bates murder before hanging up. The public and press had not been told about this possible telephone call from the alleged killer. In December 1966, an unexpected clue came to light when a janitor at Riverside City College Library – the very library Cheri Jo had been murdered near to – found a strange sinister blank verse poem that someone had inscribed into the surface of a desk found in the library basement. The handwriting and phraseology of this morbid inscription is very similar to the handwriting and wording of the letters that the Zodiac would later taunt the police and newspapers with. The poem, signed by "rh", had been written on an area just under five inches in length, in tiny letters, and it read:

Sick of living/unwilling to die

cut.
clean.
If red I
clean.
blood squirting, dripping, spitting;
all over her new
dress.
oh well
it was red
anyway.
life draining into an
uncertain death.
she won't
die.
this time
someone'll find her.
Just wait till
next time.

[signed] rh

Police could find no pupil or any other employee at the library with the initials R. H. and yet if the writer of the poem was indeed the killer of Cheri Jo Bates and the couple murdered in the summer of 1963 – Robert George Domingos and Linda Faye Edwards, it was conceivable that Zodiac had some connection with schools. Domingos and Faye had just graduated, and Cheri Jo – herself a graduate of Ramona's High School - had been killed on the campus of Riverside City College. The months wore on and the killer of Cheri Jo Bates could not be found. The teenager's remains were cremated and her ashes strewn into the sea.

In December 1968, the first of the canonical murders officially attributed to Zodiac took place, and like most of the murders perpetrated by the enigmatic killer (with the exception of the Domingos Edwards slaying, which took place on a Monday), this one took place on a weekend. The date was Friday, 20 December, 1968, and the time was approximately 11.15pm. The backdrop for this double murder was the secluded Lake Herman Road, a lonely spot known locally as a lover's lane, on the eastern periphery of Vallejo, California, where two high school sweethearts, David Faraday, aged 17, and his beautiful and petite (standing at just over five feet) 16-year-old girlfriend Betty Lou Jensen, were parked up in a Rambler Station Wagon. It was their first ever date together (and Betty Lou's first date ever), and because it was such a glacially cold December night, the heater in the vehicle was on full. It seems that the killer approached out of the darkness and, perhaps through some gesturing with his gun and the flashlight he must have carried, he herded the teenagers to one side of the car. David Faraday was shot first in the head as he left the vehicle. The .22 calibre bullet entered his skull just behind his upper right ear and lodged in the front left lobe of his brain, and this head shot caused him to die within minutes. Betty Lou tried to flee from the wagon, but was blasted five times in the back and died instantly just 35 feet from the vehicle. It was pitch black on Lake Herman Road, and so it is thought that the gunman either attached a flashlight to his weapon or pointed it at his targets with his free hand as he fired the gun with the other hand. A woman named Stella Borges, who was driving through the wintry night to pick up her grandson after his Christmas recital at Benicia High School, came upon the eerie sight of the Rambler Station Wagon parked upon Lake Herman Road with its headlights on. As the headlamp beams of Stella's Oldsmobile swept over the bodies of the murdered teenagers lying on the right side of the road, the elderly lady naturally panicked, and she drove off like a bat out of hell with her horn honking and her lights flashing to attract attention. Stella eventually alerted the law to the double cold-blooded murder. David Faraday was found holding his prized school class ring between his thumb and the third finger of his left hand, and just why he was holding the ruby ring in such a way has never been explained. Some investigators believed he had been about to offer the cherished class ring to Betty Lou as a romantic gesture because he wanted to go steady with her, and had somehow retained the ring between his fingers after he was shot, while some detectives wondered if the boy had been ready to offer it to his killer, thinking the gunman was a robber, even though it seems, from the forensic evidence, that the killer blasted David in the head from behind in a surprise attack. It's also possible that David was trying to indicate something – perhaps about the identity of the killer – by holding the ring in such a way as his consciousness was quickly ebbing away. That ring was engraved with the words Vallejo Senior High School; is it possible that the killer was somehow connected to that school? It's pure conjecture but it's also a possibility.

The killer left faint shoeprints in the frozen ground which could not be matched to any footwear, and no tyre tracks belonging to the murderer's vehicle were evident to police. Nor had the killer left any hand prints on the Rambler or even a partial fingerprint on the shell casings found at the scene.

In the summer of the following year, the killer struck again, and once more he targeted a young couple sitting in a car at a secluded location. The couple on this occasion were 22-year-old married waitress Darlene Ferrin (known by her nickname as "Dee" to closer associates and family) and 19-year-old Mike Mageau (who was single), and the venue for this slaying was a lonely poorly-lit parking lot in the Blue Rock Springs Park on the eastern suburbs of Vallejo, California – just four miles from the last double murder at Lake Herman Road. It was close to midnight, and being the fourth of July, the occasional firecracker could be heard in the distance as Mike sat next to Darlene in her brown Chevrolet Corvair. Another car entered the parking lot and rolled to a halt. Its presence made the couple nervous, but within a minute the car left the parking lot. The couple talked again for about ten minutes and as they did they heard a car approach again. It was the car that had parked up behind them earlier, and it was either a light brown Ford Mustang or a Chevrolet Corvair, just like the one the couple were sitting in. The silhouetted driver of the car, estimated by Mageau to be about 5 ft 8 or 9 inches in height, left his vehicle with a flashlight, and Dee Ferrin and Mike Mageau wondered if it might be a policeman approaching because the figure was shining a flashlight in their direction. In these cases when police did spot checks, nervous teens and people close to that age group would usually reach into their pockets, wallets, purses and handbags to produce some form of identity, and this is exactly what this couple did, but the shadowy man with the torch came to the passenger-door side of Dee Ferrin's car – and opened fire. Five shots were fired from what might have been a 9mm semi-automatic pistol with a silencer, as Mageau thought the pistol shots had sounded muffled, but of course, its possible that he had been partially deafened by the first shot being fired so close to his ear. Some of the shots went through Mageau and into Ferrin's body. The killer walked back to his car, but upon hearing Mageau's agonised groans, he returned to the Chevrolet Corvair and blasted two more bullets into each of the couple. Mageau survived, even though he had sustained four gunshot wounds, but Ferrin, who had been shot five times, was taken to hospital and pronounced dead.

People living in the area heard the gunshots and telephoned the police, and about forty-five minutes after the attack, a man claiming to be the killer made a call to the Vallejo Police Department from a phone booth at Joe's Union Station, just a few blocks away from police headquarters. A 26-year-old woman named Nancy Slover took the call from the self-confessed murderer as she sat at the police department's switchboard at 12.40am. The caller, who spoke in what Nancy would later describe as "a soft but forceful" mature voice devoid of an accent, said he would like to report a double murder at a public park. Nancy said the police had already received reports of a shooting at the park and were responding, but then the caller said: 'If you'll go one mile east on Columbus Parkway to the public park, you'll find they were shot with a 9 millimetre Luger. I also killed those kids last year.'

The 'kids last year' was a reference to the double-murder of teens David Faraday and Betty Lou Jensen at Lake Herman Road.

The chilling voice of the killer who would subsequently be known as the Zodiac stayed with Nancy Slover all of her life. His last words to her before he hung up were: 'Gooood Byyye,' and he drew out the sounds of the words as his voice went up in pitch in an eerie mocking style.

There were a number of other unnerving calls made that night, seemingly related to the murder. Around 1.30am, someone called the mother-in-law and father-in-law of Darlene Ferrin and breathed heavily down the phone before hanging up. Someone also made two telephone calls to the home of Dean Ferrin – Dalene's husband – that morning, but Dean wasn't home, and his babysitter was rather creeped out to hear the heavy breather. A further strange out-of-hours call was made to the home of Dean Ferrin's brother, but he was out the country at the time. It was beginning to look as if the killer knew Darlene Ferrin enough to know where her in-laws lived.

At the end of that month, on July 31, a man professing to be the killer of Faraday, Jensen and Ferrin sent letters containing ciphers to *The San Francisco Examiner*, *The San Francisco Chronicle*, and the *Vallejo Times-Herald*. The author of these letters provided details about the crimes that would have only been known to the killer, and intriguingly, the murderer stated in his missives that his identity was encoded in a cryptogram – a grid of 408 symbols. Detectives, newspaper staff and members of the general public attempted to crack the codes, without success. Police forensic experts applied Ninhydrin vapour to the letters to make the writer's hand or fingerprints visible but could find none. The letter to *The San Francisco Chronicle* stated:

Dear Editor

This is the murderer of the 2 teenagers last Christmass at Lake Herman + the girl on the 4th of July near the golf course in Vallejo. To prove I killed them I shall state some facts which only I + the police know. Here is part of a cipher the other 2 parts of this cipher are being mailed to the editors of the Vallejo Times + SF Examiner. I want you to print this cipher on the front page of your paper. In this cipher is my idenity. If you do not print this cipher by the afternoon of Fry. 1st of Aug 69, I will go on a kill ramPage Fry. night. I will cruse around all weekend killing lone people in the night then move on to kill again, untill I end up with a dozen people over the weekend.

The letter was signed with a circle with a cross radiating from the centre, and some thought this symbol resembled the cross-hairs and circle that are seen through the telescopic sights of a rifle. This symbol would become Zodiac's trademark. He would scrawl it on the door of a victims' car and even use it as a character in his strange codes.

A week after the receipt of the three letters, the killer wrote another taunting letter to the *San Francisco Chronicle's* editor, and in this communication he gave himself a name: Zodiac. The killer's letter began, 'Dear Editor, this is Zodiac speaking...' and the missive was a reply to a police chief's request for the letter-writer to provide proof that he was actually the killer. Zodiac included more details about the murders not known to the Press or the general public, and he stated that if his code was cracked, the police would have him. On the following day, a high school teacher named Donald Gene Harden and his wife Betty managed to crack Zodiac's cipher after working on and off it for some twenty hours. Harden and his wife had succeeded where even the cream of the Navy's cryptographers had failed. The decoded message, though, painted a very strange motive for the Zodiac's killings. The cracked code, full of similar 'typos' that have an eerie parallel to the Cheri Jo Bates confession letter, stated:

I LIKE KILLING PEOPLE BECAUSE IT IS SO MUCH FUN IT IS MORE FUN THAN KILLING WILD GAME IN THE FORREST BECAUSE MAN IS THE MOST DANGEROUE ANAMAL OF ALL TO KILL SOMETHING GIVES ME THE MOST THRILLING EXPERIENCE IT IS EVEN BETTER

THAN GETTING YOUR ROCKS OFF WITH A GIRL THE BEST PART OF IT IS THAE WHEN I DIE I WILL BE REBORN IN PARADICE AND THEI HAVE KILLED WILL BECOME MY SLAVES I WILL NOT GIVE YOU MY NAME BECAUSE YOU WILL TRY TO SLOI DOWN OR ATOP MY COLLECTIOG OF SLAVES FOR MY AFTERLIFE EBEORIETEMETHHPITI

The significance of the last eighteen letters in the decoded message is not known. Some students of cryptography believe the letters are meaningless 'leftovers' – surplus symbols used to make the cipher fit the grid it was composed within, while others believe the eighteen letters may provide some anagrammatic clue – perhaps even the real name of Zodiac or perhaps even some key to a further cryptogram he would later send to the police and newspaper – for that cryptogram of 340 symbols and letters, written in a 17 by 20 grid, has still not been decoded, even in an age when supercomputers routinely decode even the most complex ciphers. Of course, perhaps Zodiac has had the last laugh by deliberately creating a cipher full of meaningless letters and symbols peppered with a few coherent phrases, just to create the illusion of being of a superior intellect. The misspelling of the words within the decoded cipher could be attributed to sloppy work on Zodiac's behalf, and some have hypothesised that the killer made the mistakes because his pen was too thick to authentically transcribe the subtle differences between some of his symbols. It's equally possible that the misspellings arose because Zodiac's eyesight was imperfect – and some survivors of his attacks, as well as witnesses who caught brief glimpses of the killer, claimed they could see he wore glasses, even behind a hooded disguise he donned for one (daylight) attack. It's also plausible that the misspelled words are codes within the cipher; that the substituted letters may in turn spell out a valuable clue. The word 'paradice' in the decoded message from the killer was also used in several more communications with the police and newspapers, and as well as being a possible deliberate misspelling of 'paradise' it also happens to be a Welsh surname. Keep this minor possibility in mind for a future reference to Wales concerning Zodiac. Of course, there's also a possibility Zodiac may have even deliberately misspelled the words to make his cipher more difficult to crack – but why would he even have to encode his messages in the first place? It seems as if Zodiac was forever attempting to prove that he was more intelligent than everyone else, almost as if he was compensating for some feeling of inferiority in his everyday life when he was presumably working in a 9 to 5 existence. The fact that he always struck at weekends (as Jack the Ripper did eighty years before him) seems to suggest two possibilities: that Zodiac was either in regular employment and only able to indulge in his deadly pastimes on Fridays, Saturdays and Sundays – or, he was a fairly wealthy man of private means who had no need to work, and only chose weekends because that was when his victims – mostly young students – were out enjoying themselves in secluded places and open to attack.

A month after his first code was cracked, Zodiac struck again, and this time it was during the hours of daylight. It was almost a carbon copy of the 1963 murders of Robert George Domingos and his sweetheart Linda Faye Edwards. The attack took place on Saturday, 27 September, 1969, at 6.15pm, on the secluded shoreline of Lake Berryessa near Napa, California. 20-year-old Bryan Hartnell and his friend, 22-year-old Cecelia Shepherd, were relaxing on a blanket at a picturesque spot overlooking the lake. Bryan was laying on his back and Cecelia was lying on her stomach, and the couple, who had dated two years back, were reminiscing about old times. The couple's reminiscences were suddenly interrupted by a noise that sounded like the rustling of leaves somewhere in the distance. Bryan said to Cecelia, 'You have your specs on; why don't you see what the deal is over there?'

Cecelia noticed movement – a figure, some distance off, coming towards her and Bryan, and she remarked, 'Oh, it's some man.'

'What?' Bryan asked, 'Is he alone?' and he squinted over towards the area where Cecelia was looking. His eyesight wasn't too good and he didn't have his spectacles on.

'Yeah,' Cecelia answered, and then she said: 'He just stepped behind the tree!'

'What's the idea of that?' Bryan wondered out loud, and speculated: 'To take a leak?'

Cecelia looked at the tree in question with a worried expression.

'Well keep looking and tell me what happens,' Bryan told her.

Cecelia seemed to recoil in horror at what she saw next, and she gripped Bryan's arm hard and exclaimed:

'Oh my God, he's got a gun!'

The figure that approached looked sinister, menacing and deadly. It was a six-foot-tall man pointing a pistol at the couple, and he wore what looked like an executioner's hood from the medieval period. This black hood had two eyeholes in it, and over these eyeholes the gunman had attached clip-on sunglasses. The black hood went down to some sort of sleeveless black tunic, and upon this tunic there was a white symbol – the very same symbol the Zodiac had used to sign his letters to the police and the Press – a circle with a cross in the middle with the arms of the cross radiating beyond the confines of the circle – rather similar to the ancient Celtic Cross. Zodiac wore a dark blue cotton coat and dark pleated trousers, and when he addressed the couple, Bryan had the tantalising impression that he had heard the voice before somewhere, but he just couldn't place it. Thinking Zodiac was being motivated by robbery, Bryan assured him: 'Well, listen Mac, there's no strings attached; I don't have any money right now but if you need help that badly I can help you out in another way maybe.'

'Nah, time's running short,' Zodiac replied, with the gun still trained on the couple. Zodiac then claimed he was an escaped prisoner on the run from a Montana jail. He had killed a prison guard to affect his escape and now had plans to flee the country and go south to Mexico. All he needed was a car and enough money to get by. Bryan had studied sociology and psychology at college, and believed he was qualified to negotiate and perhaps parley with the 'escaped convict'. He wondered if the hooded man even had any ammo in his gun.

Bryan said to Zodiac: 'Well, man, I mean actually, I don't want to call your bluff or anything, but wouldn't you rather be stuck on a stealing charge than a threat of homicide?'

'Well just don't start playing the hero with me,' Zodiac told Bryan, 'don't try to grab the gun.'

'You know you're really wasting your time with me,' said Bryan, 'I've got a billfold and this much change and that's it.'

Zodiac pointed the gun at Cecelia and sternly told her to: 'Tie him up!' and then he turned his hooded head back to Bryan and said: 'I'd feel much better if you were tied up.' And Zodiac threw several plastic clothes-lines, cut in six-foot lengths, to Cecelia. The terrified young lady pretended to tie Bryan's wrists behind his back but simply made loose knots instead, and Bryan turned to her and whispered: 'You know I think I can get that gun; do you mind?' but Cecelia's terror-filled eyes answered his glance in such a way that Bryan realised he'd be risking her life with his well-meant intentions, as well as his own.

Zodiac then intervened, as if he knew that Cecelia had been tying weak knots, and he bound the couple up with their wrists behind their backs. 'Okay, lay down!' he barked at Bryan and then Zodiac told him: 'I've got her tied up.'

'Oh come on!' Bryan complained, 'Don't make me lay down! We could be here all night!'

'Get down! Right now!' Zodiac roared.

Bryan lay down – face down almost, as Zodiac finished tying up Cecelia. He then began to tie a length of the clothes line from Bryan's wrists to his ankles.

'Do you have bullets in there?' Bryan asked the

gunman, looking at the pistol, and Zodiac took the clip out the handle of the gun to show his captor that he really did have a loaded weapon. Zodiac then put away the gun, and Bryan turned to say something to Cecelia, who was naturally in a very anxious state. As Bryan was about to talk to his friend, he felt something go through his back. Zodiac had taken out a long-bladed knife (of approximately 12 inches in length) and was stabbing him in the back. Bryan felt no pain as the blade went in and punctured his lung because he was in shock. Cecelia almost fainted at the sight – and the sound – of the blade being plunged into her friend's back six times. But then Zodiac grabbed Cecelia, and he stabbed her five times in the back, and when she turned over, trying desperately to escape, he stabbed her five more times in the front, and seemed to go into a frenzy when he attacked her.

And then Zodiac calmly walked away. Upon reaching Bryan Hartnell's white Kharman Ghia car, the killer (presumably took off his hood,) took out a marker pen and scrawled his cross-within-a-circle symbol on the door of the vehicle, and underneath this, Zodiac wrote the word 'Vallejo; and below this he scrawled the dates of his previous murders and also the date and time of today's murder, along with a mention of the weapon used:

> 12-20-68
> 7-4-69
> September 27-69-6:30
> by knife

The couple screamed for help with their lifeblood

draining away. Cecelia made repeated attempts to roll over and free Bryan with her bound hands, and somehow she managed to help him untie himself. Bryan untied Cecelia, and he kissed her and said: 'I'm gonna try and get help.'

Bryan walked and walked and began to black out from loss of blood. He was eventually picked up by park rangers who had been alerted by a fisherman who had heard the couple's frantic screams. Cecelia was in great agony, and begged the first police officers on the scene to give her something to kill the pain. She rocked back and forth, crying and groaning. She survived for about 48 hours in hospital then passed away.

Police found size 10-and-a-half shoe prints made by a brand of footwear known as Wing Walkers at the scene of the crime, and they estimated – by the depth of the prints – that Zodiac weighed about 210 pounds. Tyre tracks found by Bryan's car indicated that the Zodiac had parked his car behind the vehicle. About an hour after the stabbings, a man telephoned the Napa Police Department and coolly claimed responsibility for stabbing Hartnell and Shepherd. The call was traced to a telephone kiosk about four blocks away from the police station, in the downtown area of Napa, and a fresh palm print – believed to be the killer's - was successfully lifted from the telephone receiver and later submitted to the FBI – but no matches with any suspects were ever made. Zodiac, whoever he was, did not have a police record, for his prints never matched any held by the police forces of America. An unidentified print of someone's hand was found on the Zodiac's first letter to the *Vallejo Times-*

Herald but again there was no match with the Napa phone booth print.

And now we come to what was possibly the final murder carried out by Zodiac, and like his previous attacks, this one occurred of a weekend, on the foggy Saturday evening of 11 October, 1969 at approximately five minutes to ten. The location was the affluent upscale Presidio Heights district of San Francisco, and on this occasion, a young couple were not targeted by Zodiac; instead, the victim was a 29-year-old English literature student of San Francisco State University who, in addition to working as a an insurance salesman, also worked as a taxi driver for the Yellow Cab Company by night to help finance his education, and his name was Paul Stine. Zodiac had hailed Stine's cab at Geary Street and Mason Street and had asked the taxi driver to take him to a destination near to the upmarket Presidio Heights district, but during the journey, Zodiac must have told Stine he'd changed his mind about his destination, for the cab pulled over in the north-eastern corner of Cherry Street and Washington Street, and here, near this intersection, as soon as the Yellow Cab halted, Zodiac reached forward and seized Stine by the throat as he prodded the taxi driver's right cheek with the barrel of his pistol. Stine tried to raise his right hand to reach over and push the gun away and as he moved the Zodiac fired, blasting the taxi driver in the back of the head near his right ear with a 9mm semi-automatic pistol, killing him almost instantly. The close proximity of the barrel of the pistol to Stine's head muffled the sound of the discharge somewhat. Zodiac lost no time exiting through the rear door of the Yellow Cab. He then re-entered the taxi through the front passenger door and whilst holding Stine's head on his lap, he removed the driver's wallet and began to tear off a large portion of his shirt, which was already soaked with warm blood. Zodiac would subsequently use a piece of this shirt to mail to the *San Francisco Chronicle* along with a letter in which he claimed responsibility for the murder of the taxi driver. Zodiac was sloppy the night he killed Stine, because five known witnesses saw him. As Zodiac was tearing a piece of the cab-drivers shirt off, three teenagers who were attending a party at a house less than fifty feet away from the crime scene could clearly see him from a third floor window. These witnesses were a 14-year-old girl and her brothers, and they watched Zodiac as he left the cab and began to wipe down both sides of the cab with the portion of Stine's shirt. Zodiac lingered even as he was watched and opened the driver's door to lean in and wipe down the dashboard. He was not successful in eradicating all of his fingerprints, and left a lot of prints on the handle and door of the cab that night. The teenagers watched the stocky stranger with the blondish crew cut turn a corner into Cherry Street, where Zodiac headed north, in the direction of the Presidio military base, and as he walked along he turned west down Jackson Street – where he actually passed two policemen – officers Donald Fouke and Eric Zelms, who were responding to the phone calls made to Richmond police station from the teenagers at the party who had reported the violent taxi 'robbery'. Through some blunder in communications, the officers had been told to be on the look out for a black male, and by the time they realised they had passed

Zodiac earlier on, the killer had vanished into the fog like a ghost. Neither policeman recalled seeing any blood on the bespectacled white male passing them that night, even though Zodiac must have had some blood on his clothes, particularly his trousers, because Paul Stine's head, which had been pouring with blood, had rested on Zodiac's lap as the killer took his wallet and tore off a strip of his shirt. Of course, it was night-time, foggy, and Zodiac wore dark coloured pants on this occasion, so the blood-staining might not have been that visible, and yet, the presence of blood on the killer would have undoubtedly helped the police tracker dogs that were quickly brought into the area – but the dogs could not track Zodiac, and he seems to have gone to ground rather quickly – as if he had lived in that classy district of mansions and expensive townhouses around the Presidio. The policemen who had passed Zodiac that night as he walked from the scene of the crime later described him as being of 'Welsh ancestry'. Why this is so has never been satisfactorily explained. No one looks Welsh, but they can certainly sound Welsh – if they open their mouths and reveal an accent. But the two policemen stated that they did not talk to the man they had passed on Jackson Street – but Zodiac later claimed they talked to him in a letter he subsequently sent to the newspapers. Did the responding patrolmen talk to the most-wanted killer in the US that night? Sadly, one of the policemen – Eric Zelms – later died in the line of duty in January of the following year when he was shot by two criminals whilst investigating a burglary – but the other officer – Donald Fouke, is still alive, and to this day he swears he never talked to Zodiac that night.

Apparently, Fouke allegedly believed Zodiac looked as if he was of Welsh ancestry because he had uncles of Welsh descent (so we must surmise Fouke believed Zodiac had a look of one of these uncles), and Fouke, incidentally, is a surname of Welsh origin. Paradice, as I pointed out earlier, is also a Welsh surname, and was used by the Zodiac in his correspondence.

Paul Stine's heartbroken older brother, Joe Stine, laid down a challenge to Zodiac: he asked the killer to make him his next victim, and in the newspapers, Joe Stine's daily routine was published in the hope that Zodiac would rise to the bait, but the killer didn't respond.

The usual taunting letters from Zodiac came thick and fast after the Stine murder. The first one, which contained a portion of the cab driver's bloody shirt, read:

This is the Zodiac speaking.

I am the murderer of the taxi driver over by Washington St + Maple St last night, to prove this here is a blood stained piece of his shirt. I am the same man who did in the people in the north bay area.

The S.F. Police could have caught me last night if they had searched the park properly instead of holding road races with their motorcicles [sic] seeing who could make the most noise. The car drivers should have just parked their cars and sat there quietly waiting for me to come out of cover.

School children make nice targets, I think I shall wipe out a school bus some morning. Just shoot out the front tire + then pick off the kiddies as they come bouncing out.

And this letter, signed with the usual circle and cross

symbol of Zodiac, was mailed to the *San Francisco Chronicle.*

The authorities were naturally alarmed at Zodiac's threat of an attack on a school bus, but thankfully it never took place. The letters went on for a few years with Zodiac claiming to have committed crimes that were later proved to be the work of other killers. Some thought that he had lost his nerve that Saturday night after his very close encounter with two police officers in the aftermath of the Paul Stine murder. He had been carrying a piece of the murdered taxi driver's shirt as well as the murder weapon when the police passed him, and had they noticed any blood stains on him he would have been challenged immediately. Had the Zodiac been arrested that night, he would, in all probability, have been put on trial and found guilty, judged to be sane and sentenced to the gas chamber. The tone of his letters to the authorities became noticeably nastier after the exceedingly close shave in the Presidio district, and those letters give one the impression that Zodiac had been really ruffled by his narrow escape that Saturday night. His usual craving for attention now extended from wanting front page coverage of his ciphers to a request for people to wear buttons (badges) with his logo on. In what was probably Zodiac's final letter, sent to the *San Francisco Chronicle* in January 1974, the writer claimed he had killed thirty-seven people without enclosing any authenticating evidence or details to validate his claim. Other letters bearing the Zodiac symbol were sent to police and the newspaper after this period, but most – if not all of these – are said to have been fake.

Who was Zodiac and what motivated him to kill? He

comes across like a man with a chip on his shoulder, a loner out to punish an uncaring society, and a person who thought he was some superhero with a name and a costume bearing a symbol that could have come straight from the pages of a Marvel or DC comic book (and there was, in fact a supervillain called the Zodiac Master, who first appeared as a foe of Batman in early 1964) and was his alter ego, like the fictional Peter Parker or Clark Kent, the archetypal conservative geek who got knocked back by every girl he approached? The typewritten confession letter written in the wake of the Cheri Jo Bates murder seems to suggest this. Zodiac was obviously someone who possessed enough intelligence to formulate ciphers, and he also seems to have had some knowledge of electronics from his schematic bomb diagrams featuring photoelectric cells etc. He also knew how to disable the engine of the car belonging to victim Cheri Jo Bates by removing specific wires to the distributor. Most of the victims were students connected to schools, colleges and universities, and these facts may provide us with a clue to Zodiac's identity. Was he a lecturer, or a teacher, or a mature student? Of course, there's also the military angle; the prints left on the ground at some of the crime-scenes were of a shoe worn by military personnel and Zodiac was described by more than one witness as having a crew cut, which was a rather square hairstyle in the mid-to-late 1960s – unless he was some military officer. Furthermore, his last known crime – the murder of taxi driver Paul Stine – saw Zodiac going to ground awfully fast in the vicinity of the Presidio – a military base.

What happened that October night after Zodiac

hailed Paul Stine's cab? It doesn't seem to have been a planned murder at all. I believe that Zodiac was stalking a couple that night in the theatre district near Mason Street and Geary Street. He was carrying his gloves – which no one would have had good cause to wear on such a typical mild and muggy San Francisco autumnal evening, and, of course, he was carrying his gun and probably his knife. I suspect that Stine somehow realised his passenger was Zodiac shortly after he had climbed into his cab, and although we will never know what conversation took place between the two men, I think Zodiac realised he'd been rumbled, and quickly decided he had to kill Stine or be captured, tried and subsequently sent to death row. In Zodiac's mind there was nothing else he *could* do but kill Stine. He had to change the destination from the original one he requested because the original dropping off point was very close to his own home or the home of his targeted couple. In the panic that ensued, Zodiac forgot his gloves, and, despite later claiming in one of his letters to the newspapers that he wore two coats of airplane glue on his fingers so he doesn't leave prints, Zodiac had to wipe down Stine's Yellow Cab that night – and yet he still managed to leave prints all over it, both inside and outside of the vehicle – and, he also left his gloves on the back seat of the cab. This hints that the murder of Paul Stine was not premeditated - that something seems to have happened in that taxi which triggered the murder. If the man who was Zodiac knew Stine personally, it would also explain why the police believed that the killer rode in the front seat with the cabby, although I personally believe the presence of Zodiac's gloves being on the rear seat of the cab indicate he was a backseat passenger. Stine was near to earning his doctorate in English Literature at San Francisco State University – so is it possible he had recognised the man who was Zodiac because he had met him as either a student or a tutor at some similar university in the past? If the killing of Stine was not premeditated, and I believe It wasn't planned at all, Zodiac has to think fast after he blasts Stine in the head, and the only option is to cover up his true motive for the killing is by disguising it as a Zodiac crime. He tears off the strip of the driver's shirt so he can use it in correspondence with the newspapers, and no one will see the forest for the trees – they will actually fall for the ploy and think Zodiac is changing his pattern. Zodiac went out of his way in the letters that followed the Stine killing to make out that he was leaving false clues in the cab when he was wiping it down, that he used coats of airplane glue so he wouldn't leave fingerprints – when in fact he had left prints all over the vehicle and had even forgotten his size 7 gloves. Had Zodiac simply walked from that cab and gone home that Saturday night, the police would have taken the prints and eventually matched them to the ones left at the other scenes of the Zodiac crimes, and they would have realised that Paul Stine had probably known the victim, and they would have looked into Stine's background and possibly made some connection which would have led to Zodiac's door. It was a stroke of evil genius for Zodiac to rip off the shirt of the man he had to kill and use it to create the impression of a deliberate pre-planned killing. That night, Zodiac must have thought he was as good as dead. He'd been forced to kill a cab driver at an intersection in a busy neighbourhood on a Saturday night with so many potential witnesses about, and he was on foot, unlike the previous times when he had killed and climbed into his car to make a quick getaway. Two police patrolmen drove past him and saw him that night, and God knows who else did and never came forward out of fear, but he had the Devil's luck when the police dispatcher mistakenly put out a description of a black male perpetrator. What's chilling in this scenario is that two people who are perhaps still living in the San Francisco area today, may even now be completely unaware that *they* were the intended targets of Zodiac that night as they left a theatre near the Mason and Geary Street area. I have no doubt that Zodiac would have become more overconfident after that night had things gone to plan. He would have gunned down the couple, and his black hood would have been donned as he carried out even more sickening and audacious crimes by day as well as night. He hinted in his letters – and in his infamous Halloween card, sent to news reporter Paul Avery, that he would kill by knife, by gun, by fire and also by rope. I think Zodiac would have ultimately hanged a couple side by side to achieve his threat of death by rope, and as a man who even provided us with schematic diagrams of bombs in his letters, it would have been easy for him to make a deadly incendiary device which would certainly kill "by fire". The Zodiac's programme of death and destruction fortunately came to a halt that night when he was, for some unknown reason, forced to kill Paul Stine in that cab in San Francisco. It had been one hell of a close-call. From then on, he had to vent his hatred for the world in his letters to the newspapers, and the editors soon tired of the hollow threats.

Is Zodiac still alive? It's possible. Ironically, Zodiac achieved the widespread 'fame' he hungered for, and has gone down in the annals of crime to join the other unknown murderers of history in that dark pantheon of infamy, and yet the man behind Zodiac, the alter ego, is unknown, and perhaps the thought of being anonymous and faceless forevermore in death has prompted the man behind the chilling persona to leave some form of confession – perhaps in the style of one of his typical ciphers - in a safe somewhere, and this confession might come to light upon the reading of a certain will. The fact that we have not yet heard of such a confession may mean two things; that Zodiac is still alive and well, or perhaps he is no longer with us and purposely remained silent, wishing to take his awful secret to the grave with him. I personally think we will know who he was in the near future, and my optimism is fuelled by a recent advance in genetic technology which will be rather worrying to Zodiac if he knows about it. A breakthrough made by groups of geneticists in Germany and other parts of the world is making it possible to generate high-definition computer images of the face of a person from his or her DNA samples, however minute they are. Hair and eye colour will also be revealed by this exciting technology. The genes labelled PRDM16 and PAX3 first hinted that this was possible several years ago, but now tremendous strides are being made in the acquisition of highly accurate "photofits" generated by a criminal's DNA – and the San Francisco Police Department and the police down at Riverside,

California (where Cheri Jo Bates was slain) have more than enough of Zodiac's DNA to see just what his face looks like, and using special software, they will be able to age the face to any age. Once this happens and the results are circulated in newspapers and posted on websites and TV shows, someone may recognise the face, come forward and finally identify the killer. There will be time-wasters who will claim they know him and there may be some dead ringers of Zodiac out there, but there's also a good chance of someone correctly identifying the murderer.

Since his last killing Zodiac must be taking enormous lengths to avoid the littlest altercation, because the interconnected police forces of the world have his fingerprints on their computers. If someone should even break into his home, Zodiac would have to have his prints routinely taken for a process of distinguishing them from the burglars' fingerprints. He must be barricaded away, trying his utmost to keep out of trouble in fact, and in a way, this is probably serving as a long-term punishment of its own.

Before the day comes – and that day might be a lot sooner than we think - when geneticists will probably unmask the Zodiac, its possible that his identity may become known in another low-tech way. It may come from a death-bed confession, a confession discovered after he has died, or perhaps the unsolved '340 cipher' of Zodiac, which has still not been cracked, is not just a matrix of nonsensical symbols and numbers designed to lead us nowhere; perhaps it really is an ingenious code that contains the name of the man who once terrorised the West Coast of the United States.

POPE JOAN

In this day and age of sexual equality, the notion of a woman disguising herself as a man to gain entry into a male-dominated career will seem absurd and demeaning to today's liberated women, but there have been numerous cases of females dressing up as men to further themselves throughout history. One such example of an upwardly-mobile female transvestite was Dr James Barry, a dashing, handsome army surgeon who served in the West Indies, South Africa and India. In 1808 he was accepted as a medical student at Edinburgh University at the age of sixteen, and ended up as a prominent surgeon. When he died at the age of 73 on July 25th, 1865, many mourned the popular old man's passing. Then came the startling revelation when Dr Barry's body was stripped naked for the post-mortem examination. Dr Barry was in fact a woman. *He* had breasts and a vagina. Furthermore, the post-mortem revealed that 'Mr Barry' had given birth to a child in her youth, but what became of the scion is a secret that the unidentified woman took with her to the grave.

Another bizarre case of a woman masquerading as a man is said to have taken place around AD 864 at Rome. The first mention of this incredible and heretical tale is to be found in an obscure manuscript in the Vatican Library at Rome. In a yellow, timeworn tome that is now hidden from the light of day, a 9th century Roman scribe named Anastasius Bibliothecarius tells the story of a woman who, after passing herself off as a man - was elected Pope! The scribe's account is today classified by the Vatican as a blasphemous, apocryphal fable, but other writers after Bibliothecarius have also recorded more detailed accounts of 'Pope Joan' - as she was allegedly known. In the 11th century, Martinus Scotus, a monk from the Abbey of St Martin of Cologne in Germany, wrote:

In AD 854, Lotharii 14, Joanna, a woman, succeeded Leo, and reigned two years, five months, and four days.

A 12th century scribe known as Sigebert de Gemlours, also writes of the controversial event:

It is reported that this John was a female, and that she conceived a child by one of her servants. The Pope, becoming pregnant, gave birth to a child, whereof some do not number her among the Pontiffs.

The 13th century scribe Stephen of Bourbon also alludes to the Pope Joan incident in his religious work, *De septem donis Spiritu Sancti* ('Of the seven gifts of the Holy Spirit') but he was very reticent about the exact details of the story. The only reliable and detailed account of the Pope Joan episode is contained in the pages of *Chronicron pontificum et imperatum* (The Chronicle of the popes and emperors), written by the 13th century annalist Martin of Troppau. He writes:

After Leo IV, John Anglus, a native of Metz, reigned two

years, five months and four days. And the pontificate was vacant for a month. He died in Rome. He is related to have been a female, and when a girl, to have accompanied her sweetheart in male costume to Athens; there she advanced in various sciences and none could be found to equal her. So, after having studied for three years in Rome, she had great masters for her pupils and hearers. And when there arose a high opinion in the city of her virtue and knowledge, she was unanimously elected Pope. But during her papacy she became in the family way by a familiar. Not knowing the time of the birth, as she was on her way from St Peter's to Lateran she had a painful delivery, between the Coliseum and St Clement's Church, in the street. Having died after, it is said she was buried on the spot.

And where is this spot where Joan was irreverently interred? It was said to have been indicated by a large stone slab, inscribed with a very concise summary of the blasphemous woman who laid beneath it. But because the stone was becoming an embarrassment to the church, Pope St Pius V (1566-1572) had it removed and broken up. After the Pope Joan foozle, all papal candidates were forced to undergo a brief physical examination to prove their gender. In 1557, a century after the advent of the movable type which had made the mass-production of books possible, the Catholic Church drew a list of censored writers and their books. One of the first scribes to appear on the list of prohibited books, or the *Index Librorum Prohibitorum* as it was officially known, was Giovanni Boccaccio, an Italian writer. His book of one hundred licentious stories, *The Lives of the Decameron*, which took ten years to write, happened to mention the story of Pope Joan, and so the papacy immediately placed the book on the Index. Boccaccio later reissued a sanitised version of his epic tome, minus all the sinning monks and nuns, and the Council of Trent subsequently forgave him and struck the book off the Index. But with the Reformation in full swing, the Protestant pamphleteers saw the Pope Joan story as excellent propaganda, and error-laden printed accounts and word-of-mouth tales of the 'Popess' were soon circulating Europe, and with each telling of the story, the details became more sordid. In England, it was said that Joan's first lover had been a Benedictine monk, and her second paramour had been a cardinal, and she had ended up copulating with Lucifer himself. Because of the bitter anti-Catholicism that swept western Europe, the story of Pope Joan was distorted until it bore no resemblance to the original account, and as the Vatican is still withholding most of the intriguing references about the incident in its subterranean library, we simply don't have the necessary information which would enable us to determine if the female Pope ever existed.

THE THING IN BERKELEY SQUARE

Long before Mayfair's Berkeley Square was synonymous with nightingales (thanks to Eric Maschwitz's famous song), the place was invariably associated with a rather nasty ghost that was alleged to inhabit number 50, a four-storey townhouse that dated back to the 1740s. It was once the London home of Prime minister George Canning (1770-1827), but it seems very unlikely that the well-documented supernatural goings-on at number 50 are anything to do with his spirit, as Canning died at Chiswick. No one seems to know just what haunted number 50, because few who encountered it lived to tell the tale, and those who did survive were always left insane by the supernatural confrontation.

All we can do is piece together the fragments of anecdotes and accounts that concern the Berkeley Square entity.

In 1840, the 20-year-old dandy and notorious rake Sir Robert Warboys heard the eerie rumours about the Berkeley Square "Thing" in a Holborn tavern one night, and laughingly dismissed the tales as 'unadulterated poppycock'.

Sir Robert's friends disagreed with him, and dared him to spend a night in the haunted second-floor room in Berkeley Square.

Warboys raised his flagon of ale in the air and announced: 'Ha! I wholeheartedly accept your preposterous harebrained challenge!'

That same night, Sir Robert visited the haunted premises to arrange an all-night vigil with the landlord. The landlord tried to talk Sir Robert out of the dare, but the young man refused to listen, and demanded to be put up for the night in the haunted room. The landlord finally gave in to Sir Robert's demands, but stipulated two conditions; if the young man saw anything 'unearthly' he was to pull a cord that would ring a bell in the landlord's room below. Secondly, Sir Robert would have to be armed with a pistol throughout the vigil. The young libertine thought the conditions were absurd, but agreed to them just to get the landlord out of his hair.

The landlord handed Warboys a pistol and left as a clock in the room chimed the hour of midnight. Sir Robert sat at a table in the candlelit room and waited for the 'Thing' to put in an appearance.

Forty-five minutes after midnight, the landlord was startled out of his sleep by the violent jangling of the bell. A single gunshot in the room above echoed through the house. The landlord raced upstairs and found Sir Robert sitting on the floor in the corner of the room with a smoking pistol in his hand. The young man had evidently died from traumatic shock, for his eyes were bulged, and his lips were curled from his clenched teeth. The landlord followed the line of sight from the dead man's terrible gaze and traced it to a single bullet hole in the opposite wall. He quickly deduced that Warboys had fired at the 'Thing', to no avail.

Three years after Warboys' death, Edward Blunden and Robert Martin, two sailors from Portsmouth, wandered into Berkeley Square in a drunken state and noticed the 'To Let' sign at number 50. They had squandered most of their wages on drink and couldn't afford lodgings, so they broke into number 50. Finding the lower floors too damp, the sailors staggered upstairs and finally settled down on the floor of the infamous room.

It proved to be a serious mistake. Blunden told his friend he felt nervous in the room, and felt a 'presence', but Martin told his shipmate he'd been at sea too long, and was soon snoring.

A little over an hour later, the door of the room burst open, and the enormous shadowy figure of a man floated towards the sailors. Martin woke up and found himself unable to move. He was paralysed with fear. Blunden tried to get to his feet, but the entity seized him by the throat with its cold, misty-looking hands and started to choke him.

Martin suddenly gained enough courage to enable him to spring to his feet. He tried to confront the apparition, but was so horrified by its deformed face and body, he found himself fleeing from the house. He encountered a policeman in the square outside and told him of the vaporous assailant that was throttling his friend. The bemused policeman followed the distressed sailor into number 50 and when the two men entered the room up on the second floor, there was no sign of Blunden. They searched the entire house, and found the missing sailor's body in the basement. His neck had been broken and his face was contorted in a terror-stricken grimace.

Documentary evidence for the aforementioned incidents is very scant, but the eminent psychical researcher Harry Price unearthed a great deal of data on the Berkeley Square bogeyman while investigating the case in the 1920s. Price scoured periodicals and newspapers from the mid 18th century onwards for a reference to the ghost of Berkeley Square, and discovered that in the 1790s, a gang of counterfeiters and coin-clippers had used number 50 as their headquarters. Price speculated that the criminals had invented the ghost to disguise the true nature of the bumps in the night: the printing presses churning out bank notes. But the theory could not explain how the ghost was heard decades after the counterfeit gang had been detected and thrown into prison. Price discovered more intriguing references to the ghost. In 1840, several neighbours of number 50 Berkeley Square heard a medley of strange sounds emanating from the haunted house; bumps on the stairs, dragging noises as if heavy objects were being moved around, jangling of signal bells below the stairs, and the tramping of footsteps. Price read that one of the braver neighbours who had grown weary of the noisy spectre obtained a key and dashed into the house one night during the creepy cacophony. There was no one in the house. Down in the kitchen, the signal bells were still bouncing on their curled springs.

Price found another thought-provoking account of the ghost in Notes and Queries, a magazine published during the 1870s. An article in the publication by the writer W. E. Howlett stated:

The mystery of Berkeley Square still remains a mystery. The

story of the haunted house in Mayfair can be recapitulated in a few words; the house contains at least one room of which the atmosphere is supernaturally fatal to body and mind. A girl saw, heard and felt such horror in it that she went mad, and never recovered sanity enough to tell how or why.

A gentleman, a disbeliever in ghosts, dared to sleep in number 50 and was found a corpse in the middle of the floor after frantically ringing for help in vain. Rumour suggests other cases of the same kind, all ending in death, madness, or both as a result of sleeping, or trying to sleep in that room. The very party walls of the house, when touched, are found saturated with electric horror. It is uninhabited save by an elderly man and his wife who act as caretakers; but even these have no access to the room. This is kept locked, the key being in the hands of a mysterious and seemingly nameless person who comes to the house once every six months, locks up the elderly couple in the basement, and then unlocks the room and occupies himself in it for hours.

Price continued to research the history of number 50, and learned that the house had been empty for remarkably long periods, yet the address was one of the most desirable ones in London, so why had the house been left vacant for so long? Had the rumours scared off prospective occupants, or had the ghost itself frightened them away? Price could not answer this question, nor could he draw any firm conclusions to the whole case. His final surmise was that a particularly nasty poltergeist had been active at number 50 in the 1840s, but doubted that the 'thing' was still at large.

But there have been many ghostly encounters at number 50 in recent times. In January 1937, Mrs Mary

Balfour, an octogenarian lady of a stately Scottish family, moved into a flat in Charles Street, which lies adjacent to Berkeley Square. One night Mrs Balfour's maid summoned her to come to the kitchen situated at the rear of the flat. The maid was staring intently through the window at the rear of a house diagonally opposite. It was the rear of Berkeley Square. The maid drew Mrs Balfour's attention to one of the rear windows of number 50, where a man stood dressed in a silver-coloured coat and breeches. He wore a periwig and had a drawn, morose ashen face. The two women thought he had been to some New Year fancy dress party, because his clothes were centuries out of date. The man moved away from the window, and Mrs Balfour and her maid were later shocked to learn from a doctor that they had sighted one of the ghosts of number 50 Berkeley Square. The doctor told them that number 50 was currently unoccupied, but workmen in the building two months back had seen the phantom of a little girl in a kilt on the stairs.

Stories of the haunted house continue to circulate today in Mayfair. Late at night, faces are said to peep out from the upper windows of number 50, which is now occupied by a firm of antiquarian book sellers. Will the 'thing' ever make a comeback? Only time will tell.

MURDER REPEATS ITSELF

On 27 May 1817, the body of a murder victim - 20-year-old Mary Ashford was found in a flooded sandpit at Erdington, a village lying five miles outside of Birmingham in England. Exactly 157 years afterwards to the very day and hour of the Ashford murder, history repeated itself in a most brutal and chilling way when 20-year-old Barbara Forrest was strangled and left in the long grass near to the children's home in Erdington where she was employed as a nurse. This may seem nothing more than a coincidence, but more intriguing similarities and parallels between the two murders came to light when the police were investigating the Barbara Forrest murder. As a police archivist officer read through the Ashford murder of 1817 he shook his head in disbelief. Whit Monday had been on 26 May both in 1817 and 1975 - the year of the Barbara Forrest murder. Like Ashford, Barbara Forrest had been raped before being murdered and both victims were found within 300 yards of one another. Ashford and Forrest shared the same birth date, and the coincidences didn't stop there. Both girls had visited their best friend on the evening of the Whit Monday to change into a new dress for a local dance party. After each murder a suspect was arrested whose name was Thornton, and in both instances, this Mr Thornton was charged with murder but subsequently acquitted.

Let us take a closer look at these uncanny coincidences. At 6.30 a.m. on 27 May, 1817, a labourer on his way to work in Erdington came upon a heap of bloodstained clothes belonging to a woman, near to Penn's Mill. He informed the police and during a search of the area around the suspicious find, they saw two tracks of footprints made by a man and a woman which led towards a flooded sandpit.

The police followed the two sets of footprints and saw that they ended at the edge of the water around the pit. The pit was searched and the corpse of a well-known and well-loved local girl named Mary Ashford was recovered. Her arms were heavily bruised and her clothing was bloodstained. Police made enquiries with the locals and soon established Miss Ashford's last movements on the previous day. On Whit Monday - the 26 May - Mary had travelled from Erdington to Birmingham to sell dairy produce at the local market. She had then made arrangements to visit a friend's house where she would change into a new dress. Then she and her friend - Hannah Cox - would go to the Whitsuntide dance at the Tyburn House Inn in the evening. Mary had arrived at her friend's house at six in the evening. She changed into the new dress and then went to the dance with Hannah, and the two girls seemed to have enjoyed themselves, and they'd had no shortage of male admirers, although for a majority of the evening, Mary had been in the company of a young bricklayer named Abraham Thornton, while her friend had been dancing with a boy named Benjamin Carter. The dance ended around midnight, and the foursome headed towards their respective homes as far as a place known as the Old Cuckoo, which lay just a short distance from Erdington village. Hannah and Benjamin then separated from Mary and Abraham and went off in another direction.

Later on, about 3.30 a.m., Mary Ashford was seen walking towards the home of Hannah Cox's mother. A witness mentioned that the girl was 'walking very slowly and alone'. At the house of Hannah's mother, Mary took of her new dress and changed into her working clothes. She told Hannah she was going home then said goodbye to her friend and left the house at 4 a.m. On two more occasions that morning Mary Ashford was seen. A Joseph Dawson testified that he had set eyes on the girl in Bell Lane around 4.15 a.m., and about ten minutes after that, Mary had been seen again in that same lane by Thomas Broadhurst. Both witnesses noted that Mary had been alone in Bell Lane.

Not long after these inquiries into Mary Ashford's last movements, the police interviewed Abraham Thornton, who seemed in a state of shock after being told that Mary had been murdered, probably by strangulation - after being raped.

Thornton told detectives: 'I cannot believe she is murdered; why, I was with her until four o'clock this morning.'

Thornton seemed sincere enough and apparently didn't understand that he was the chief suspect in the murder investigation. However, he soon understood the situation when he was taken into custody later that day and searched. Detectives grilled him about every detail of events which unfolded after he had left Tyburn House Inn with Mary. Thornton admitted that he'd had sexual intercourse with Mary, but he denied he had raped and murdered the girl. In a deposition the bricklayer stated that when his friend Benjamin Carter and Mary's friend Hannah Cox had left them, he and Mary had strolled hand in hand over a field to a stile. The couple sat talking for about fifteen minutes then went to the Green at Erdington where Mary went into her friend's house to change her dress. Abraham had waited for quite some time but Mary did not come out so he went home alone. Thornton's statement was backed up by three other witnesses who had seen him at that time. One witness, a gamekeeper named John Haydon, had even chatted to the young man for over quarter of an hour. The police continued their investigation into the murder of Mary Ashford, but came up against a brick wall. No one had seen the murder victim and Abraham Thornton together after they had been sighted at the stile at the top of Bell Lane at three in the morning, a fact which provided the police with a real headache.

Thornton was brought to trial in August that year at the Warwick Assize Court before Mr Justice Holroyd. Hundreds of people who believed Thornton had killed Mary Ashford had waited outside the courthouse from six in the morning. All of them hoped they'd be the first to hear that a verdict of guilty had been reached, but they were to be disappointed. After just six minutes of deliberation, the jury returned a verdict of 'not guilty'. In modern English law, that verdict would have been final but in the early 19th century an ancient law existed which enabled Mary Ashford's brother William to appeal against the jury's verdict and thus demand a second trial. This was duly done and upon 17 November 1817, Abraham Thornton once again stood in the dock, this time before Lord Ellenborough at the Court of the King's Bench. By now, interest in the Mary Ashford murder had reached fever pitch in every corner of Britain, and the Fleet Street news hounds were delighted at a dramatic turn in the case. Legal history was made when Lord Ellenborough allowed Thornton to take advantage of an archaic law called 'Trial by Battel'. This ancient right necessitated Thornton renewing his plea of 'not guilty' before throwing down a gauntlet from the dock. This signified a challenge to William Ashford for a fight to the death, unless one of them surrendered or was incapacitated during the fight.

There were objections to the Trial by Battel option, but Lord Ellenborough proudly enunciated to the court: 'It is the law of England!'

If Ashford accepted the challenge and won, Thornton would be executed immediately, but if Thornton won, he would have to be freed and would no longer have to appear in court in connection with the Ashford murder.

Abraham Thornton held what resembled a heavy leather mitten with a trailing feather attached, and invoked the ancient English law. He declared he was innocent and that he was ready to defend his innocence with his body. He then lifted the gauntlet above his head, then hurled it down from the dock as the pressmen scribbled furiously.

William Ashford's counsel disputed Thornton's right to Trail by Battel and criticised Lord Ellenborough for allowing such an alternative to a proper second trial, but the protestations came to nothing. Because William Ashford had not responded to Abraham Thornton's challenge by 21 April in the following year, the latter was thoroughly discharged. He would no longer have to stand trial for Mary Ashford's murder, but because of the adverse publicity, no one would employ the bricklayer, so he later emigrated to the United States.

To this day, criminologists have tried in vain to determine who murdered Mary Ashford. Now for the facts of the eerie case which has strange echoes of the Ashford murder.

On 27 May, 1975, 20-year-old Barbara Forrest was found dead in the long grass of a ditch near Erdington. She had been strangled and raped, and her body, which was partly clothed, had lain undetected for over a week. Barbara had worked at the nearby Pype Hayes Children's Home. Her facial features bore an almost identical similarity to Mary Ashford, and like Mary, Barbara had also been strangled after being raped. The police made inquiries and later arrested Michael Thornton, a Birmingham child care officer who worked at the home where Barbara had also worked. Like the Thornton who stood accused of murdering Mary Ashford in 1817, Michael Thornton was tried for the murder of Barbara Forrest, and he too was later (and quite rightly) acquitted. Both murders had taken place around the same time of day, and, furthermore, both victims had been to a friend's house to change into a new dress before going out on the evening of Whit Monday to a dance.

Stranger still, days before each victim was murdered, they made prophetic remarks about their impending fate. The week before Mary Ashford was murdered, she told Hannah Cox's mother that she had 'bad feelings about the week to come', but was unable to elaborate on her unfounded sense of dread, and ten days before Barbara Forrest was raped and then strangled to death, she told a colleague at work of a strange premonition. Barbara's words had been: 'This is going to be my unlucky month. I just know it. Don't ask me why.'

Were the 'twin' Erdington murders just a spate of uncanny coincidences, or were more sinister forces at work?

THE TITANIC'S FROZEN WOMAN

There are many sane and respected people around the world today who intend to have their bodies 'put on ice' when they expire. Their frozen corpses will be stored in liquid nitrogen at a temperature of minus 196 degrees centigrade until a future time when advances in medical technology will allow the deep-frozen dead to be resurrected. These attempts at cheating death through freezing are practical examples of the relatively young science of applied cryonics. The Cryonics Society of California is a pioneer in this field and started freezing newly-dead bodies in 1967, but there are now cryonic storage societies starting up in other parts of the world. Many scientists still regard the prospect of cryogenic immortality as a slim and laughable chance, because it is still difficult if not impossible to freeze human tissue fast enough to avoid vital-cell destruction. This problem will undoubtedly be resolved in the not-too-distant-future, and already rudimentary human embryos have been successfully frozen at sub-zero temperatures. Moral watchdogs are concerned at the pace of progress in cryonics, and recent legislation in Britain has limited the period scientists can hold the embryos in cold storage.

We don't have to look to cryogenics to see examples

of deep-frozen mammals; nature has already beaten us to it. In the summer of 1977, a perfectly-preserved specimen of a six-month-old baby mammoth was disinterred by a bulldozer from permafrost in the Yakutsk Republic of the former USSR. This baby mammoth, nicknamed Dinah, is over ten thousand years old. In 1900, a larger Russian mammoth was found in Berezovka standing upright in the Arctic permafrost. The frozen beast was so perfectly preserved by the sub-zero temperatures that the ancient buttercups it had been eating when it died were still stuck to its tongue. No reason has ever been given to explain why the mammoth died so suddenly it never had a chance to swallow the flowers, but the beast seems to have been literally frozen in its tracks.

Human bodies that have been frozen naturally in Arctic conditions have been reported from time to time. In August 1984, scientists chipped through five feet of gravel and permafrost on Beechley Island, which is situated at the entrance to Canada's Wellington Channel. What the excavating scientists came upon was breathtaking - three graves containing the bodies of sailors who had died in 1846. One of the corpses was perfectly preserved. The body was subsequently identified as that of seaman John Torrington of the ill-fated Franklin Arctic expedition. Sir John Franklin had left England in 1845 on a mission to find the Northwest Passage, a long-sought sea route from the Atlantic to the Pacific by way of Canada's arctic islands. The British Government and its Admiralty were confident that Franklin would find the Passage, and they gave him two ice-region ships named *Erebus* and *Terror* which had been completely overhauled and refitted for the expedition. Franklin and his men perished in the Arctic Circle before they could find the Northwest Passage, but the fate of the ships is unknown. However, in 1851, the captain and crew of a brig named Renovation were astounded to see two full-sized ships perched on top of a huge iceberg in the North Atlantic. Two old seadogs on the Renovation identified the ships through a telescope; they were the frozen wrecks of *Erebus* and *Terror*. The 19th century ice-bound wrecks were allegedly seen once more in the early 1950s still embedded in a berg.

There have also been more sinister reports of people frozen in ice. The following story was buzzing across the Internet in the late 1980s and was even reported in a BBC radio bulletin in Britain.

According to the story, in March 1988, towards the end of the Cold War, a Russian destroyer was on manoeuvres in the North Atlantic, about 800 miles south of Iceland, when a lookout on the ship with high-powered binoculars spotted an iceberg on the horizon. There was nothing unusual about an iceberg being in that area of the ocean in March, but what excited the lookout was the curious dark spot he could see on the iceberg. As the berg floated nearer to the destroyer, the lookout zoomed in on the dark spot, and sighed in disbelief; the dot was the figure of a woman lying on a ledge, covered in a thin layer of ice. She was dressed in a black jacket and a long black dress, and was lying on her back.

The captain of the destroyer immediately dispatched a motorboat to take a closer look. Two divers left the boat and swam over to the ledge of the iceberg to take a closer look at what was obviously the frozen corpse from some sea disaster. Three more men, including a physician, came off the ship and spent almost an hour freeing the body from the ice. The woman, who looked about twenty-five to thirty years old, was perfectly preserved, except for one ankle, which was blackened by the tissue-destroying ice crystals. However, the out-dated clothes she wore indicated that she had been frozen for a long time, perhaps fifty years or more. The corpse was put into a body bag and taken on board the Russian destroyer, where it was put in refrigeration until the ship returned to the Soviet Union.

The corpse was then transferred to a military hospital in Leningrad and slightly thawed to just under room temperature. Even the lipstick on the woman's face looked fresh, and the woman looked as if she was only sleeping. Suddenly, the woman's eyes flew open. It seemed to be just a reflex action, and not a sign of life. The blue eyes were slightly bloodshot, but looked animated. All of the scientists present recoiled in shock. The eyes then rolled upwards and the eyelids of the corpse flickered, then closed. One report said that the scientists tried unsuccessfully to resuscitate the corpse by firing a high voltage current through its chest, but the lungs were full of ice and the other internal organs were damaged beyond repair.

In the pockets of the woman's coat, several papers and belongings were found. A brooch, a purse with old money that dated to the early 1900s, and a number of documents which stated that the woman had been a passenger on the *Titanic* liner, which vanished below the waters of the Atlantic after hitting an iceberg 350 miles southeast of Newfoundland in 1912.

It was surmised that the woman had probably fallen or jumped overboard from the stricken vessel, and had probably somehow been swept onto one of the icebergs drifting through the waters in the area where the *Titanic* went down. The story was reported in some Russian satellite states, but the Soviet Union allegedly hushed up the strange find because the Russian destroyer that found the ice-bound corpse had been involved in electronic eavesdropping on very-low-frequency broadcasts from American submarines. According to further reports that leaked out of the crumbling USSR in 1990, scientists removed the frozen woman's ova cells and were attempting to clone her.

BEWARE THE IDES OF MARCH

Although the Romans were the most level-headed and fearless people the world has ever known, they were very superstitious and quite obsessed with prophecies and omens. Arguably the most famous prediction in history is the one concerning the fate of Julius Caesar, made by the seer Vestricius Spurinna: 'Beware the Ides of March.' This warning was made in 44 BC. That year the oligarchic republic was collapsing, and Pompey, the champion of the Roman nobility had been killed in a battle. Julius Caesar, his father-in-law and conqueror, at the age of 55 had been declared dictator for life, and he dreamed of a Pax Romana stretching from Parthia to the western shores of Spain. Then came a terrible omen which even made Caesar shudder. In the city of Capua, Roman settlers unearthed the tomb of Capys, the city's founder, and discovered a bronze plaque which was inscribed with the chilling warning: 'When once the tomb of Capys is brought to light, then a branch of the Julian house will be slain by the hand of one of his kindred.'

It wasn't widely known at the time, but a relative was

involved in an assassination plot against Caesar. This person was Marcus Brutus, who was commonly believed to have been a descendant of Lucius Junius Brutus, who had routed an earlier monarchy of Rome. Marcus Brutus was cruelly goaded into joining in the conspiracy to assassinate Caesar by sixty conspirators who scrawled graffiti on the statue of Lucius Brutus which read: 'Your posterity is unworthy of you.' This message to Brutus was ambiguous, because it also intimated that he was the son of Caesar, and many thought that this was so, including Caesar himself. There were more 'omens' which intimated that something dire was in the offing. Wild birds fluttered and roosted in the Forum, and strange vision of fiery human-like figures were seen fighting. Caesar killed a wild animal, and when it was cut open, it was seen to have no heart. The respected augur Vestricius Spurinna told Caesar that a monstrous evil would manifest itself and threaten his life on the Ides (the fifteenth day) of March. Caesar never took the prophecy seriously, but as the 15th of March approached, many strange incidents took place around him. On the evening of 14th March, Caesar remarked to his wife that the best death would be the swiftest one, and no sooner had he ended the sentence when there was a loud unearthly howl somewhere outside. Later that evening while he and his wife Calpurnia were in bed, the couple were awakened by a tremendous howling gale which blasted open the doors and windows. Calpurnia awoke screaming and told Caesar that she had just suffered a vivid bloody nightmare about his fate. In the dream she had seen their home crumble and had been cradling her dead husband in her arms She begged him to postpone tomorrow's Senate meeting, and Calpurnia gave Caesar great cause for concern, because he had never known her to be superstitious. On the following day, Caesar, feeling confident and assuming all the so-called omens were but tricks of his mind, laughingly told his augur: 'Well Spurinna, the Ides of March have come.'

'Yes Caesar, come but not yet gone.' Spurinna replied. It was still only midday after all.

Within minutes, Caesar had entered the Senate chambers and was distracted by Tillius Cimber until the other assassins had assembled close by. Then Cimber gave the signal to attack by baring Caesar's neck. The first blood was drawn by Casca, and Caesar grabbed his sword and shouted for help, but none came. The gaggle of assassins closed in, daggers drawn, ready to strike, when Brutus was allowed through. He stepped forward and stabbed Caesar in the groin.

Struck with horror and despair, Julius Caesar gasped, 'You too, my child?' He knew by then that there was no hope of escape, and in a final act of pride, he covered his face with his robe and fell at the foot of Pompey's statue, with his blood ebbing away from the 23 stab wounds he'd sustained.

Caesar's heir, the Emperor Augustus was another leader who consulted seers. When Augustus built a temple of Peace he asked the famous Oracle at Delphi how long the structure would stand. The answer he received was seemingly nonsensical at the time: 'Until a virgin gives birth to a child and yet remains a virgin.'

Augustus interpreted the answer as an indication that the temple would last forever, but at the time of the birth of Jesus of Nazareth, the Temple of Peace suddenly collapsed on its foundations for no apparent reason. Furthermore, shortly before the temple crumbled, Augustus consulted another prominent prophetess known as the Tiburtine Sibyl. He asked her whether he should accept the title of God of Nations which had been conferred on him from the Senate.

As the Sibyl muttered an unintelligible phrase in a trance-like state, a meteor flashed across the sky. The seeress suddenly broke out of her trance and stated: 'A Child has just been born who is the true God of the World. He is of humble birth and from an obscure race. He will work miracles but will be persecuted as a result. In the end though, he will be victorious over death itself, rising from where his killers entombed him.'

THE AKASHIC RECORDS

Throughout the history of human civilisation there have been individuals who have claimed to be the possessors of arcane knowledge that had allegedly been accessed from unknown sources. The masons, Mystery schools and various other esoteric groups have professed to possess secrets of the occult; but where did these secret societies get their clandestine information from in the first place?

Some of the occult knowledge was probably carefully passed from generation to generation by initiates of the fabled Ancient Wisdom; this being a vast collection of books about cosmic law, the hidden powers of mankind and other mystical matters, supposedly written by the scientists of a super-civilisation in antediluvian times.

But for centuries, occultists have claimed that there is another source of hidden knowledge called the Akashic Records. These records are said to contain data on everything in the universe; every thought and deed of every life-form from the beginning of the cosmos to the present.

The word 'akashic' derives from the Sanskrit akasha, meaning the fundamental etheric substance of the universe and of which the records consist. The substance is said to fill all space and to link every atom of animate and inanimate matter.

The Akashic Records are therefore like some colossal databank (similar to the Net but unimaginably more extensive) that contains information about every person and event from the dawn of time to the present day. The Western counterpart of these records would be the Book of Life, where all details about a person's conduct are recorded by their attendant angel.

If you think the notion of vast amounts of information existing in the ether is a bit far-fetched, consider this: gigabytes of data are passing through you and surround you at this very moment as you read these words. TV, satellite and radio signals carrying pictures, music, chat, classified and encoded military information, messages from mobile phones etc, are radiating through your body at the speed of light. This modern-day continuous chatter of the electromagnetic spectrum is a good analogy when referring to the Akashic Records. The same thing happens in both cases; unless you know how to tune in and decode the signals around you, they are undetectable and of no use.

How then, do you tune in to access the records? Mystics use meditation or visualisation techniques where you simply picture a blank chalkboard and wait for the information you need to appear on it.

Sometimes it would seem that the records are unconsciously accessed at random by people who believe that they have been inspired. For instance, Mozart claimed that he often heard new symphonies playing in his head which didn't seem to be of his making, while Sir Paul McCartney has always maintained that his most popular song, *Yesterday*, came to him from the depths of his sleep. Many writers and poets, such as Samuel Taylor Coleridge and Charles Dickens, have made the same curious assertions about novels and poems that seemed to have been dictated to them from some invisible author in their unconscious minds. In fact, Coleridge dreamed the whole of his poem *Kubla Khan* and simply wrote it down in the morning.

Scientists have also made many discoveries in the time-honoured tradition of 'sleeping on the idea'. In 1863, a young German scientists named August Kekule experienced such a dream of discovery while dozing on a bus. The scientist dreamt that he was watching chains of carbon and hydrogen atoms slithering about like snakes. Suddenly, one chain formed a type of loop which instantly revealed to the dreamer what the molecular structure of benzene was. Kekule awoke excited; he had been wracking his brain trying to work out the structure of benzene for months and now all had been revealed to him in a dream.

Of course, all the previous cases could be rationalised as the products of a fertile subconscious. However, if the Akashic Records do exist on some higher plane of existence, then the information they contain could often be accessed by more than one person simultaneously. It is often said that when the time is ripe, ideas, inventions and discoveries usually appear in different parts of the world at the same time. For example, in 1900, three scientists in Holland, Germany and Austria Hugo de Vries, Carl Correns, and Erich von Tschermak respectively independently discovered the laws of genetics on the same day.

In 1876 the same thing happened when Alexander Graham Bell patented the telephone. Another inventor named Elisha Gray sent a detailed description of his telephone to the US Patent Office a few hours after Bell's invention had been patented. More and more patents for a telephone poured into the office and, within few years, there were some 600 lawsuits over the Bell telephone patents.

But how would something new as the telephone be a part of the Akashic Records? Some occultists maintain that because the records are universal, they therefore contain the history of other planets in the cosmos that are more technologically advanced than Earth. The scientists of these older worlds will have progressed further in physics than Earth's scientists and will doubtless have long accomplished telephonic communication and other technological advancements. Thus all such achievements would be recorded in the Akashic repository.

How could the Akashic Records store such a phenomenal amount of universal data? No one seems to have an answer to that question but that doesn't mean that there isn't an explanation, simply that it is not known, or perhaps not recognised for what it is, at the present moment. After all, a laser hologram is a not dissimilar concept, yet this would have baffled scientists of the 1950s completely. We now know that if a photographic plate containing the interference patterns of an object that has been recorded as a 3-dimensional hologram is shattered, the whole 3-D image can be recreated by shining a laser through one small sliver of the smashed plate. All the information about the total image of the object has been recorded somehow onto every point of the plate. This discovery was not made until 1965 and was totally unexpected, so who are we to dismiss the possibility of something similar on a far grander scale?

The Akashic Records are reputed to exist as a network of 'etheric space' which science has yet to discover. All the same, most scientists would no doubt scoff at the concept of this mysterious ethereal archive. Yet Einstein himself once expressed how science is unable to work out just what empty space actually is with a very profound remark. He said, 'What does a fish know about the water in which he swims all his life?'

OLD TESTAMENT UFOS

Within the unimaginable depths of the universe there is a small family of worlds circling about a star we call the Sun; it is just a single star among the billions upon billions which are shining in the cosmos. Against the awesome backdrop of the infinite blackness of space, our world is just another planet; nothing more than an insignificant speck on the cosmological scale of things, but it is our home, and as of yet we have found no other planets which are remotely like Earth. The history of our world is a story which is still largely incomplete. Just a few centuries ago, the most learned historians knew virtually nothing about events beyond 3,000 years ago. These students of the past had a surplus of legends about the origin of man and his world, but the fables and myths were seemingly at variance with the fossilized bones of dinosaurs and apelike beings. These archaeological finds clashed severely with the beliefs and religions of people who took the Hebrew Bible's account of Genesis as a literal authentic history of the world. If prehistoric monsters roamed the Earth in the past, why were they not mentioned in the Book of Genesis? The halcyon tales of the Garden of Eden only mention Adam and Eve; there is no reference to the now-extinct races of ape-men and men-apes such as the Neanderthals, the Cro Magnon people, and other sub-human anthropoids.

Despite the conflicting evidence of the fossil records, the Church attempted to circumvent the problem by seriously asserting that the Devil had maliciously fabricated the fossils of ancient plants and animals and had planted them in rocks to disprove the Biblical scriptures. In fact, by meticulous analysis of the Book of Genesis, the Archbishop of Armagh (1581-1656) even came to the conclusion that God had created the world at 9 am on October 23, 4004 BC! Some writers and thinkers have conjectured that there is a theological no-man's land where the Biblical view and scientific version of man's history can co-exist. One of the earliest attempts to reinterpret the books of the Old Testament as a terrestrial account of alien visitations can be found in *Yezad*, a 1922 science fiction novel by George Babcock. Babcock's sci-fi treatment of the Old Testament was branded by many as sacrilegious, while others thought his concept was preposterous.

In the early 1950s, the Old Testament was once again interpreted from a scientific angle by the distinguished academic and Freudian psychiatrist Immanuel Velikovsky. After his extensive researches into Israelite history, Velikovsky proposed that certain parts of the Bible's Old Testament were factual, and he offered many outrageous theories to describe Biblical events as misinterpretations of cosmic incidents.

Velikovsky argued that Earth had been involved with a near-collision with Venus. The effects of this hypothetical planetary near-miss on the Earth's axis and rotational speed would have been responsible for the account in the Book of Joshua 10:12-13: 'The Sun stood still in the midst of Heaven and did not go down about a whole day.'

Why did Velikovsky think Venus was the culprit? Well, until the second millennium BC, that planet was not grouped by astronomers with the rest of the planets; it was in fact always described as a menacing comet-like body which was said to have rained fire down on the Earth in the past. The Aztecs called Venus 'the Star that smoked' and claimed that it once passed by the world blazing, and killed many people in its wake. The Peruvians called Venus 'Chaska' - which means wavy-haired. Strangely enough, the Greek myths tell how a blazing star named Phaeton almost destroyed the world with fire before being transformed into the planet Venus. The Jews also regarded Venus in a similar manner for some reason, and a passage in the Talmud states: 'Fire is hanging down from the planet Venus.' Venus - the nearest planet to ours - was also classed as a dangerous fire-spitting planet by the Egyptians, Assyrians, Babylonians, Arabs, Hindus, Chinese, and even the Samoans. Velikovsky strongly backed up his wandering planet hypothesis with more historical references to our nearest planetary neighbour in his controversial book, *Worlds In Collision* (1950), but predictably, the historians and astrophysicists ridiculed the work. The Biblical fundamentalists also attacked the book for equating the works of God as mere cosmic cataclysms. But other writers came along with even more controversial interpretations of the historical events which have allegedly inspired the world's religions and cultures.

In 1967 a book called *Chariot of the Gods?* was published, and within the space of five years it had become a best-seller in 38 countries and was translated into 26 languages. The author of the book was Erich Von Daniken, the managing director of a Swiss 5-Star Hotel. The claims made by Von Daniken in his work were bold and blasphemous. Von Daniken had been educated at the College of St-Michel in Fribourg, where even as a student, he had occupied all of his spare time studying ancient holy writings. His lengthy research led him to the following conclusions: Humanoid aliens from a remote galaxy had visited the Earth around 10,000 years ago, apparently after an intergalactic war. These 'sons of the stars' created the human race in their own image by tinkering with the genes of the primates. The alien visitors so overawed their creations with their far superior technology that they were worshipped as gods. Evidence, such as artefacts and relics of the visiting ancient astronauts have been uncovered by archaeologists but unrecognised. Many of the fabulous stories in the Bible and other sacred books are actually accounts of the ancient spacemen intervening in human affairs.

Von Daniken was heavily criticized by theologians, archaeologists, social anthropologists, cultural historians, astronomers and astrophysicists, but his first book sold five and a half million copies and captured the imaginations of people the world over. *Chariots of the Gods?* spawned a deluge of books with the same theme of ancient astronauts, many of which became bestsellers. Today, Erich Von Daniken still holds dearly to his beliefs, although he bravely and honestly admits there were some errors in his books. In 1985, he wrote a book about the errata of his works entitled, *Did I Get It Wrong?* and he even asked his readers to consider if he had misconceived the whole ancient astronauts theory in the first place.

Could there be at least a grain of truth in the claims of Von Daniken and the other writers who say God was an astronaut? Let us analyse the Bible in our quest for ancient spacemen. The Christian sacred book is actually a collection of books, divided into two parts: the Old Testament and the New Testament. The former contains thirty-nine books (according to the Protestants), plus a supplement of fourteen books known as the Apocrypha. These are books of doubtful authority, but are included in the Greek (Septuagint) and Latin (Vulgate) versions of the Old Testament, but are usually viewed as non canonical or of little value by most Christians and Jews. The Old Testament was compiled during a period ranging from the 13th century to the first century BC. No original manuscripts have actually survived, and the present versions are based on two main sources: the Septuagint - a Greek translation made from the Hebrew in Alexandria in about 250 BC - and the Massoretic Text, which resulted from the collaborations of a group of Jewish scholars, beginning in the sixth century after Christ. This group of scholars assigned themselves to the task of preserving the Hebrew versions then available, and the Massoretic Text was finally finished at the end of the 10th century.

The Septuagint became the accepted Old Testament of the Christians, and the Massoretic Text became the Hebrew canon. There were, however, even more versions of the Old Testament; they were the Samaritan Pentateuch - fourth century BC text preserved by the Samaritan community - and a Latin translation by St Jerome (begun in 382 AD) called the Vulgate, which is the authorized Roman Catholic version.

The New Testament of the Bible was most probably written in Greek during the first century. Without a doubt, the New Testament is riddled with mistakes, but none of them are significant enough to affect the essential doctrine of the texts. These errors occurred through numerous textual changes which were accidentally introduced through poor copying, misinterpretations that were added, and accidental - and deliberate - omissions. Some of these alterations were made for political and religious reasons. The great British scientist Isaac Newton became an atheist after learning Hebrew. After retranslating the Bible from the original Hebrew texts, he discovered that in the fourth century, during a bloody power struggle within the Christian Church, key passages in the Bible were altered by the Christian leader Athanasius. Newton was devastated to learn that the text was falsified by Athanasius to elevate Christ on a level with God and the Holy Spirit in the doctrine of the Holy Trinity. Newton decided that Jesus then, was just another prophet like Moses, and thought the worshipping of Christ as God's equal was nothing short of idolatry. This illustrates the problem of authenticity faced by modern theologians. If we take the Bible literally, as it is intended to be taken, according to Christians, then its scriptures are open to some intriguing interpretations. In Genesis, we are told that:

In the beginning God created the heaven and the Earth. And the Earth was without form and void; and darkness was upon the face of the deep. And the Spirit of God moved upon the face of the waters...

Further on another passage reads:

And God said, Let the Earth bring forth grass, the herb yielding seed, and the fruit tree yielding fruit after his kind, whose seed is in itself, upon the Earth: and it was so. And the Earth brought forth grass, and herb yielding seed after his kind, and the tree yielding fruit, whose seed was in itself, after his kind: and God saw that it was good.

If we are to interpret the aforementioned passages not as some sacred account of creation, but as a primitive allegorical interpretation of an real higher intelligence transforming a cratered, barren planet into an oasis, we would see striking parallels with the far-sighted plans the scientists of today have for 'terraforming' planets in out solar system which are at present too hostile for us to survive on. The late astronomer and astrophysicist Carl Sagan once put forward an ingenious plan for terraforming (making a planet hospitable) the currently infernal world of Venus. Sagan calculated that if we bombarded Venus with 1000 rocket-loads of blue-green algae, some of the hardy one-celled organisms would reproduce in the upper atmosphere before crashing down to the surface, which has a temperature of 900 degrees Fahrenheit. This incredibly hot temperature is nothing to some algae that thrive in boiling hot springs on Earth. Rocket-loads of the tough algae cells released into the thick cloud cover continually over a period of years would ultimately allow a flourishing colony of cells that would convert the carbon-dioxide in the Venusian atmosphere into oxygen. After several hundred years, enough oxygen would be formed on Venus to cool down the planet and vastly reduce the Venusian greenhouse effect. This in turn would allow the significant amounts of water vapour which is known to exist in the atmosphere of Venus to fall as rain. The end product would be a cycle of rainfall and the formation of rivers and lakes on the planet. Sagan's plans are not pipe dreams; computer simulations have determined that a terraforming programme for Venus is entirely feasible if enough time, money and technology is provided for the project, which would literally reap astronomical profits. A transformed Venus would not only become a second Earth for humanity to colonise, it would present unprecedented territorial ownership disputes among the nations of Earth.

As Venus has no tectonic plate system like Earth, it would be earthquake free. Secondly, the Venusian day lasts 243 Earth days; that would be 243 days of continual sunshine in the planet's tropical belt, which entails obvious advantages over Earth's tourist industry. Venus would become the ultimate retreat for this planet's millionaires, and the ultra-novel extraterrestrial holiday location would require a sizeable workforce from Earth. The prolonged period of sunshine on Venus would probably necessitate subterranean or air-conditioned dwellings where artificial night could be simulated. Another possibility at stimulating a localised form of night could work by orbiting inflatable reflective myelin mirrors around the planet. The shadows of these mirrors falling on the surface of Venus would create an oasis of darkness which the inhabitants would experience as a solar eclipse effect. Alternatively, perhaps anyone tiring of the eight-month day could even journey to the dark side of Venus, where the stars would be on view for as long as there were clear skies. Of course, no one is entirely sure what resources lie beneath the Venusian crust, but as the planet is almost a twin of the Earth in size and gravity, we must surmise that there will be radioactive ores, gold, silver and many other precious metals and minerals present. This brings us back to the problem of who would own these resources. When NASA landed its first astronauts on the Moon, the Soviet Union, China and many other nations frowned at America planting the tinfoil flag of the Stars and Stripes in the lunar soil. The other nations of the world argued that a united banner of humanity should have been planted there instead. This suggestion outraged NASA and the American government, which had spent billions of dollars and lost a number of astronauts in order to reach the Moon. If an American company as successful as Microsoft financed the Venus terraforming venture, there would be similar squabbles amongst the Terran leaders of our much-hyped 'Global Village'. In fact, it is highly likely that wars would rage over the possession of the new world. Perhaps even a war of independence for the new Venusians who wish to become autonomous and free from the Earth governments. Going back to the Biblical texts of Genesis; is it possible that a similar war over planetary possession was fought when the gods transformed the Earth from a lifeless sphere 'without form and void' into the Garden of Eden? Curiously, American Charles Fort (1874-1932) the great student of the unexplained and collector extraordinaire of bizarre newspaper clippings and reports, once made a profound statement in 1919 in his Book of the Damned, an incredible examination of the holes and contradictions in our scientific understanding of the universe. Fort wrote:

I think we are property. I should say we belong to something. That once upon a time, this earth was No-Man's land, that other worlds explored and colonised here, and fought among themselves for possession, but that now it's owned by something. That something owns this earth - all others warned off.

Did Fort hit on a truth? It would explain all the tales in Apocrypha and other religious works about the ancient conflict called 'The War In Heaven' which was fought by dissenting factions of angles, led by rogue Archangel Lucifer against his master, Yahweh, the God who made a lifeless world fertile and created Homo Sapiens to tend to his Garden of Eden. In the Book of Isaiah 14:12, it says of Lucifer:

O Shining star, son of morning, how you have fallen from the heavens... For you said in your heart, I will go up to the heavens; I will raise my throne above the stars of God...

Most people equate the name 'Lucifer' with Satan,

however the Bible implies that this is not the case, and the name Lucifer is only mentioned in one passage of the Old Testament.

According to the Book of Job 26:11-13, when Lucifer, 'the Boastful Angel' and his followers rebelled, Yahweh destroyed their dwelling places a place in the heavens called 'Rahab', which was reduced by God to 'stones of fire'. The Book of Enoch hints that Rahab was an actual world in the sky which God smashed. In some accounts, Rahab is curiously connected with the mythical planet Phaeton, which was said to have been destroyed by a catastrophe millions of years ago. Is there any physical evidence that Rahab once existed?

Each planet in our solar system is somewhere between 1.3 and 2.0 times as far from the Sun as the next nearer planet. The one exception in this numeric relationship is the fifth planet Jupiter; it is 3.4 times as far from the Sun as Mars. This inconsistent gap puzzled astronomers for years, especially after Uranus was discovered in 1781. It was quite obvious that a planet was missing which should have been orbiting between Mars and Jupiter. Astronomers scanned this gap in the orbits for years, hoping to discover the absent planet, but in 1801, the first fragment of the missing planet was discovered by stargazers. It was a carbonaceous chunk of rock, 620 miles in diameter, and it was named Ceres. By 1807, more enormous fragments were spotted, and as the century progressed, it became clear that there were thousands of chunks of something spread in a belt around the sun between the orbits of Mars and Jupiter. Today, it is known that there are at least 100,000 asteroids in the belt, and the debate still rages over just what the asteroids are the remnants of. Some astronomers think they are leftover material from the birth of the solar system which never formed into a planet, while others think the asteroids are the remains of a world which exploded in the distant past. What force could destroy an entire planet? Cometary collisions, and even geological catastrophes could have been responsible. Water from the planet's oceans seeping down through faults in the crust to the core would be sufficient to generate a super-heated blast of steam that would blow a planet into oblivion. This scenario was witnessed on a small scale here on Earth in 1883 when seawater seeped into the active volcano on the East Indian island Krakatoa. The ensuing blast destroyed the island, killed 36,000 people, and hurled fragments over an area of 300,000 square miles.

The evidence for the demolished world of Rahab could then, be the hundreds of thousands of chunks floating about between Mars and Jupiter, but in the search for an extraterrestrial angle on the Bible, we must now turn our attention to the chronicled events which allegedly happened here on Earth.

One thing which does seem absolutely certain in the Old and New Testaments, is that something unearthly caused a stir in the Middle East, in the time of Moses and in the period Jesus was on Earth. let us begin with the Old Testament. Whatever way we look at it, something that was literally not of this world commanded Moses to lead the Israelites out of the bondage of the Pharaoh and through the wilderness to the Promised Land. It all began when Moses was eighteen years old, according to the Talmud. The sight of the wickedness being inflicted upon his people by the Egyptians moved Moses to tears, and it culminated in him killing an overseer who was beating a Hebrew labourer. Moses was saved from execution by an angel and transported instantly to Ethiopia where he fought as a general. Soon after the death of Kikanus, Moses was crowned king and Queen Adonith became his wife. However, Moses abdicated and journeyed to Midian, where he married Zipporah, the daughter of Jethro, and for forty years lived as a shepherd. Scriptures then give a strange account about Moses's encounter with an unearthly entity:

Moses was minding the flock of his father-in-law, Jethro, Priest of Midian. He left the flock along the side of the wilderness and came to Horeb, the mountain of God. There the angel of the Lord appeared to him in the flame of the burning bush. Moses noticed that although the bush was on fire, it was not itself being burned up; so he said to himself "I must go across to see this wonderful sight. Why does not the bush burn away?" When the Lord saw that Moses had turned aside to look, he called out to him out of the bushes "Moses, Moses." And Moses answered "Yes I am here." God said "Come no nearer; take off your sandals; the place where you are standing is holy ground."

This passage has been interpreted by researchers looking for scriptural spaceships as perhaps some account of bush silhouetted against a lit-up spacecraft which had landed on the secluded mountain. The 'Lord' warning Moses to keep his distance has also been construed as the amplified intercom voice of the captain or pilot of the landed ship advising Moses to keep out of range of harmful radiation emanating from the craft. The Lord told Moses to deliver the Israelites out of bondage and lead them to the Promised Land 'flowing with milk and honey'.

Aided by his elder brother, Aaron, Moses finally led the 600,000 Israelites out of thraldom and embarked on the epic forty years of wandering to Canaan. In the Book of Exodus XIII,21 it is written:

And Yahveh went before them by day in a pillar of cloud, to lead them the way; and by night in a pillar of fire, to give them light; to go by day and night. He took not away the pillar of the cloud by day, nor the pillar of fire by night, from before the people.

The pillar has been the subject of much speculation to scholars, critics and theologians over the centuries. One Biblical scholar, M .Daniel-Rops, asserts that the pillar of cloud - the visible sign of Divine Presence in the eyes of the Hebrews - was nothing more than a side effect of the 'Qadim', a sirocco-like wind of Arabia, which raised opaque clouds of spiralling dust. But Mr Daniel-Rops neglects to explain how this whirlwind of sand kept going for forty years, and how it became highly luminous and fiery upon nightfall. What we can assume, without the risk of being sacrilegious, is that the pillar of cloud and light was not of this Earth, and definitely not a product of weather conditions. Something from above was intervening in the affairs of the Hebrews, and it was not some mass hallucination affecting the thousands of Israelites and the Egyptian nation; something real and tangible was taking place.

The Pharaoh was well aware of the reality of the

Hebrew Lord when he decided to send his cavalry and chariots after the fleeing Israelites. Faced with the obstacle of the Red Sea, Moses could lead his persecuted people no further, but at the Lord's behest, Moses suddenly stretched out his hand towards the river, and the waters parted. A tremendous wall of seawater moved off to the right, and another water-wall roared off to the left, exposing a vast tract of dried seabed stretching from one shore to the next. Moses and his people fled across the dry path to the safety of the other side, but when the Egyptian army tried to follow them across the seabed of the Red Sea, the water came thundering back down on top of them and they were drowned.

No natural phenomenon can account for the parting of the Red Sea, but if we are open-minded enough to entertain the hypothesis that extraterrestrials were responsible, we could imagine some potent antigravity forces pushing back the waters. We can already manipulate liquids at a distance with electrostatic forces. Many computer printers utilise this affect by using electrical fields to manoeuvre jets of charged ink around paper. If you let a thin stream of water run from a tap, then comb you hair and place the comb inches from this stream, the static electricity in the comb will actually bend the flow. If the static charge was greater, the water would flow at right angles, and if the electricity was charged further by a Van de Graff generator, you would be able to draw up gallons of water from a swimming pool. To part the Red Sea would take millions of watts of power, but that would easily be expendable to a space faring race. Two more incidents mentioned in Exodus give the impression that something akin to a spaceship landed on Mount Sinai:

And the Lord came down upon Mount Sinai, on the top of the Mount; and the Lord called Moses up to the Mount; and Moses went up.

Also, we read:

And it came to pass on the third day in the morning that there were thunders and lightnings, and a thick cloud upon the mount, and the voice of the trumpet exceeding loud; so that all the people that was in the camp trembled, And Moses brought forth people out of the camp to meet with God, and they stood at the nether part of the Mount. And Mount Sinai was altogether on a smoke because Yahveh descended upon it in fire; and the smoke thereof ascended as the smoke of a furnace, and the whole Mount quaked greatly.

Scripture then records that Moses advances towards the landing of Yahveh, but is given a stern warning by the Lord not to let anyone near the landing site. Only Moses is allowed to proceed. Yahveh says to the leader and prophet: 'And thou shall set bounds unto the people round about, saying, Take heed to yourselves that ye go not up into the Mount, or touch the border of it: whosoever toucheth the Mount shall be surely put to death: there shall not an hand touch it, but he shall surely be stoned, or shot through; whether it be beast or man it shall not live.'

Intriguingly, after an undefined period of time has elapsed, Yahveh lifts his exclusion zone from around the mountain, and Moses is allowed to take Aaron and seventy elders with him as he goes up to get a closer look at the mysterious cloud-pillar, although they all maintain a respectful distance from the supernatural sight. But then they see the awe-inspiring figure of Yahveh:

And they saw the God of Israel and there was under his feet as it were a paved work of sapphire stone...

Standing on a blue scintillating platform, they actually see the elusive but powerful God who co-ordinated the Exodus of the Jews after sending ten plagues against Egypt, the last of which resulted in the death of the Egyptian first-born (and may have only affected the Pharaoh's family). The celestial deity instructs Moses to construct a large tent of specific dimensions with the aid of the craftsmen in the encampment. The Hebrew lawgiver was told that the tent would be a 'Dwelling Place' for Yahveh and would also serve as a rendezvous where Moses and Aaron could meet with the extraterrestrial host. The specialized enclosure, also known as the Tent of Reunion, later served as the shelter of one of the most enigmatic objects in history: the Ark of the Covenant.

The Ark of the Covenant was an ornate chest of acacia wood which accompanied the Israelites throughout their nomadic wanderings. The Ark contained Aaron's rod, a pot of manna, and the broken stone tablets of the Decalogue - or Ten Commandments. It was 2.5 cubits (3 ft 9 ins) in length and 1.5 cubits (2 ft 3 ins) in height, and was carried by poles at the longs sides. Bezaleel, a Judahite artisan who was highly skilled at working in metal, wood and stone, was the principal architect of the Ark, but it was built to plans revealed to him by God, not to his own designs. The instructions imparted from Yahveh were very intriguing indeed. The poles used to carry the Ark were to be made of acacia and overlaid with gold leaf. In order to transport the Ark, these poles were to be carefully inserted into specially made receiving rings mounted on the sides of the chest. The poles were to remain in the rings at the sides of the Ark and never to be removed. The instructions for transporting the Ark of the Covenant were equally specific. Only the Kohathites - a clan of Levi - were allowed to carry the Ark and the holy things associated with the tabernacle. God warned that anyone else who touched those things would meet a swift death. What potent power did this Ark contain to be so jealously guarded? It was soon discovered why there were so many precautions regarding the handling of the Ark; as it was being transported by oxen, the beasts of burden stumbled, an a man named Uzzah who was not a Kohathnite or of the clan Levi - instinctively reached out to steady the Ark in case it toppled off the cart - and he was struck down dead by a tremendous bolt of energy (2 Samuel 6:7). The religious interpretation of this tragic event is that God smote Uzzah for being disobedient to his conditions, but one freethinking French writer, the late Robert Charroux, has conjectured that the Ark of the Covenant seems suspiciously like some high-voltage condenser which may have been a part of apparatus for communicating with the heavenly Yahveh. Erich von Daniken has also opted for this startling possibility, and the idea was also partly used in the 1981 Spielberg film, *Raiders of the Lost Ark*.

The fate of the Ark is not known. Some scholars have concluded that it was captured by the Babylonians in 587 BC, when the destruction of Jerusalem and the Temple was completed by Nebuchadnezzar. Yet, for some unknown reason, the Ark was not recorded in the list of the Babylonians' stolen booty. The current theory is that the Ark is in Ethiopia, because of an old legend, which goes as follows. The Queen of Sheba once visited King Solomon and was highly impressed by his wisdom (that is mentioned in the Book of Kings). She had an affair with him and when she returned to her nation, the Queen discovered she was having Solomon's child. The queen subsequently gave birth to a son, who was called Menelik, meaning son of the wise one. Upon adulthood, Menelik travelled to Israel to seek his father, who welcomed him with honour. Solomon gave so much attention to his illegitimate son, the elders complained and demanded that Menelik should return to Ethiopia. Solomon agreed, but only on the condition that all of the elder's oldest sons would accompany Menelik. The elders had to agree with the King, and Azarius, the oldest son of Zadok, the high priest of Israel, went to Ethiopia with Menelik - after stealing the sacred Ark of the Covenant. When Menelik reached Ethiopia, Azarius revealed the Ark, but Menelik believed that the theft would not have been successful without God's consent. And so, it is said that to this day, the Ark of the Covenant is under lock and key in the Church of St Mary of Zion in Axum. Should a thorough investigation ever get underway and successfully trace the Ark, it will be interesting to see if it is just an acacia chest - or something more hi-tech.

In other sections of the Bible there are other fascinating descriptions of fantastic events which have parallels with the modern UFO era. One apparent close encounter with a craft from the sky takes place in the Book of Ezekiel. Ezekiel was one of the Jews deported to Babylon during the first exile of 597 BC. His call to be a prophet came in Babylon and his entire prophetic ministry was carried out there. By the River of Babylon - the Khobar - Ezekiel was sitting, in a sad mood, on the 'fifth day of the fourth month of the fifth year since the captivity' (the year 593 BC) when he suddenly saw what he assumed to be a 'chariot of Yahveh' coming towards him through the sky. In a state of shock the prophet stood transfixed, looking skywards at the strange craft:

And I looked, and behold, a whirlwind came out of the north, a great cloud, and a fire unfolding itself, and a brightness was about it, and out the midsts thereof as the colour of amber, out of the midsts of the fire. Now as I beheld the living creatures behold one wheel upon the earth by the living creatures, with four faces. The appearance of the wheels and their work was like unto the colour of beryl [a greenish sheen] and they four had one likeness: and their appearance and their work was as it were a wheel in the middle of a wheel. When they went, they went upon their four sides, and they turned not when they went. As for their rings, they were so high they were dreadful, and their rings were full of eyes [portholes?]. And when the living creatures went, the wheels went by them: and when the living creatures were lifted up from the earth, the wheels were lifted up. Withersoever the spirit was to go, they went, thither was their spirit to go; and the wheels were lifted up over against them: for the spirit of the living creature was in the wheels.

Ezekiel goes on further to say that above the discs, there was another amazing object which he enigmatically alludes to as 'something that had the appearance of the likeness of the glory of Yahveh.' In earlier books of the Old Testament, the glory of Yahveh is always referred to as pillars of could or fire. Perhaps that was what Ezekiel was seeing above the landed object he could hardly describe in his limited language.

There are other accounts of possible UFOs in the Old Testament. The outstanding narrative concerning the adventure of Elijah when he is taken up by a 'whirlwind' - the same description Ezekiel uses for his UFO. Then there is the incredible tale related in a 4th century apocryphal work known as The Vision of Isaiah:

After taking Isaiah to Heaven, the angel was requested to return the prophet to earth. Isaiah said: 'Why so soon? I have only been here two hours.' The angel said: 'Not two hours, but thirty-two years...do not be sad, you will not be an old man.'

This seems like the well-documented effects of time-dilation. If Isaiah had been onboard a spacecraft capable of travelling near to the speed of light, time for him would run slower compared with someone back on Earth. Einstein was one of the first scientists to predict this curious effect, and in the 1970s, an experiment was carried out to prove the time-dilation theory. Two highly accurate atomic clocks were synchronized so they both had the same read-out, right down to the last decimal place. One clock was put on the supersonic airliner Concord, and flown from London to New York and back, while the other clock remained on the ground. When the read-outs from the clock on the ground and the travelled clock were compared, it was seen that the clock from Concord had somehow lost microseconds. In short, with a risk of oversimplification, the faster an object moves through space, the slower it moves through time compared to a stationary object. Simple extrapolation and a modicum of mathematics will tell us that if you were to embark on a two-hour trip into outer space at a speed close to the velocity of light, you would return to find your friends and family decades older than when you left, while you would only be two hours older. This complicated effect was only predicted by Relativity Theory in the 20th century, so how did the author of the Vision of Isaiah know about it?

As we have seen from our brief tour of the Old Testament, there is more to the biblical tales of pillars of clouds and whirlwinds. If they were contemporary accounts of visitations from extraterrestrials, are there any similar accounts of this superior race's activity in the New Testament? That question is addressed in the next chapter.

WAS JESUS AN EXTRATERRESTRIAL?

The gospel of St Matthew opens the New Testament with a frightening visit from a skyborne being who descends from the starry heavens to proclaim a sensational message to terrified shepherds attending their flocks:

Behold, a virgin shall be with child and shall bring forth a son, and they shall call his name Emmanuel, which being interpreted is, God is with us.

This event - if it happened at all - would have occurred between four and eight years before the era which came to bear Christ's name Anno Domini - which is Latin for 'in the year of our Lord.'

Like his death and alleged resurrection, the birth of Jesus of Nazareth is cloaked in mystery. Just as the pillar of light led the Israelites through the wilderness to the Promised Land in the Old Testament, another enigmatic object served to guide those with wisdom to the birthplace of a carpenter's son in the New Testament. The ufological angle certainly seems to fit the account of this guiding light in the sky which is depicted on millions of Christmas cards all over the world. It is sung about in carols, it shines down from the tops of Christmas trees, and foil imitations of it twinkle over Nativity scenes. But just what was the Star of Bethlehem? Is it just a myth or did the starry messenger really exist in the skies of Judaea? For centuries, theologians and scientists have argued over their interpretations of the celestial event, which was recorded only by the apostle Matthew. In the second chapter of his gospel, Matthew tells us: "When Jesus was born in Bethlehem of Judaea in the days of Herod the King, behold, there came wise men from the East to Jerusalem, saying, 'where is he who is born King of the Jews? For we have seen his star in the East and have come to worship him.' "

According to Matthew, Herod summons the mysterious Wise Men and tells them that if they should find the newborn king, they must divulge the child's whereabouts to him. Later, the Wise Men see the guiding star in the East and it leads him to the stable where the babe Jesus is sleeping.

In the 17th century, the great German astronomer Kepler, sent shockwaves through the Christian world when he suggested that the star the Wise Men had followed might have been nothing more than a conjunction of the planets Saturn and Jupiter. However, it is now known that no such conjunctions were visible in the Holy Land during the period St Matthew mentions, which historical scholars reckon is around 4 or 5 BC. After Kepler's heretical attempts to explain away the Star of Bethlehem as a natural phenomenon, many other scientists also tried to formulate theories to rationalize the stellar oddity. Halley's Comet was blamed but astronomers have calculated that the comet had already visited and left the heavens before Christ's birth. Another theory proposed that the star that hovered over the stable was actually a distant star that had exploded - or gone supernova, to use astronomers' jargon. Such explosions do occur from time to time and can remain visible in the sky for weeks, even during the daytime.

Now, it is recorded in ancient Chinese texts that such a supernova explosion did occur - around 4 BC. Chinese astronomers of the time recorded that a star flared up in the constellation of Aquila the Eagle, just below the bright star Altair. What's more, it has been computed that, to anyone standing at the South Gate of Jerusalem, the brilliant star would appear to be over Bethlehem.

The American scientist A. J. Morehouse, who discovered the Chinese record, therefore believes that the Star of Bethlehem is still in the sky, but it is very faint.

Opponents of Morehouse's theory have pointed out that the exploding star of 4 BC occurred too late to be associated with the birth of Christ. Also, such a bright spectacle in the night sky would hardly have gone unnoticed by Herod and the other inhabitants of Judaea. Moreover, a supernova cannot hover in the sky as the star of Bethlehem did over the manger.

Just as enigmatic as the Star are the Wise men who followed it. Matthew simply states that they were from the East without specifying what countries they came from, and, contrary to popular belief, St Matthew does not actually say there were three of them. In fact, according to the early versions of the Nativity in Medieval times, there were twelve Wise Men! Whatever their number, most Biblical scholars agree that the Wise Men were students of astrology, which was very popular among the Jewish community at the time. This theory was strengthened by the discovery of the Dead Sea Scrolls in 1947. Among the timeworn Hebrew and Aramaic texts - some of which date back to the birth of Christ there are astrological charts depicting signs of the Zodiac and mystical texts referring to the influence of the stars and the planets on the newly-born. The Scrolls also mention an unnamed individual who lived at the time of the Jesus who was known as the Teacher of Righteousness.

In the end, despite all the conjecture and historical research, we are still no nearer to uncovering the truth about the most mysterious herald in history - the Star of Bethlehem. If it wasn't a comet, nor a planetary conjunction, then surely there is only one logical hypothesis which can explain a light in the sky which behaves as if it is controlled by an intelligence: the Star of Bethlehem was a spacecraft; and if we can accept this explanation, we must ask: what was it doing hovering over the stable where Jesus was born?

The Christians have longed claimed that the arrival of Christ at Bethlehem had been predicted centuries before. In the Book of Micah 5:2 (written in the 8th Century BC), it states that the Messiah - Hebrew for "the anointed one" - would be born in Bethlehem, and in the Book of Isaiah 7:14 (also written in the 8th century BC) scripture specifically asserts that the person who will come as God's representative in the flesh would be born of a virgin. In the Book of Malachi 3:1 it is foretold that someone would go ahead of the Messiah to prepare the way. Most Christians have interpreted this as being John the Baptist. In Isaiah 9:1-2 it predicts that the Messiah would live and work around Galilee in a northern province remote from the centres of power, and that he would heal people. The Book of Zechariah foretells that the long-awaited Messiah who would restore his people to a position of power and prosperity which they enjoyed under David and Solomon would ride into Jerusalem humbly, on a donkey, and not on the war-horse of a military conqueror. In that same book a passage eerily maintains that the Messiah will be betrayed to his enemies for thirty pieces of silver. This prophecy seems to have been fulfilled by one Judas Iscariot.

There are more amazingly accurate predictions in Psalms, the 19th book of the Old Testament. Crucifixion - execution by nailing the condemned to a cross - was unknown to the Hebrews until the Romans came to power, yet in Psalm 22 there is a graphic description of the way the Messiah will be put to death, hundreds of years before Jesus of Nazareth was crucified. The passages say his hands and feet will be pierced, and that his executioners would mock him and gamble for his clothes. All of the incidents foretold by the Jewish scriptures, if applied to the life of Jesus, are astoundingly more accurate than the prophecies of Nostradamus.

Little is known about the early days of Jesus, especially the circumstances of his conception and birth. Traditionally, March 25 is held as the Day of the Annunciation, when the angel Gabriel announced to Mary that she would give birth to the Messiah. Curiously, in May 1999, Israeli historians researching ancient copies of the Apocrypha told the newspaper *National Midnight Star* that one translation of the Virgin Mary's conception after a visitation from God described a chilling tale which sounded very similar to the accounts of people who had undergone gynaecological examinations in UFO abduction experiences. When reporters pressed the codex researchers to comment further on their intriguing claims, but the historians were evidently advised by the religious authorities to withhold further interpretations of the timeworn texts.

Even the hardened scientific sceptic, philosopher and historian H. G. Wells - who was not at all impressed by Christianity - once wrote of Jesus:

Christ is the most unique person in history. No one can write a history of the human race without giving first and foremost place to the penniless teacher from Nazareth.

In this age of scientific and medical marvels, it is possible through the techniques of artificial insemination to produce a child in the womb of a woman who is a virgin. In Japan and America, scientists are making rapid progress with the development of artificial wombs which will allow the development of a fertilized egg into an embryo and finally a nine-month-old baby. These 'baby hatcheries' were described in 1932 within the pages of Aldous Huxley's far-sighted novel *Brave New World*, although Huxley confidently assured his shocked readers that cloning and mechanical wombs were three centuries away. In 1962, the year before Huxley died, the English physicist Francis Crick and American biochemist James Watson, shared the Nobel Prize in medicine and physiology for discovering the double-helix structure of DNA - the genetic code of the human body. Five years later, the British biologist John B Gurdon cloned a South African clawed frog. Eleven years after that, British Doctor Patrick Steptoe and his colleagues overcame the problem of sterility in women by producing the first test-tube baby outside the womb in July, 1978. Twenty years after that, scientists had cloned sheep and higher mammals, and it was recently claimed that cloned humans in America and Korea had been allowed to develop to an embryonic stage before being destroyed.

Envisage then, a superior race from another world steering the affairs of mankind. This higher race implants the embryo of Jesus into a peasant woman's womb so she becomes a surrogate mother. Jesus is born in an obscure village, and as he grows he probably becomes aware of the psychic superhuman talents he possesses. He works in a carpenter's shop in Nazareth until he his thirty, then embarks on a three-year mission which will sow the seeds for the most momentous sociological and philosophical revolution in world history. Immediately the authorities realise that he is not an average prophet, for he raises three dead people: a young girl (Matthew 9:1819), a young man (Luke 7: 11-15), and a man named Lazarus (John 11: 1-44). The Jews believed that only God could control the weather to induce storms and stop them, so they were amazed when Jesus stopped a storm (Matthew 8:23-27). There are also accounts of Jesus - or Yeshua - as he was known - walking on water, exorcising evil spirits from possessed people, healing the sick and crippled, restoring the sight of blind people, turning water into wine, and feeding the multitudes (on two different occasions).

All of these supernatural acts proved Jesus was no ordinary human being, and he himself said the

Kingdom or realm he came from was 'not of this world'. He also maintained that his father was in the heavens, and he spent many lengthy periods in the vast isolation of the Sinai Desert, where he may have received the instructions for his revolutionary programme to change civilization. Perhaps this was the rendezvous point for meeting his extraterrestrial kin. There are many instances of luminous objects descending onto Jesus and shining rays at him. All of these incidents are interpreted as religious omens among the primitive people of the time, but what can we make of them? For example, in Luke 3: 21-22, it is recorded:

Now, when all the people were baptised, it came to pass, that Jesus was also being baptized and praying, the heaven was opened. And the Holy Ghost descended in a bodily shape like a dove upon him.

What was this thing which resembled a luminous dove? We are none the wiser now. Nor can we explain the significance of the following episode, mentioned in detail in Matthew 17: 6-9:

Jesus took Peter and John and James and went up into a mountain to pray. And as he prayed, the fashion of his countenance was altered, and his rainment was white and glistening. And behold, there talked with him two men, which were Moses and Elias; who appeared in glory, and spake of his decease which he should accomplish at Jerusalem. But Peter and they that were with him were heavy with sleep: and when they were awake, they saw his glory, and the two men that stood with him. And it came to pass as they departed from him, Peter said unto Jesus, Master, it is good for us to be here; and let us make three tabernacles; one for thee, and one for Moses, and one for Elias: not knowing what he said. While thus he spake, there came a cloud, and overshadowed them: and they feared as they entered into the cloud. And there came a voice out of the cloud, saying, 'This is my beloved Son: hear him.' And when the disciples heard it, they fell on their faces and were sore afraid, And Jesus came and touched them and said Arise and be not afraid. And when they had lifted up their eyes, they saw no man, save Jesus only. And as they came down from the mountain, Jesus charged them, saying, Tell the vision to no man until the Son of Man be risen again from the dead. And they kept it close, and told not man in those days of the things which they had seen.

Why did Jesus ask the disciples to keep quiet about the incident? How did Peter, John And James know the figures with Jesus were Moses and Elias, who lived a thousand years before they were born? And what mysterious process was going on during the miraculous transformation of Jesus, which made his face and clothes 'brighter than the sun'? What mysterious forces were at work on the summit of that mountain? Was Jesus being 'recharged' by some energy source hidden in the cloud which hovered overhead? So many intriguing, but alas, unanswered questions.

Of course, the ultimate proof that Jesus was no ordinary Earthman came with his physical resurrection, which was mentioned in all four gospels and referred to in Corinthians 15: 3-7. Mark relates that Jesus of Nazareth was scourged and treated brutally by the Roman guards, who crowned him with thorns, mocked him, then crucified him at the ninth hour (3 p.m.) of the day. Jesus had to be buried before the Sabbath began at 6 p.m., so that his corpse should not profane the holy day. A secret disciple of Jesus named Joseph of Arimathea, bravely asked the Roman Governor Pontius Pilate if he could bury Christ. Pilate was surprised that Jesus had died so quickly, and after checking with his centurion to see if Christ had indeed passed away, he allowed Joseph to take charge of the preacher's body.

Joseph wrapped the corpse of Christ in a fine linen; this cloth was afterwards rumoured to feature a miraculous imprint of the body of Christ, and some think the burial cloth is still around as the famous Turin Shroud. The shrouded body of Jesus was hurriedly laid in a sepulchre hewn out of a rock, and the entrance to this tomb was sealed with an enormous stone. There can be no doubt that at this point, Jesus was not faking death, although some researchers have claimed that he had not died on the cross, but had only swooned. But the facts say that was not possible, for a Roman scourging was so terrible and traumatic, many victims died before being crucified. Then there is the graphic account of John, who says a soldier named Longinius thrust a spear into Jesus's side while he was on the cross and that 'blood and water' came out. This is a medically accurate description of what happens when the pericardium is pierced, and such a wound is always fatal.

Shortly before dawn on the Sunday morning following the Jewish Sabbath (which is a Saturday), Mary Magdalene went to visit the tomb where Jesus was laid to rest, and noticed that the heavy stone had been rolled back. In John 20: 1-9 it states:

The first day of the week cometh Mary Magdalene early, when it was yet dark, unto the sepulchre, and seeth the stone taken away from the sepulchre. Then she runneth, and cometh to Simon Peter, and to the other disciple, whom Jesus loved, and saith unto them, They have taken away the Lord out of the sepulchre, and we know not where they have laid him. Peter therefore went forth, and that other disciple, and came to the sepulchre. So they ran both together: and the other disciple did outrun Peter, and came first to the sepulchre. And he, stooping down, and looking in, saw the linen clothes lying, yet went he not in. Then cometh Simon Peter, following him, and went into the sepulchre, and seeth the linen clothes lie, And the napkin that was about his head, not lying with the linen clothes, but wrapped together in a place by itself. Then went in also that other disciple, which first came unto the sepulchre, and he saw, and believe. For as yet they knew not the scripture that he must rise again from the dead.

The events of that first Easter morning soon came together like a mystical jigsaw puzzle. The Jewish Council, the Sanhedrin, trembled when they heard the news of the empty tomb. They heard strange accounts of how, in the early hours of that Sunday morning a being in 'snow-white clothes' with a light on its head as bright as lightning had descended from the low oppressive clouds and terrified the Roman soldiers guarding the tomb of Christ into stupefaction. This strange figure - assumed by the Jewish priests to be a heavenly being - an angel of some order - proceeded to push away the stone blocking the tomb's entrance with superhuman might. It was later revealed that two unearthly-looking men dressed in white clothes had been seen at the entrance of the tomb by Mary

Magdalene, Mary the mother of James, and Salome. The three women said one of the eerie figures said: 'Be not affrighted; ye seek Jesus of Nazareth, which was crucified. He is not here...he is risen. But go your way, tell his disciples and Peter that he goeth before you into Galilee; there shall ye see him, as he said unto you.'

The enigmatic men in white later vanished into the skies as mysteriously as they had appeared. Did they return to some mothership in Earth orbit? The ship that had been interpreted as the Star of Bethlehem?

The resurrected Jesus later reappeared to his faithful disciples, but seems to have undergone a 'transfiguration'. Although he was apparently solid and tangible enough to eat food and to allow the disciples to touch his wounds, doors did not have to be opened before he could enter a room full of people. He bi-located on several occasions (allowed himself to be seen in several places at once simultaneously), and seemed slightly different. Some people who had been familiar with him prior to the crucifixion did not recognize him immediately; in fact even Mary Magdalene mistook him for a gardener. Luke mention this intriguing facial metamorphoses when he relates the two disciples' walk to Emmaus, seven miles outside Jerusalem. Christ joins them but says 'there eyes were holden that they should not know him'. The disciples told the bemused Jesus about the crucifixion and of the empty tomb he had been laid in. Jesus then revealed his identity be expounding the scriptures concerning himself. The overawed disciples shared their evening meal with him, and he blessed them and broke the bread. He subsequently performed a vanishing act, and the disciples hurried back to Jerusalem to tell of their emotional and heart-lifting encounter with the risen Christ. The eleven Apostles, meanwhile were giving their accounts of meetings with the returned Jesus, when their Lord suddenly appeared in their midst.

After the ghostlike Christ had instilled faith into his followers, he is said to have 'ascended' into heaven. The Christian Bible doesn't go into any detail about what this ascension was like, but we possess thought-provoking accounts of the event in the Apocryphon Jacobi, and the Epistle of the Apostles. These books, which were suppressed by the Church for centuries, give us a full description of the Ascension. They tell us that at the ridge, east of Jerusalem, known as the Mount of Olives, where Jesus often prayed and meditated in the evenings, there was a great stir. The resurrected Jesus of Nazareth was talking to his followers, when his words were interrupted by a clap of thunder and lightning. The roll of rumbling thunder shook the entire mountain, and a chariot descended through the clouds. The Jews of old called this chariot a Merkaba - a celestial vehicle of the angels which is mentioned in the ancient Kabbals. The texts describe how Jesus entered the Merkaba and was welcomed by the angels within who were dressed in 'white apparel'. One of these heavenly beings said to the apostles:

Men of Galilee, why stand ye gazing up into heaven? This same Jesus, which is taken from you into heaven, shall so come in like manner as ye have seen him go to heaven.

And the Apostles watched in wonderment as Jesus

rose higher and higher into the heavens until he and his angels in the Merkaba were lost to sight.

Today, the Christians assert that Jesus was God incarnate, while the Jews maintain that he was merely a prophet. Whoever Jesus was, there can be no doubt that he was a most extraordinary, and possibly extraterrestrial being. How else can we explain the miracles he performed, the transfiguration, and eventually regeneration after being executed on the cross? Then there is the futuristic philosophy Jesus propounded which predates the doctrines of Communism formulated by Marx and Engels by centuries. Jesus said that it would be easier for a camel to pass through the eye of a needle than for a rich man to enter the kingdom of heaven, and he also said that in his kingdom, the underdog and the wretched would be put first (which enraged the self-righteous Pharisees). He told his astonished followers that pacifism was the only way to live; if their enemy should strike them, they must turn the other cheek, ready to be hit again. This seemed to be the exact opposite of the Old Testament's suggestion of 'an eye for an eye' and more in keeping with Ghandi's philosophy of non-violence which lay nine centuries in the future. Jesus also preached that those who wished to follow him would have to love their enemies and pray for them, and abandon all worldly wealth. The strange philosophy of Christ seems so alien to the selfish nature of the human race; was this because Christ was an alien? Because the whole subject of Jesus and his teachings is still surrounded with so many blind dogmas and taboos, it is difficult to see beyond the religion and analyze just who or what the carpenter from Nazareth really was. The extraterrestrial interpretation does not denigrate Christ in any way, but shows him in another, wider role in the cosmos. The next time you gaze up into the night sky at the stars, consider that somewhere out there, for all we know, an interstellar Christ may be preaching the word of Yahveh to the multitudes of some alien world.

EXECUTION IN A RAILWAY TUNNEL

Housewife Maria Cunningham, of Wirral, England, will never forget the Halloween of 1996, when she visited London with her twelve-year-old son, Jason. In the morning they went to Madam Tussaud's and later paid a visit to her sister in the Kensington district of the capital.

Just after nine o'clock that night, Maria and her son boarded the London to Liverpool train at Huston Station. As the train entered a tunnel, Maria, Jason, and several other passengers, were startled and horrified to see the flashing image of a man convulsing in the throes of death in an electric chair, just beyond the window-panes of the railway carriage. The disturbing image could not have been projected on to the wall of the tunnel by some hoaxer, because the witnesses all agreed that the man in the chair had looked three-dimensional and completely solid. The deeply disturbing image had been so detailed and vivid, that Mrs Cunningham had even seen sparks of electricity around the metal wristbands fastening the man to the chair. The same terrifying apparition was later seen by tourist in the same railway tunnel in 1999. The electric chair has never been used in Britain, but there are rumours that a London gangster was tortured in an access tunnel off that stretch of railway line in the 1950s. It is alleged that he was wired to an electrical transformer to make him talk.

When I gave out an account of this strange story on a radio station (where I was an invited guest talking about the supernatural), I received a call from a Wirral man called Freddy Ryden. In 2000, Freddy and four friends decided to go to London to look for work in the construction industry, and minutes before their train pulled into Huston, they all saw the distinct image of a man bound by metal bracelets to what seemed to be an electric chair. On this occasion, the man's face was obscured by a dark vapour, but Freddy and his friends could clearly see the body violently convulsing as sparks fizzed from the bracelets on his hands.

The Liverpool men informed a guard about the electrocuted man as soon as the train pulled into the station, but the guard said that it was impossible for anyone to be sitting in a chair in that stretch of tunnel, as there were simply no vaults or passages where the figure could be situated.

To deepen the mystery further, I received a newspaper cutting from a listener to the radio programme I had been featured on, and the clipping was about the ghost in the electric chair, published in the *Daily Mirror* in the late 1990s. Here is the gist of the article:

A twenty-two-year-old Watford housewife, Karen Woo, was taking the tube to London for a spot of sightseeing with her family and her eight-year-old nephew Kaitian, when she decided to take his photograph. Only after the snapshots had been developed did Karen realise that she had captured a strange apparition on film. Behind her nephew, framed by the window of the tube train, in the inky blackness of the tunnel, was the clear image of a man being executed in an electric chair. Karen said, "My husband's family was visiting from Malaysia and wanted a picture of them all travelling on a tube train. I had the photos developed a few months later and was completely astounded because I'd never seen anything like it before."

A bouncer also got in touch with me to tell how he had been on the train out of Huston Station, when he and two friends were suddenly startled by the appearance of an alarming moving image in the windows of their carriage – a man was shaking violently in what seemed to be an electric chair. The figure wriggled and shook with such a ferocity it was as if the observers were watching a speeded-up film. A few seconds later the startling apparition went out "like a light being switched off" and the bouncer looked at the faces of his shocked friends in silence for a moment. "What the hell was that?" asked the bouncer's friend, and the bouncer asked one of the staff on the train if the man in the electric chair was some gimmick, but although the train employee shrugged, he seemed to know what the bouncer was talking about, which deepened the mystery.

So many independent witnesses, all describing the same apparition, lend weight and credibility to the sightings, and we can only speculate as to their significance.

THE MYSTERY OF THE
MARY CELESTE – SOLVED?

One of the greatest mysteries of history is the enigma of the *Mary Celeste*, and that ship has many connections with Liverpool, England. In 1863, the *Mary Celeste* - then sailing under her original name - *The Amazon* - is said to have collided with a brig in the Straits of Dover, sustaining serious damage. Several crewmen serving on the ship at the time were said to have Liverpool relatives, and there are some who even claim that The Amazon came to Liverpool just before the American Civil War. I would not be too surprised if she did, as my city was then one of the greatest ports in the world, and Liverpool's wealth and reputation was largely based on trade with America, particularly the southern states. I have related the folklore, theories and urban legends of the *Mary Celeste* in volume two of *Haunted Liverpool*, but after much research, I believe I may have finally solved this hoary, almost supernatural, maritime puzzle. Here are the facts to begin with.

On 5 November 1872, the two-masted sailing ship *Mary Celeste* left Pier 44 on New York's East River, bound for Genoa, Italy with a cargo of whale oil, fusel-oil (from spirits distilled from potatoes and grain), and one thousand, seven hundred and one barrels of undrinkable denatured alcohol. Because of bad weather, the ship had to drop anchor at Staten Island for two days. An exchange of signals took place between the *Mary Celeste* and another ship three hundred miles southeast of New York, and then the most mysterious vessel in history pointed her bows to the east and headed across the Atlantic.

At the helm of the ninety-six—foot-long ship was New Englander Captain Benjamin Briggs, a thirty-seven-year-old master mariner of enormous maritime experience who came from a seafaring family. The first mate, a veteran of the American Civil War named Albert G Richardson, was a highly competent and trustworthy man. The cook and steward of the *Mary Celeste* was Brooklyn-born Edward Head, and the remainder of the crew consisted of four men, two of whom had a mysterious background. They were two Germans known as the Lorenzen brothers, who claimed to have lost all their belongings on their last voyage when their ship was wrecked. The other two people on the ship who were journeying into the unknown were the captain's wife, Sarah Elizabeth, and her daughter, two-year-old Sophia Matilda.

Eight days after the *Mary Celeste* had set sail for the wine merchants H Mascerenhas & Co of Genoa, the English brig *Dei Gratia* left New York, bound for Gibraltar with a cargo of petroleum. At the wheel was Captain David Reed Morehouse, a man who had dined with Captain Briggs shortly before the *Mary Celeste* set sail.

On the afternoon of 5 December, John Johnson was at the wheel of *Dei Gratia* when he sighted a vessel five miles off the port bow. It turned out to be the *Mary*

Celeste, and she was not only sailing erratically, she also appeared to be deserted. The *Dei Gratia* closed in on her, and Captain Morehouse surveyed the ship. He noticed that the rigging was fouled, and parts of it had been blown away. When the *Mary Celeste* was just four hundred yards away, Morehouse shouted to her but no reply came, and he decided to allow his first mate, Oliver Deveau and two crewmen to board the deserted ship. These men soon discovered that there wasn't a soul to be found onboard the *Mary Celeste*. Although the ship was in a far better condition than most seagoing vessels, and there was a six months' supply of food and water on the ship, she had obviously been abandoned in a hurry. The crew had left the *Mary Celeste* so suddenly, they had even left their tobacco, pipes and oilskins behind. The three men from the *Dei Gratia* looked at one another uneasily in the eerie silence.

Superstitious mariners across the globe regarded the eerie incident as some kind of paranormal occurrence. Some believed a giant squid had surfaced from the depths of the Atlantic to pick off the people onboard the *Mary Celeste* with its writhing tentacles, but that outlandish version of events could not explain why the squid would also take the ship's papers, the sextant, chronometer, the bill of lading, the register, and other documents from the captain's cabin. The ship's lifeboat was missing, yet the six months' worth of food and water, plus the crew's tobacco and pipes had been left behind.

The compass had been deliberately destroyed, and the wheel had not been secured with rope - the normal procedure when abandoning a ship. The other mystery concerning the *Mary Celeste* was the unusual route her captain had chosen. Instead of taking the most direct route towards the Straits of Gibraltar, Captain Briggs had steered his ship around the northern coast of Santa Maria in the Azores, coming within a few miles of the islands. Briggs had brought the *Mary Celeste* over sixty miles off course to skim the coastline of a small tropical island. From the information recorded in the ship's log, we know that something significant happened just after eight o'clock on the morning of 25 November 1872, and it took place within the waters of Santa Maria Island.

At the time of the *Mary Celeste* mystery, the Azores had an infamous reputation that stretched back a decade. In 1861, the American Civil War began, and the conflict impacted heavily on Liverpool, because sixty per cent of cotton from the American South came through our city. Under international law, Britain was required to remain neutral, yet Liverpool quickly supported the Confederate states, because the Union was blockading the South's exportation of cotton to Lancashire mills.

In June 1861, a cunning confederate spy from Georgia named James Dunwoody Bulloch arrived in Liverpool, where he made secretive arrangements with local shipyards to build warships for the South. One of these vessels - the *Enrica* - was built by the Laird brothers of Birkenhead, then taken to the Azores, where she was refitted as an armed Confederate cruiser. The Confederate flag was raised, and the *Enrica* was renamed the *Alabama*.

Many of the ship's crew were Liverpool men, and many more Liverpudlians were employed to transfer ordnance to ships on the islands of the Azores, including Terceira and Santa Maria. When the South lost the war, Confederates such as Bulloch were warned that they would be hanged if they tried to return to the United States, so they remained in exile. Bulloch stayed in Liverpool, and is buried in Toxteth Park Cemetery. Some exiles settled on the islands of the Azores, and from these former Confederate island naval bases, the ex-soldiers resorted to gun-running and piracy to survive. I believe that the *Mary Celeste* became involved in the schemes of these gun-runners.

On 13 December 1872, the *Mary Celeste* was brought to Gibraltar under the remarkable expert hands of a three-man skeleton crew from the British brig Dei Gratia. The brig's captain, David Morehouse, claimed the deserted *Mary Celeste* as salvage. There's nothing unusual about a claim for salvaging an abandoned ship on the high seas, but this claim was seen as unique and somewhat sinister, as the *Mary Celeste* was not dismasted or waterlogged - in fact she was completely seaworthy. Mr Solly Flood, the Admiralty Proctor at Gibraltar, virtually accused the crew of the *Dei Gratia* of murdering the *Mary Celeste*'s crew, and he got in touch with Colonel John Austin of the Royal Engineers.

Colonel Austin, incidentally, was a close friend of two people who have surfaced in my research before - General Sir Charles Warren, and my prime Jack the Ripper suspect, Colonel Claude Reignier Conder. Warren and Austin had drawn up the plans for the fortifications of Gibraltar just a few years before. Four captains of the Royal Navy, a Colonel of the Royal Engineers, and the Marshal of the Vice-Admiralty

Court suddenly descended on the *Mary Celeste* as she lay berthed in the harbour at Gibraltar. Derelict ships had been brought into Gibraltar before, but none had ever received this much attention. The *Mary Celeste* was inspected inside and out from nose to stern. Surveyors from the Army were called in, and port workers and the curious were kept away from the *Mary Celeste* by soldiers. When a part-owner of the vessel named James Winchester heard about the military involvement surrounding his derelict ship, he immediately sailed from New York to Gibraltar. When he arrived, Winchester saw the ship crawling with the red-coated soldiers of the Royal Engineers. Winchester had a disliking for the English, because many of them had supported the South during the Civil War he had fought in, and he shouted, "By God, I know I have English blood in my veins, but if I knew where it was, I'd cut them open and let it run out!"

With Winchester was his friend Captain Shufeldt, a former Union Navy Commander who had fought for the North in the Civil War. Shufeldt also seemed angered by the British soldiers. As the two Americans looked on, Royal Engineers dived on the *Mary Celeste* to inspect the hull. Colonel Austin, meanwhile, crouched near the huge cast-iron oven hob in the ship's galley. It had been lifted from its four stone blocks and placed a distance away. The hob was so heavy it took four men to shift it. Austin mentioned the out-of-place hob to Solly Flood, and also drew attention to the fact that nine of the *Mary Celeste*'s one thousand, seven hundred and one barrels were inexplicably empty and bone-dry. Had something been removed from those barrels? Had they contained rifles? After the Civil War, American rifles, ammunition and gunpowder had been illegally exported to Europe in the cargo holds of merchant ships. These rifles and bullets had been upsetting the balance of various power struggles in Europe, and the British Intelligence Service knew this, so many ships from America were randomly boarded and inspected by Britain at the gateway to the Mediterranean - Gibraltar.

Under maritime law, a person who salvages an abandoned ship is entitled to a substantial share of the vessel's total worth. Captain Morehouse, his first mate, and two crewmen were given a salvage award of £1,700 for bringing the deserted *Mary Celeste* into Gibraltar. The ship of mystery was kept at Gibraltar for three months as the court of enquiry tried to unravel the fate of her captain and crew. It was said that the *Mary Celeste* had originally been called the Amazon, and that she had allegedly visited English ports on many occasions, including Liverpool. The court considered many scenarios in an effort to solve the mystery of the missing crew, but no theory fitted the facts.

Over one hundred and thirty years have passed since the *Mary Celeste* conundrum, and during that time many badly thought-out theories have been churned out again and again. One unrealistic hypothesis was that Captain Briggs heard the barrels of alcohol 'boiling' in the hold and feared that the ship was about to explode, so he and his crew took refuge in a lifeboat that was tethered to the ship by a rope. Denatured alcohol has never been known to have boiled in the cargo hold of a ship on the transatlantic runs, and Briggs was a master mariner of great experience who hailed from a greatly respected sea-going family. He would never have put his wife, child and crew in unnecessary danger by ordering them to leave a seaworthy vessel to crowd into a small lifeboat adrift on the high seas.

The truth behind the *Mary Celeste* enigma lies in another direction. Britain's Intelligence Service suspected many Europe-bound American ships of gun-running. In 1872 there was a Carlist war raging in Spain, and it was fed by many rifles and gunpowder from the United States gun smugglers. There were also rumblings of unrest in other parts of Europe, and gun-runners were doing a roaring trade as a result. The Royal Engineers, stationed at Gibraltar knew this, and they also knew that some of the gun-runners had bases in the Azores, where the Confederate rebels from the American South - and Liverpool - had fitted the infamous Alabama warship with guns. The Captain of the *Mary Celeste* had visited an island in the Azores on the morning on which her crew vanished into obscurity.

What was the point of the rendezvous? Nine barrels that never contained alcohol are emptied there, the ships papers are removed, along with the crew, and a huge cast-iron galley stove is removed from its blocks - seemingly because someone had to gain access to something that had been stored under it. A skeleton crew then steers the ship on a course that points it away from the island and they abandon the *Mary Celeste* and return to the island on her lifeboat. The *Mary Celeste* is subsequently scrutinised by four captains of the Royal Navy, a Colonel of the Royal Engineers, and the Marshal of the Vice-Admiralty Court. In 1884 at a

Liverpool society dinner, the Mayor mentioned the strange case of the *Mary Celeste*, which had just been featured in the Cornhill Magazine. One man at the table not only had a thorough knowledge of the ship and its crew, he knew the Azores like the back of his hand. The man was Captain James Dunwoody Bulloch, the Georgia-born spy who commissioned the Alabama warship to be built at Laird's in Birkenhead. In the Civil War he had taken the Alabama to the Azores from Liverpool with a crew that was mostly from Lancashire. People around the dinner table, and Mr Radcliffe, the Mayor, noted that Bulloch had tears welling in his eyes.

"Whatever became of the *Mary Celeste*'s crew?" someone asked.

Bulloch became pale. He shook his head and muttered, "It's all in the past now." Bulloch then left without making an excuse, and without uttering another word. Today, he rests under a fine towering tombstone in Liverpool's Toxteth Park Cemetery on Smithdown Road.

THE ULTIMATE MYSTERY

This is a bizarre story about guilt, curiosity and deadly knowledge which could possibly change your view of the world and yourself, and even turn you insane. In Liverpool, England, there is a certain series of streets near Goodison Park which infer specific words. The streets: Oxton, Wilmslow, Eton, Neston, Andrew, Nimrod, Dane, Wilburn, Ismay, Lind, Lowell, Index, Arnot, Makin, and so on, spell out, very distinctly, the words 'Owen and Williams'. In actual fact, Owen and Williams was the name of the firm of builders who built those very streets. A major shareholder in this firm was a Lancashire millionaire named Henry Williams.

Williams had become a millionaire after his father had died and left him his fortune. He felt immense guilt over his sudden wealth, which rumour has it may have been brought on after he heard a sermon by a Welsh Presbyterian minister in 1886. Around this time, Mr Williams' behaviour became very erratic. He became completely fixated with the concept of death and started spending most of his time in and around hospitals. Specifically, he started to visit a particular hospital in Liverpool on a regular basis. In one instance he went over to a dying girl and sat with her, holding the sick little girl's hand as she passed away. Mr Williams softly stroked her frail hand, as if in a daze, he repeatedly urged, "What can you see?" The staff became concerned by the eccentric man's persistent questions and eventually an alert nurse beckoned the doctor on the ward to literally throw Mr Williams out of the hospital grounds.

As the weeks went on, Williams' obsession with dying and what lies beyond the present life intensified. He talked at length with priests, vicars and ministers of every denomination and found that none of them could answer his question: what was it like after death?

It was not until he visited an equally unconventional man, a Dr McCheyne, and discussed the nature of death and the next world with him, that Mr Williams saw a potential solution to his inquiry. Dr McCheyne suggested something that today would have had him struck off the medical register. The eccentric doctor stated that he was confident that he had the means to stop Henry Williams' heart for a set period of time. He went on to claim that he could then revive him. He explained that he believed that this borderline between life and death, when the heart ceased beating and the brain became starved of oxygen, was the moment when many patients who were later resuscitated had reported intriguing glimpses of the 'next world'.

Amazingly, Williams became excited beyond belief at the prospect of his curiosity being satisfied once and for all, and hurriedly agreed to the highly unethical and dangerous experiment. Attended by a nurse, Dr McCheyne used ether and a solution of cocaine to bring Williams's heart to a halt. That part of the experiment ran smoothly, it was the restarting of his heart that became problematic. As Williams turned bluer by the minute, Dr McCheyne massaged his heart in utter desperation. There was still no response and

Dr McCheyne became distraught as the clock ticked away. If left much longer, the brain would suffer irreversible damage and death would inevitably occur.

The nurse became increasingly anxious. She was all too aware of just how illegal an operation they were involved in, and shuddered at the fact that Dr McCheyne could well be imprisoned for such an unethical experiment and that she too could be tried for aiding and abetting him. After six seemingly endless minutes of electrified suspense and grim foreboding, the nurse detected a faint pulse in Henry Williams' wrist. His heart started to beat again, feebly at first, but gradually getting stronger. As he regained consciousness, the millionaire's body went into spasm, and he then proceeded to vomit, violently and uncontrollably.

Some thirty minutes later, Williams was calmer and was able to relate a very strange tale indeed. He described how he had travelled along a tunnel towards a bright and startling light, which is an overused description we hear regularly nowadays from people who have had a near-death encounter. Williams went on to explain how he had then found himself walking up large stone steps that were flanked on each side by huge pillars. At the top of this staircase there had stood a being, an amorphous snow-white column of immense power which gave off a terrific roar that sounded like a gigantic waterfall. He stated that it was God, claiming that he could not explain how he knew this, just that he had sensed it with an indisputable certainty.

Williams proceeded to give details about the figures he had seen coming down the stairs; they were faceless people draped in long, flowing gowns. These presences were in a limbo of some sort, but again Williams could not explain how he knew this. He claimed that at the top of the steep staircase, he communicated with God, which he described as feeling as if he was a vortex of life-giving energy. Williams went on to describe how he had told the force that he had come to Him for knowledge.

It was at this stage of his account that Williams became anxious. He stuttered as he explained how God had duly given him an overwhelming reply, which he described as the answer to everything -the meaning of life - contained in a single sentence of just seven words. The nurse and doctor waited and watched, enthralled by what they were hearing.

Apparently, the next thing that Williams had known was that he was alive again and recovering in the doctor's private room. As he sat up, he stared back at his dumbstruck companions with his eyes wide. He became visibly agitated as he struggled to remember what the all-important knowledge he had received from the other side had been.

Just moments later, with a look of sheer horror on his face, he slowly recalled what the momentous message had been, and animatedly recited the compact sentence to the nurse and doctor.

Events then took a very sinister turn. Within just one week, the nurse had allegedly committed suicide and the doctor was certified as insane. Williams is said to have told his secret to only six other people, each of whom supposedly also died within the year. Only one man who heard those seven mind-boggling words is said to have survived, a psychical research scientist, Sir

Oliver Lodge.

Williams was also committed to a lunatic asylum and died from an epileptic fit eighteen months later. When the strangely linked deaths became public knowledge, religious mania was blamed. A persistent rumour circulated at the time, that the seven words of the so-called, 'ultimate answer' were written on seven separate pages and placed in a secret place.

I published an account of this strange story in the fifth volume of my Haunted Liverpool series, and received many letters, from priests, theologians, and the downright curious who wanted to know what the Ultimate Answer was which had driven people insane. One morning in 2004 at my office I received a long letter from a man named Patrick, who was a dealer in antiquarian books, and he told me how he had come into possession of a leather-bound notebook written by an unknown gentleman of the Victorian or Edwardian era in 1975. The notebook was full of essays about the author's thoughts about metaphysical aspects of life and the universe, and sixty-seven pages into the work, this freethinker began to relate the story of one Dr McCheyne, and of his experiments to glimpse the next world by 'killing' a subject and then resuscitating him. McCheyne had told the writer of the book that he had unravelled the very nature of human existence – why we are all here and what 'reality' really was. The writer claimed that the person reading the book was the only real living person in existence, and that everything else was nothing but make-believe. He maintained that every person in existence was one and the same as the person reading the book, and that this one person, through unimaginable loneliness, had created everyone else in the world, and then to fool itself into thinking it was not alone, it had hypnotised itself into forgetting that it was the only thing in the universe that existed. This is known as solipsism in the sphere of philosophy. In other words, you reader, are the only thing that exists, no matter how real you think everyone else is. Just as you create realistic people in your dreams that seem to have a life of their own, the people in this world were created by you. The book ended with the words: 'Yes, reader, only you exist in this lonely universe, and all the people you see and hear about are but phantoms created by you to ease your terrible lonely existence. When you "die" you will merely wake up from a dream within a dream that you have created. This is the Great Truth which you have unknowingly hidden from yourself since time began, and now that you know that only you exist, you may surely lose your mind.'

Well, when I read this, I admittedly felt a little dizzy, but surely it's all the ramblings of a paranoid solipsist – I hope!

Other books by Tom Slemen

Haunted Liverpool series
Haunted Liverpool Casebook
Murder On Merseyside
The Pellew Street Horror
Beasts, Banshees & Bogeymen
Jack the Ripper – Secret Service
Tales of the Talking Picture
Tall Tales for Little People

All of these books are available from Amazon.

Printed in Great Britain
by Amazon.co.uk, Ltd.,
Marston Gate.